Y 50666

GW01418276

LO'   F'   FIELD

THE EMISSARY
G. D. Birla, Gandhi and Independence

by the same author

POETRY
Poems 1942–67
The Taj Express
Open Sea
Death Valley

GENERAL
Colours of War
The Turf (edited)

TRAVEL
Time Was Away
The Gulf of Pleasure
South to Sardinia

AUTOBIOGRAPHY
Blindfold Games

CRICKET
Australia 55
Cape Summer
Through the Caribbean
Australia 63
West Indies at Lord's
The Cricketer's Companion (edited)
Ranji

ALAN ROSS

THE EMISSARY

G. D. Birla, Gandhi and Independence

COLLINS HARVILL
8 Grafton Street, London W1
1986

William Collins Sons & Co. Ltd
London · Glasgow · Sydney · Auckland
Toronto · Johannesburg

BRITISH LIBRARY CATALOGUING IN PUBLICATION DATA

Ross, Alan
The emissary: G. D. Birla, Gandhi and
independence.
1. Birla, G. D.   2. Politicians, India –
Biography
I. Title
954.03′5′0924   DS481.B54

ISBN 0 00 272067 1

First published by Collins Harvill 1986
© Alan Ross 1986

Photoset in Linotron Baskerville by
Rowland Phototypesetting Ltd
Bury St Edmunds, Suffolk
Printed in Great Britain by
St Edmundsbury Press Ltd, Bury St Edmunds, Suffolk

While at times I feel disappointed, I also feel that I am amply compensated in having to defend Englishmen before Bapu [Gandhi], and Bapu before Englishmen. It is a very interesting task. I would have no heart to do it, but the more I discuss Bapu with Englishmen and *vice versa*, the more I believe that it is a tragedy that these two big forces in the world cannot combine. I think it will be a service to the world when they do. And this conviction cheers me up.

G. D. Birla, in a letter to C. R. Rajagopalachari
3 July 1937

I think Queen Mary would find G. D. Birla better company than J. R. D. Tata if she wishes to invite one of them to lunch. Tata is a pleasant enough fellow to meet, but I have not found him communicative, and as a casual acquaintance he is much the same as any other wealthy young man who has had a conventional education and turns himself out well. Birla, on the other hand, is a less conventional type. He has plenty to say, and whatever one may think of Marwari businessmen and their ways, he is well worth talking to. I think Queen Mary would have a very dull lunch with Tata and quite an interesting one with Birla.

Lord Wavell to Mr Amery
The Transfer of Power
vol. IV page 1021, document 535

CONTENTS

ILLUSTRATIONS

AUTHOR'S NOTE

I would like to express my gratitude to the many people in India who assisted me in my researches into the writing of this book. Particular thanks are due to Mr and Mrs B. K. Birla, for their hospitality and attention to detail; to Mr Shyamlal Pareek, former secretary to G. D. Birla; and in London, to Mr Ramesh Kumar.

Although it was only in the later part of his life that Ghanshyamdas Birla was generally known as "G.D." I have, for convenience, and to distinguish him from other family members, referred to him almost throughout by his initials. His employees called him "G. D. Babu".

PREFACE

The career of G. D. Birla, who died in London in 1983 aged eighty-nine, offers a remarkable "alternative" history for someone like myself, born in India and whose family, in one way or another, has been involved in Indian affairs since 1790. To most Indians Birla, as a public figure, needs no introduction. Not only had he, by the time of his death, created a vast industrial empire, but he had long been the most articulate and shrewd advocate of Indian industrial expansion. He was known as an intimate for over twenty years of M. K. Gandhi, to whose causes Birla had been the main financial contributor, as he had also been to the nationalist movement. He was respected as the unofficial emissary of the Mahatma and an honest interpreter, in the disappointing years leading up to Independence, of Gandhi's thinking to the British Government and of British intentions towards Indian political aspirations. It was in his house that Gandhi was assassinated.

In later life Ghanshyamdas Birla became, in addition to being a philanthropist on an almost unprecedented scale – builder of temples and hospitals, creator of schools, technical colleges and a university – a profound thinker on most aspects of India's economic problems, travelling the world to study techniques and setting up co-operative enterprises. No visit was complete without a meeting with the head of state, commemoratively photographed.

All this is well enough known in his own country, as is Birla's work as a co-founder and President of Harijan Sevak Sangh, the organization that fought to free untouchables from the iniquities of the caste system.

Nevertheless, capitalists, on so grand and unrepentant a scale, tend to be regarded with suspicion in an ostensibly socialist society. As a result the name Birla is as much associated in a slightly resentful if reluctantly admiring way with industrial power and wealth as with the freedom movement or philanthropy. That is in the nature of things. The unostentatious private life of G. D. Birla and his family, a characteristic of Marwaris generally, differentiated him from the run of Indian millionaires, certainly as envisaged by the popular imagination. Ultimately as rich as most Maharajahs in their heyday, G. D. Birla could scarcely have lived in a more dissimilar style.

G. D. Birla was born in 1894, five years later than my own father, and his youngest son, B. K. Birla, was born in the same year as I was and in the same Alipore district of Calcutta. These coincidences of propinquity, of no relevance in themselves, were a source of pleasure, restoring a sense of intimacy with my own Bengal childhood. The writing of this biography has been, in a sense, a form of self-education, the period covered by it almost exactly the same as if I had been writing about my own family.

For thirty years my father, as a director of Shaw, Wallace & Co., and Chairman of the Indian Mining Association, and G. D. Birla worked within walking distance of each other, and within sight of Howrah Bridge. They were colleagues, on different sides and representing different interests, in the Bengal Legislative Assembly. And, while between 1915 and 1945 their business lives must have touched at many points, their private lives existed in parallel. It is the other parallel that, in writing about G. D. Birla, I have tried to discover.

There is no shortage of information about how the British spent their time in India, whether as civil servants, soldiers or in industry. My father arrived in India just before the 1914–18 war and apart from war service in Mesopotamia remained there until he retired in 1946. My mother's family on her father's side, the Fitzpatricks, served without break in India between the arrival of John Fitzpatrick as a cadet in 1790 and the death of Vere Fitzpatrick in Calcutta in 1942. Fitzpatricks were mainly Army surgeons, though one was in the Police and another Governor of the Punjab. My mother's mother was the daughter of Edward Budd who first went to India as the captain of a sailing ship of the East India Company. He married an Armenian who had huge indigo estates and they had five children, one of whom married a Burmese girl and disappeared into Burma. If each Anglo-Indian family had its own particular history and individual ramifications, the general nature of their activities scarcely varied. As a child in India, and as an adolescent with Indian connections, Indian history for me was the history of the British presence.

About Indian families of the same period almost nothing has been written in English. The British in India had virtually no contact, except officially, with Indians and little curiosity. G. D. Birla was neither prince, nor politician nor peon, the three categories most familiar to those who spent their working lives in India. Yet it was Indians of his generation, deprived in their formative years of both freedom of expression and power, who would ultimately demand and take responsibility for the country's future. The British knew little about them. As far as they were concerned all Indian political activity, in so far as it affected the status quo, was subversive, and industrial competition to be discouraged. Birla was not by nature subversive, but he was determined.

The story of G. D. Birla is that of an exceptional man coming from an unexceptional family who by his vision and endeavour changed their whole history. It begins in the small village of Pilani, a hundred miles out of Delhi in the desert of Rajasthan. Symbolically, it will have its ending there, too, for it is in Pilani, more than anywhere else, that G. D. Birla made an indelible mark on the map of India.

A. R.,
New Delhi – Pilani – London,
1984–6

15

Pilani

The drive south-west from Delhi takes three hours, by bus
nearer to five. For an hour suburban traffic, bullock carts,
motor rickshaws, bicycles, stick like burrs to the car, gradually
detaching themselves as the road opens up. Soon sand dunes
appear, their ribbed hollows alternating with low, fleshy hills.
For miles on end there is only stone, sand, the occasional white
temple on an outcrop of rock. The road feels rubbery in the
heat, telegraph poles the only uprights in the flat, pressing
blue.

At intervals you pass small villages, thatched huts and tin
shacks leading out like spokes of a wheel from a central hub,
empty except for a large tree and a well. In the shade of the
tree camels munch superciliously, certain here of their own
superiority over the assortment of horses and donkeys over-
taken en route.

Through Bhiwani, a blur of brass pots and pans, of stalls in
a bazaar blocked by bullock carts, and then at Loharu you
cross the single-line railway track that joins Rewari to Sadulpur
and passes through the rocky Aravallis. Branch lines continue
on into the heart of Rajasthan, to Ajmer and Jaipur, and on
the western extremity to Bikaner, the Headquarters of the
Camel Corps, but Pilani has no railway. Instead the road aims
itself like a sword through thorn trees and scrub, squares of
swaying brown millet ranged along oblongs of silken wheat.
Buffaloes, goats, sheep swim out of the haze, and then the
desert, with its shifting contours and glinting stone, takes over
again.

This is the entrance not only to Pilani, but to Shekhavati,
a bleak area of Rajasthan dotted with abandoned Rajput forts.
For the most part the forts have outlived their usefulness, but

the towns of the area, scattered on either side of the Aravallis, still retain the great mansions – *havelis* – that Marwari merchants built for their families between 1750 and 1930. The merchants have mainly departed for the cities, but, in varying states of repair or dilapidation, the family houses remain, their painted walls testimony to the habits, beliefs and mythology of the past.

The Birla *haveli*, built in 1864 when Ghanshyamdas's grandfather Shivnarain returned from Bombay with the first spoils of trading, is in better condition than many, inhabited by family retainers and acting in part as a museum. The ochre of its exterior walls, across which elephants parade and horses charge, has faded to a soft sepia. The Birla frescos mostly record traditional subjects, but others, especially the later ones among the score of *havelis* from Surajgarh in the north-east to Sri Madhopur in the south of Shekhavati, have many of the characteristics of Bengal company paintings. Thus, while in a Mukundgarh *haveli* of 1859 the elaborately decorated arches and lintels contain images of Krishna and Ganesha, a fresco in Chirawa, painted in 1929, illustrates Rajputs, Pathans and police in British-designed uniforms.

The inner and outer courtyards of the Birla *haveli*, part whitewashed under elaborately decorated balconies and brackets, contain scenes of merchant activity, as well as of military action and local flora and fauna. In Fatehpur, built twenty-five years later, the ceiling of the Nand Lal Devra *haveli* is encircled by gilded portraits of Mughal emperors and Europeans of both sexes, with lapdogs, bottles, smoking equipment and arms. In the Nagar Mal Somani *haveli* in Islampur richly accoutred camels and horses enact scenes from the Rajesthani tale of Dhola and Maru.

If elephants and camels outnumber other animals on *haveli* walls, some of the earliest *havelis* are rich in birds and mythical beasts. In others, at Mandawa for example, the emphasis is on Rajput military skills on horseback and on *shikar*. Wrestlers, acrobats, Rajputs at their daily ablutions, families taking the air in their carriages, railway trains and scenes from the Ramayana and the Mahabharata, Europeans courting and tailors and carpenters at work, British troops on parade with brass bands, and even a memsahib staring crossly at a horn gramophone, are other examples, ranging from the literal to caricature, of an art that began in India in the Ajanta caves of Maharashtra nearly 2000 years ago and which takes in the painted rock temples of Karnataka, the Hampi temples and palaces, the Orissa maths and the Mattancheri Palace at Cochin.

Outside the village walls the sand brushes like a tide up to the first huts. The sky shines like steel, now deepening, now shedding the last remnants of colour. Dust swirls over thorn bushes. There is nothing, beyond the glint of stone and the drab, canvas-coloured earth, to soothe the eye except the indigo saris and magenta skirts of working women and the wine-red and orange puggrees of the men swaying by on camel trains.

It was not surprising therefore that long-absent Marwari merchants should, as acts of compensation to their families for their neglect, have built these high-walled, fortress-like structures – embodiments of financial security and respectability – and having secured them against the elements and intruders, lavished such care and imagination on the decoration of their interlocking courtyards, their hanging balconies and archways, their walls and doorways.

As they have faded, so have many of the frescos taken on a melancholy beauty in keeping with the decline of their situations. It was the style of the *haveli* to turn its back on the desert and the street, glimpsed only through slits in the upper storeys, and to bathe in the light of private courtyards overlooked by interior verandas. Scarcely a *haveli* today is inhabited as a main residence by its original family – the Birla one is no exception – but neither time nor neglect can quite suppress the lyrical flights of fancy that make these painted walls of Shekhavati vivid reminders of the past. In the last light of day the colours glow, merchants and Mughals, gods and *gopis*, elephants and tigers, sahibs and saints, rehearsing once more the rituals that relate them to their era.

It is in keeping that the Birla *haveli*, the initial landmark and cornerstone of Birla prosperity and the birthplace of Ghanshyamdas, should – despite the proximity of elegant new Birla country properties – still give off an air of priority.

The decisive moment in the rise of the Birlas came when Ghanshyamdas's grandfather, Seth Shivnarain Birla, declined the offer of the position, previously held by his father, as accountant to a wealthy banking family, the Ganeriwalas, with a Head Office in Hyderabad. The post involved dealings with East India Company officials and factory owners in the cantonments of Ajmer and Mhow, and Shivnarain, only sixteen when his father died, must have been tempted by the prospect of financial security.

He chose instead to strike out on his own, an assertion of independence foreshadowing the many similar decisions to be taken later by his grandson. Bombay had been a centre of Marwari migration since 1800, followed shortly by Calcutta, in both places Marwaris acting as agents, contractors and bullion brokers.

It was to Bombay, in 1862, that Shivnarain made his way by camel. The nearest railway station at the time was Ahmedabad, itself a twenty-day journey by camel from Pilani. The country was rough and waterless and, though most people travelled in caravans rather than singly, there was constant danger of dacoits. The camel was always a favourite animal with Ghanshyamdas. "People these days do not look upon the prospect of a long journey by camel with any enthusiasm," he was later to write, "but the animal always fascinated me by its endurance, patience and stupidity."

Seven years went by before Shivnarain, lodging initially in the houses of already established Bombay Marwaris and dependent on their support, felt he could return with enough money to lay the foundations of a dignified *haveli*, to which in due course he would add a temple to Shiva and a well. Had Shivnarain stayed where he was, happy to accept the limited if comfortable prospects open to him as a clerk in a provincial concern, the history of the Birlas might have been very different.

By the time Ghanshyamdas was born in 1894 the Birlas had

become "affluent", to use the term G.D. himself used much later when describing his childhood in *Ve Din*. Marwaris, though coming on the business scene long after the Parsis and Gujaratis, had made up for lost time by successful speculation, especially in the opium and cotton markets. The alliance between the warrior Rajputs and the merchant Marwaris worked to their mutual advantage, the former providing security and the latter finance. Eventually, as a consequence of the Opium War in China, and trade restrictions imposed by the British, the Marwaris found themselves obliged to move out of Rajasthan and develop new outlets.

Shivnarain's first trading adventures had been in seed and bullion, enterprises in which his only son, Baldeodas, had joined him in 1875 at the age of thirteen. Marwaris, unlike the constantly feuding and disunited Rajputs, were sustained by the kind of family feeling common to Jews and Quakers, to the latter of whom G.D. liked to compare them. As a result of this instant support most Marwaris, instead of feeling alienated on arrival in the big cities, found themselves among friends, offered not only useful business contacts but also lodgings.

The Birlas, father and son, thrived, to an extent that, four years after the birth of G.D., an import–export branch was set up in Calcutta. Each return to Pilani over the intervening years resulted in extensions to the *haveli* but no relaxation of the austere disciplines that were characteristic of Marwaris. The day began at 5 a.m. with exercise and prayers and continued with religious rituals and readings; a routine that G.D. carried out to his dying day.

When Ghanshyamdas was born, on the auspicious Ramnavami – the birthday of the Hindu God Lord Rama – Pilani had only 3000 inhabitants and was known mainly for its huge banyan tree. There were two elder brothers, Jugal Kishore, born in 1881, and Rameshwardas, born in 1892.

During G.D.'s early years his family, though better housed and fed than the majority of villagers, lived in a manner scarcely distinguishable from the poorest. They had their own camels and cows but few household refinements. Neither

G.D.'s father, Baldeodas, nor grandfather, Shivnarain, were often at home, the small retail shop started by Shivnarain in Pilani as an alternative to accountancy soon being handed over to Baldeodas and then disposed of when Baldeodas joined his father in Bombay.

G.D., therefore, was left in the charge of women and to his own devices. He has described in *Ve Din* the main Pilani characters of those days: Swami Charandas, a temple mahant with medical and scholastic inclinations, the alms collector Kaniram Tola, the wrestler Qamaraddin Ilahi and his humiliation at the hands of the camel driver, Giglia, who had never wrestled before, the local witch Brajli.

Belief in witchcraft and ghosts was widespread, a Birla ancestor being rumoured to ride a white horse at night to protect the *haveli*.

Like most desert areas of Rajasthan, Pilani was dependent on heavy rainfall during the monsoon, but in 1899, when G.D. was five, there was drought on an unprecedented scale. The scene, with dead camels, bullocks, buffaloes and cows littering the landscape and whole families dying of starvation, was one that G.D. never forgot.

More relevant even to the future of the family was the Bombay plague of 1896 which decided Shivnarain and Baldeodas, conferring in Pilani at the height of the epidemic, to establish a branch in Calcutta. While G.D. was doing his first lessons at the local open air *pathshala*, his eldest brother Jugal Kishore was setting up the firm of Baldeodas Jugal-kishore, later to become Birla Brothers.

Such education as G.D. received was rudimentary. In the cool season classes were held in the market, in the hot weather in the shadow of a wall, and in the rainy season not at all. There were no books and lessons were confined to arithmetic and the alphabet. One day the teacher disappeared without warning, taking off, it was rumoured, with a local widow. The school closed down.

Eventually a white-bearded Rajput, Kan Singh, was found to replace him and classes continued in a room in the Birla *haveli*. Kan Singh knew no English, could scarcely read Hindi and was little more knowledgeable about mathematics than his pupils.

His successor, Ramvilas from Bhiwani, was half Kan Singh's age, and progressive in outlook. He introduced elementary English, largely for its commercial usefulness, and was able to discuss religious texts in the evening with Shivnarain. This worked to everyone's advantage and Ramvilas remained in Pilani to the end of his life.

Ghanshyamdas, however, was sent off at the age of nine to live with Jugal Kishore, now established in Calcutta. Jugal Kishore, absorbed in his own business affairs, rarely concerned himself with G.D.'s activities. Attendance at the Vishuddananda Saraswati School dwindled from the spasmodic to the nominal, G.D. setting off in the morning with his books and satchel and returning in the evening, having spent the whole day roaming about Calcutta. He soon knew the city as well as any rickshaw wallah.

This period of day-dream ended with recall to Bombay for a course in book-keeping, a private tutor being engaged to improve G.D.'s English. This attention to English among business families was uncommon at the time, particularly among Marwaris with traditional outlooks and religious backgrounds.

His course over, G.D. returned to Pilani and the intelligent supervision of Ramvilas. He began to take an interest in Hindi literature, but no sooner had he passed his lower primary examination than his father sent for him to start his apprenticeship in the business in Bombay. He was thirteen.

From now on, G.D.'s education was carried on after office hours. At Pilani he had begun to read for pleasure, acquiring at the same time a curiosity about the world that encouraged him to study languages, science, philosophy and religion on his own account. Aware that his own lack of formal education had proved no obstacle to success, G.D. later came to distrust the academic life pursued for its own sake. As a consequence of his own experience he urged, in the educational institutions he later founded at Pilani and elsewhere, that students of engineering and science combined theoretical work with periods in his own mills and factories.

In Bombay, while being instructed in family business methods, G.D. continued his self-education. Always preferring to learn on his own rather than be taught, he bought books, newspapers, and dictionaries, patiently improving his English and Sanskrit and learning history and geography through biographies and travel books. He was also, on one of his return visits to Pilani at the age of fourteen, married. His bride's name was Durgadeviji, and a year later their son Laxminiwas was born. Photographs taken at this time show G.D. elegant in a variety of outfits, ranging from kurtas and dhotis to business suits and riding breeches. A neat moustache gives him a faintly military air, making him look older than his years. G.D. from his boyhood had a chameleon-like ability to look the part and blend into his surroundings. Always appropriately turned out, he could within the space of hours change from the disciple of Gandhi to the successful broker, from the Marwari in native dress to the westernized magnate.

The Bombay business had begun to change its pattern, the declining trade in opium being replaced by forward trading in cotton, wheat, rape-seed and silver. G.D., because his English was better than that of either his father or his brother Rameshwardas, was made responsible for negotiations in gold and silver with such long-established brokers as Montagu and Sharp.

Not long after the birth of G.D.'s son his wife contracted tuberculosis. G.D. hurried back to Pilani but she died four months later. The son went to the maternal grandparents to be looked after and G.D. returned to a solitary life in Bombay.

The two Birla brothers were taken up by Chunilal, one of the most powerful bankers and businessmen in Bombay, who began to conduct his foreign transactions through their firm. Not content with having his own bank, however, Chunilal started gambling heavily on silver. The market collapsed, Chunilal and many others losing all their money. Chunilal, prosecuted by the government, won his case but committed suicide soon afterwards. Ghanshyamdas, though he was to launch many large-scale enterprises in his own career, learned enough from this brief but hectic period never to take unnecessary risks. One of the hallmarks of his future entrepreneurial style was that adequate funds should be available in advance for all likely contingencies.

With the death of his wife, followed closely by the Chunilal disaster, Bombay began to lose its charm for G.D. His reading was also taking him into areas outside business and domestic concerns. "The Russo-Japanese War [in 1904/5] had created a wave of enthusiasm among the Asiatic nations," G.D. wrote in his *In The Shadow of the Mahatma*, "and India did not escape this surge. As a child my sympathies were definitely with Japan, and the ambition of seeing India free began to excite me."

This early stirring of political interest was not regarded as conducive to business by the rest of the family, who had no history of such frivolous involvement. Nevertheless, by the time Ghanshyamdas, at the age of sixteen, left for Calcutta to join J.K., he was not only reading Marx and Tilak, but reassessing Marwari business methods and social concepts.

The British up to this time had been a spectral inheritance in G.D.'s imagination rather than an intrusive presence. But when, leaving his brother to his own highly profitable dealing with China and Japan, G.D. decided to start his own broking business, the situation rapidly changed. The British, who dealt only with approved buyers, saw no reason to accommodate an inexperienced Marwari, even one who quickly began to make handsome profits through the selling of textiles on the free market. The social slights he experienced brought home to G.D. that there was one rule for Europeans and another for most Indians. He admired British business methods, honesty and organizational capacities but not their racial arrogance. "I was not allowed to use the lift to go up to their offices," G.D. wrote, "nor their benches while waiting to see them. I smarted under these insults and this created within me a political interest."

These private frustrations, scarcely assuaged by rapidly escalating successes in business, almost led G.D. to disaster. He had, like most Marwaris starting up in the city, initially shared lodgings and business premises with others from his state, in G.D.'s case the Kali Godown in 18 Mullick Street, off Harrison Road. Facilities were virtually non-existent, whether for cooking or washing, and a single room served a variety of purposes. In 1911, in partnership with Prabhudayal Himatsingka, a young law student, and Ram Kumar Jalan, he extended this informal association by the founding of a club, the Bara Bazaar Youth League.

Marwaris had been the principal sufferers in the recent communal clashes, so that while the club was ostensibly sporting in character, one of its aims was to provide instruction in physical combat and the use of firearms. Meeting initially in Rankumar Rakhit Lane, the members instigated political discussions as well as setting up facilities for wrestling and rifle-shooting. G.D. took an active part in all aspects of the club's activities as well as providing financial support.

In March 1913 the Marwari Relief Society was founded, with premises in Cotton Street. Primarily a charitable organization devoted to social work, its leading members tended to be successful businessmen, among them his eldest brother Jugal Kishore. Since there were outlets for various forms of recreation, the club came to be patronized by Bengal revolutionaries like Bipin Ganjuli, eager to practise and instruct others in useful terroristic disciplines.

The Rajasthan Club, the name under which all these social, sporting, and political activities became combined, grew increasingly radical in character. Visiting political activists were invited to address them, among them Lokmaniya Tilak, who came to Bengal in 1916. The more established and conventional members preferred to abstain from involvement in these discussions but rousing oratory of the kind practised by Tilak had a heady effect on the younger ones.

Although G.D. was himself only twenty-two in 1916, his six years in business on his own had made him rich. The years of the 1914–18 war, in which Indians from the princely states and British India fought in their thousands in France and elsewhere, brought great profits to those who traded at home. In 1912 G.D. had been encouraged to re-marry, his second wife Mahadevi giving him two sons and three daughters, as well as selfless devotion, until her death in 1926.

This secure family background did not prevent G.D. from taking part in such political activity as was going. M. K. Gandhi, just returned from South Africa, had paid a visit to Calcutta in 1915 when G.D., among others from the Bara Bazaar Youth League, had fêted him, unyoking the horses from his carriage and themselves hauling him up to Bhupendra Nath Basu's house, where Gandhi was staying.

Gandhi's appearance and his apparent insignificance, compared to other leaders of the liberation movement, initially was disconcerting. His message of non-violence was also not one which, at that time, they wished to hear. But they listened, even if, their heads filled with Tilak's encouragement to action, they did not heed.

In 1916 G.D.'s daughter Chandrakala was born, but he was to see little of her for several months. One of Bipin Ganjuli's friends from the Rajasthan Club had taken advantage of his employment with Rodda & Co., the armament importers, to divert part of a consignment of arms. Two crates containing revolvers and cartridges were hidden in a warehouse prior to distribution when news came that the police had got wind of their disappearance.

The crates were moved from place to place, including at one stage to G.D.'s own house in Zakaria street. Realizing that there was no hope of saving them a friend of G.D.'s, Devi Dutt Saraf, dressed himself up as a coolie, put the crates on his head and dumped them in the Hooghly.

The police, unable to get their hands on the culprits, made up for their failure by wholesale arrests of suspects. Houses were searched and incriminating letters discovered. Among those who suffered were Prabhudayal Himatsingka, interned in Dumka for four years, and Phool Chand Chowdhury, sent to the Punjab for five years, both stalwarts of the Bara Bazaar Youth League.

Ghanshyamdas Birla was on the wanted list, but luckily, the day before the police came to search his rooms, he had left for a holiday in Ootacamund. Word was sent to him there that a warrant for his arrest had been issued.

G.D., therefore, went underground, making his way across country up to the edge of the Great Thar Desert in western Rajasthan. He spent weeks, dressed sometimes as a *saddhu*, in the Pushkar valleys, where the most sacred lake in India spills between steep rocks, and where camels still race in the great October *mela* for horses, camels and bullocks. Although Ghanshyamdas had never sought austerity for its own sake and was already established in a comfortable family house, his disciplined way of living, the principles and rituals instilled into him at an early age, made him peculiarly fitted for such an interlude.

During G.D.'s absence efforts were successfully made on his behalf to establish that his links with the revolutionaries had been more social than political, and that though he may have connived at terrorist activities he had never taken part. The warrant for his arrest was eventually withdrawn and he was free to return to Calcutta. The profits, during a period of immense inflation, had continued to accrue. Opium, silver, jute, gunny and latterly real estate dealings had increased the joint Birla assets in Bombay and Calcutta out of all recognition during the four years of war. What had been an assortment of individual firms in scattered unimpressive premises was, in 1918, amalgamated under the registered title of Birla Brothers.

The Birth of an Industrialist

In the same year, 1918, G. D. Birla, in association with his father-in-law Mahadeo Somani, made the important switch from trade to industry, setting up the first Indian-controlled jute mill. A steel plant had been set up in 1907 at Jamshedpur in West Bengal by J. N. Tata, the Parsi cotton millionaire, but none of the great Marwari merchant families had ever contemplated risking the fortunes made from broking by speculating in industrial ventures.

It is some evidence of the finance available to G.D. that he felt able to take this step, since in the short term industrial development offered none of the pickings that came from commodity broking. The Tatas had come near to ruin in the early days of Jamshedpur and few of the more established and orthodox Marwari firms gave G.D.'s enterprise encouragement. Nevertheless, it was this determination, at a ridiculously early age, to lay the foundations of an Indian industry that resulted, by the time Independence came thirty years later, in the Birlas being able to rival the Tatas for industrial supremacy.

It was not easy going. The impact of British rule, its draining of Indian wealth to support the British economy, was felt more in the villages than in the cities, but Indian industry had to cope with many handicaps, including lack of tariff protection. The benefits that derived from political stability, improved irrigation and the opening up of the country by rail were largely offset by a financial and legislative structure that inhibited Indians from exchanging a secondary role for an innovative one. The Birla jute mill was a case in point.

It was Marx who observed that "England has broken down the entire framework of Indian society" as well as that the

British intruder "broke up the Indian hand-loom and destroyed the spinning wheel". In a sense Marx might not have appreciated, G.D. would have agreed with both propositions and also have approved of them.

It was not only in late nineteenth-century India that heavy industry lagged behind consumer industries. The same situation occurred in Russia, Japan and Brazil. But though over half India's manufacturing revenue came from cotton, jute, food and tobacco, by the time the 1914–18 war had broken out India could not only meet the demand from the railways but export coal from the Bengal coalfields.

India's lack of chemical and electrical industries can be put down to subordination of Indian to imperial interests and foreign control of raw materials, but there is no doubt that until G. D. Birla began to think in different and more ambitious terms the inhibitions against heavy industry tended to be psychological and traditional. There was no lack of a potential labour force and problems created by the caste system were never crucial. The crucial factor was foreign investment.

The pattern of investment and employment in Bombay and Calcutta was totally different. At the time G.D. left for Calcutta to start up independently, nearly 100 of the 130 textile mills in the Bombay presidency were Indian owned, whereas in Calcutta, where jute rather than cotton was grown, almost every mill was foreign owned. It was in this near monopoly that G.D. had to make the first dent, and in a situation where European firms commanded managerial and technically skilled staff beyond the reach of any Indian competitor.

If imperial governments by their nature lack the sense of identity necessary to give a powerful stimulus to local industry and tend to operate cautiously within huge financial margins, individual European firms had no inhibitions in fending off competitors.

Andrew Yule, the largest managing agency in Calcutta at the time of G.D.'s proposed entry into mill ownership, was no exception. The company did its best to hinder Birla Brothers by gratuitously buying up land adjacent to plots already bought for the proposed mill, forcing the Birlas to go further south towards Budge-Budge. Here, on an idyllic curve of the Hooghly, with fishing boats tied up in the reeds, their nets taking on the brilliant green of the rice fields beyond, the first Birla jute mill came into operation.

As an experiment G.D. had bought a derelict cotton mill in Delhi a year earlier, more or less to train himself in industrial management. In Calcutta, where the stakes were in earnest, he found major obstacles. The exchange rate between the pound and the rupee was manipulated so as to make the cost of importing of new machinery prohibitive, and the Association of Mill Owners denied him, as an Indian, membership.

G.D., having successfully floated shares for an entirely Indian-owned jute and cotton business, found the Imperial Bank initially refusing to provide capital. When they were eventually prevailed upon to do so it was at a provocatively high rate of interest compared to that charged to British firms. Transport charges, too, especially for river traffic, were raised steeply, in a further attempt to dissuade Indian intrusion into what had been a British preserve.

G.D. was not deterred, and the family, sceptical beforehand, closed ranks behind him. Birla Jute got safely off the ground and the first step in redeeming earlier humiliations by the British had been taken. Henceforth, as far as business was concerned, G.D. would never need to deal as less than an equal.

Meanwhile, with the idea of modernizing his Delhi cotton mill, G.D. had ordered new textile machinery from England. While this was on its way G.D. chanced to meet the Maharajah of Gwalior at a fund-raising occasion, where each donated five lakhs of rupees, for the Hindu University at Benares. The meeting led to friendship and the proposal from the Maharajah that it might be to their mutual advantage if Birla Brothers could set up a textile mill in his state.

Despite the fact that raw cotton was not available anywhere near Gwalior and that climatic conditions were far from ideal for the working of a cotton mill, G.D. did not hesitate. The Maharajah offered to put up part of the money at normal interest rates and G.D. really arranged for the machinery destined for Delhi to be switched to Gwalior. On 9 August 1921 Jiyajeerao Cotton Mills Limited was incorporated and, after harvesting was completed on the selected ninety *bighas* of cultivated land, building was started. A year later the mills, Indian owned, managed and worked, went into production, eventually becoming one of the largest composite textile mills in the country.

It was in Gwalior that G.D. really put himself through the business of learning how to run a mill. He determined from the outset that he would come to know more about the techniques, mechanics and cost of production than any of those he employed. To this end he devoted himself to mastering the work of each department in turn, working long hours at even the most manual of tasks. It was this meticulous attention to details of cost accounting and production methods that characterized all his subsequent enterprises.

Numerous mills in different ownerships were established outside Bombay and round Ahmedabad, but, despite the encouragement to buy Indian, retailers preferred imported cloth, made from Indian-grown cotton, to the home-produced variety. While Jiyajeerao began to show steady profits a number of Bombay factories went to the wall.

A Romantic Attachment

"Such connection as I have had with politics is in the economic field," G.D. wrote, "but I sought to prevent the growing distrust in India entertained of Gandhiji's high motives and the passionate distrust which Indians felt in regard not merely to the English in India but towards British statesmen and the British Parliament."

When G.D. first met the Mahatma in 1915 he was twenty-one, a successful Marwari broker with a romantic attachment to the cause of Indian independence. By the time their correspondence began in 1924 the broker had become a leading member of the Calcutta business community, the proprietor of jute and cotton mills, and a member of the 1921–2 Fiscal Commission. He was already rich enough to have given considerable sums to social, educational and religious institutions, and to have aligned himself with nationalist leaders, convinced that Indian industry and commerce could only thrive ultimately in a free India.

S. R. Das, later to become Chief Justice of India, described a meeting with G.D. at that time. Das was acting as a junior in the case the Birlas brought against the Zamindars of Mauza Pujali who, under harassment from Andrew Yule & Co., had reneged on an agreement over the purchase of land for the mill at Budge-Budge.

He was a very slim young man of my age. He was dressed in what I gathered later was the usual evening dress for the Birlas, namely, a fresh dhoti, a well-pressed silk punjabi, and a black sleeveless woollen jacket which was then known as a Jawahar coat. He was wearing a pair of chappals. He was very soft spoken and courteous. . . . He had an impressive face which one could not overlook even in a big gathering of men.

It was, curiously enough, G.D.'s difficulties within his own community that led to the start of his correspondence with the Mahatma. The Birlas, as a result of their progressive views on such matters as the remarriage of widows, the veil, and the dowry system, were being ostracized by more orthodox Marwaris. It was to Gandhi that G.D., more in hope than expectation, turned for advice.

The correspondence thus initiated runs to four volumes, each of nearly 500 pages, and was published in 1977 under the title of *Bapu: A Unique Association*. It is, even so, far from being a complete record of Gandhi's letters to G.D. and G.D. kept few copies of his own part of the correspondence. Sometimes the letters are a direct exchange between Gandhi and G.D., on other occasions Gandhi answered through his secretaries Mahadev Desai and, on Desai's death in 1942, Pyarelal Nayar, G.D. addressing his letters to them equally. The published volumes also contain a number of letters to and from successive viceroys and other public figures. The last letter is dated 30 October 1947, three months before Gandhi's assassination in G.D.'s house in Delhi.

There are few important events of these twenty-three years which could not be discussed in terms of these letters, even though there are gaps, either because the two were together, or, as in 1931 and between 1942 and 1944, Gandhi was in gaol.

While the Birlas had been progressing from the simple Pilani family that Shivnarain had left on camel-back for Bombay, to become, a mere half century later, wealthy enough for G.D. to be a financial mainstay to Gandhi and the Indian nationalist movement, events had conspired to draw a few Indian business leaders much closer to political activists than might otherwise have been the case.

The Indian National Congress, launched by A. O. Hume, a domineering but dynamic retired East India Company official, in 1885, had in its earlier years been modest in its aspirations, concerned mainly with passing annual resolutions dealing with political, administrative and economic grievances. Greater powers were also demanded for central and state legislative bodies, political rights being requested, in Gokhale's presidential address of 1905, merely for those considered to be educationally qualified.

What Congress in its first twenty years essentially stood for was greater Indianization of the Civil Service and Army as a means of increasing racial equality. Hume had left for England in 1892, disappointed at the general lack of progress and at his failure to persuade Muslims and the peasantry into active co-operation. In England Hume continued to campaign through the British Committee's journal *India* but Congress itself was in decline. In 1900 Curzon, always hostile, announced "The Congress is tottering to its fall, and one of my great ambitions, while in India, is to assist its peaceful demise."

It was Curzon himself who unwittingly revived Indian nationalism by his largely unpublicized decision, in 1905, to partition Bengal. The idea may have originated in administrative convenience but most educated Bengalis felt both suspicious of the motives and insulted. The result was an increase in militancy, including isolated acts of terrorism, a boycott of British goods, and a resurgence of intellectual patriotism. Rabindranath Tagore, who later was to be a beneficiary of G.D.'s financial support, initially provided stimulus and inspiration but as his moderating influence faded, so too did his own involvement in a cause – the removal of the British from Bengal – for which he had little stomach.

While G.D. was moving between Calcutta and Bombay, a child in years but already learning the business, extremist movements were losing their impetus elsewhere, in the Punjab especially. The deporting from the Punjab in 1907 of Lala Lajpat Rai, destined to become one of the two or three most powerful influences on G.D., effectively muffled them.

A year earlier the All-India Muslim League had been founded, its objectives the representation and advancement of political rights for Muslims. In December 1907 the Indian

35

National Congress, meeting at Surat, split, the extremists, led by Tilak, Lala Lajpat Rai, and Bipin Chandra Pal, seceding after their advocacy of extending the boycott had been defeated by the moderates under Gokhale.

By the time G.D. had returned to Calcutta to start his own jute and gunny-broking business, revolutionary terrorism in Bengal was back in full swing. *Swadeshi* dacoities to raise funds and the random assassination of traitors and officials were monthly occurrences, the outbreak of the 1914–18 war, with British troops in India reduced to 15,000, offering an opportunity for disruption on an unprecedented scale. German and Turkish military and financial help for the revolutionary movement was promised but never materialized. More important, the Indian nationalist leaders, allowed back in Congress in 1915, decided in favour of supporting the British war effort. The Defence of India Act, which resulted in the rounding up of political suspects and imprisonment without trial, finally removed the last threats of a *coup d'état*.

When Gandhi returned from South Africa in 1915, his fame, as a result of his successful *satyagraha* – or civil disobedience – activities on behalf of Indians there, had preceded him. He, too, supported the British war effort, on the assumption that the price for Indian co-operation was political reform. A year later, the Muslim League and Congress, meeting separately at Lucknow, attempted to resolve their differences by demanding eventual dominion status for India, Congress allowing the principle of a separate electorate for Muslims, and both parties agreeing on the distribution of seats.

While the Birla brothers, individually and then jointly, were making fortunes in Calcutta, Gandhi was establishing his ashram at Ahmedabad and taking up workers' causes. His vigilance was social rather than political. He successfully intervened on behalf of the indigo workers at Champaran and the textile workers at Ahmedabad, in the latter case by a fast which resulted, on its fourth day, in mill-owners accepting a 35 per cent wage increase.

In 1919, the war over, the Government of India Act, based on the recommendations of Edwin Montagu, the Secretary of

State, and Lord Chelmsford, the Viceroy, came into effect. Montagu had declared in the House of Commons on 20 August 1917, that British policy would be directed at "the gradual development of self-governing institutions, with a view to the progressive realisation of responsible government in India as an integral part of the British Empire". Regarded at the time as a statement of generous intent, promising India a broader electorate and Indians a substantially greater say in their own affairs, the Act by the time of its passing appeared less of a radical departure than had been envisaged. In any case, whatever merits it had, were swiftly obscured by the hasty processing of the Rowlatt Report into a Bill in March 1919. The terms of this, which were never in fact applied, allowed for detention without trial and roused universal opposition among both Hindus and Moslems.

Gandhi's immediate and successful organization of a country-wide *hartal* and his close workings with prominent Muslims to co-ordinate peaceful but practical protest were followed brutally soon by the massacre at Jallianwalla Bagh. This took place on 13 April, an unarmed crowd of country people congregating in Amritsar for a fair and ignorant of the ban on meetings being gunned down on the orders of General Dyer. Over 400 were killed.

Gandhi, though unwell at the time, had been on his way to the Punjab by train when he was served with a written order outside Palwal station prohibiting him from crossing the state boundary. Declining to leave the train voluntarily he was taken off and put into police custody.

News of Gandhi's arrest caused crowd disturbances throughout the country, especially in Bombay, to which station Gandhi was returned and then released.

It was now, in the wake of martial law and the violent repression that followed the civil disobedience – *satyagraha* – that he had set in motion, that Gandhi began to have second thoughts. "A Satyagrahi obeys the laws of society intelligently and of his own free will, because he considers it to be his sacred duty to do so," Gandhi wrote in his autobiography,

It is only when a person has thus obeyed the laws of society scrupulously that he is in a position to judge as to which particular rules are good and just and which unjust and iniquitous. Only then does the right accrue to him to the civil disobedience of certain laws in well defined circumstances. My error lay in my failure to observe this necessary limitation ... I realized that before a people could be fit for offering civil disobedience they should thoroughly understand its deeper implications.

It was to educate the people in the implications that Gandhi founded a corps of volunteers, issued leaflets and spoke at meetings all over India. His calls for non-violence, however, were no more heeded by his followers than were his pleas to the Government for mercy. Disappointed, Gandhi went on a penitential fast, at the same time suspending *satyagraha* "as people had not learnt the lesson of peace". The clinching factor for Gandhi had been the burning alive of twenty-two policemen by *satyagrahi* peasants, fired on during a procession at Chauri Chaura, in Uttar Pradesh. The sudden halting of a movement that was on the verge of creating anarchy caused dismay among the imprisoned Congress leaders, though they mostly came round to Gandhi's view that the time had not been ripe.

As Gandhi ruefully observed, he was blamed for events in the Punjab by the Governor, Sir Michael O'Dwyer, and Punjab activists equally, the latter asserting that it was the suspension of civil disobedience that had resulted in martial law and the Jallianwalla Bagh killings.

The humiliations inflicted on Indians as a result of what happened at Amritsar, for which no government apologies were forthcoming, totally changed Gandhi's attitude towards the British. "When a Government takes up arms against its unarmed subjects, then it has forfeited its right to govern." He called now for the removal of the British and complete self-government for India.

The Indian National Congress, which had only marginally been involved in the political activities of the previous months, had held special sessions at Calcutta and Nagpur in the autumn of 1920. Gandhi, imposing his own views on non-co-operation and meticulously drafting a revised constitution, ensured that henceforth Congress participation would be central to any debate about the future of India.

The boycott of foreign cloth and the burning of imported cloth were the first steps in more aggressive moves against British rule. At the same time Indians were encouraged to produce khadi by hand-spinning and hand-weaving at home.

As the movement spread, so did the leadership advocate stronger measures against the British, including non-payment of taxes. One by one the leaders were arrested and within a year only Gandhi was not in gaol.

His turn came on 10 March 1922, when he was arrested on a charge of sedition, based on three articles he had contributed to *Young India*. The trial at Ahmedabad was courteously conducted. Gandhi, pleading guilty, made things easy by inviting for himself the highest penalty, "for what in law is a deliberate crime, and what appears to me to be the highest duty of a citizen". He received six years, a sentence the Judge, C. N. Broomsfield, proposed with reluctance and with the hope that circumstances would soon allow it to be reduced. In fact, Gandhi, after being operated on for appendicitis, was released on 5 February 1924, having served under two years. The first letter in *Bapu*, from Gandhi to G.D., is dated 7 February 1924.

How closely the political developments of the previous years had involved G.D. is not clear. He never wrote about the wartime period or discussed it in public. Having returned from his enforced absence over the Rodda & Co. arms affair in 1916 it is safe to assume that his business activities kept him fully occupied. Political unrest, strikes and sabotage were as much hindrance to him as a mill-owner and trader as they were to the authorities. Yet the earliest letters that G.D. exchanged with the Mahatma reveal a keen awareness of the nature of the political struggle that was going on, if no great concern with the details. Gandhi was no stranger by then to prison and G.D., though he admitted many disagreements with Gandhi, confessed that "always there was the belief that he must somehow be right in a sense that I could not grasp". Gandhi's relationship to Congress, his reaction to events in the Punjab, his advocacy of civil disobedience and then its suspension, must therefore have closely been studied by G.D. in Calcutta. It was, though, always Gandhi as a religious character, "his sincerity and search for truth" – that attracted Birla, not his power as a political leader. In politics Gandhi played a more ambiguous and sophisticated game.

Early Letters

It was in no mood for reconciliation or to practise Gandhian *ahimsa* that G.D. had described to Gandhi the behaviour of the Marwari community towards his own family. He got a typical reply, "when both parties are in the wrong it becomes difficult to decide how much one is to blame more than the other. I have therefore thought out a simple plan – to do good even to the evil doer." However disconcerting such quixotic views might have been to a young Marwari aggrieved over communal bigotry, they were consistently held and acted upon by Gandhi, even to the extent of advocating, on the eve of Independence, that a Muslim should be made Prime Minister of India.

The contents for 1924 in *Bapu: A Unique Association* show eleven letters from Gandhi to G.D., and one from G.D. to Gandhi. On 21 April Gandhi is already writing "Bhai Ghanshyamdas, Your letters are pouring in." In the next paragraph he observes, "I hold the Hindus alone responsible for these continuing attacks on Hindu women. The Hindus have grown so unmanly that they are not able to defend the honour of our sisters. I am going to write a lot on this subject." On 13 May, writing from Juhu, outside Bombay, Gandhi is acknowledging the receipt of 5000 rupees, at the same time expressing anxiety about differing attitudes to the Marwari problem among members of G.D.'s own family.

Ten days later Gandhi is writing from Birla House, Pilani, "even if we fail to realize the objective, we must not abandon the path of non-violence". G.D., in one of the longest and most carefully thought-out of his earlier letters, answers him on 11 June, now himself in Pilani, "You might have gathered from this letter that I have come to my native place in Rajputana.

I am sure you already know that this area excels in the production of quality Khadi. This is not due to the non-co-operation movement; this has been the case from years earlier."

G.D. goes on to express wry pleasure at Gandhi's reduced support from those he considered unsuitable followers and at the hostility towards him among Arya Samajists and Swara-jists.

At the Sirajganj Conference the Swarajists have openly declared themselves in favour of violence and have thereby torn the mask of non-violence off their faces. . . . It is quite probable you are reduced to a minority but the work will from now on be marked by purity of conduct which will release an amount of strength to the cause.

Despite G.D.'s allegiance to the concept of non-violence in Gandhi's presence, he confesses that when he is away from him doubts return. "Supposing somebody kills another for the good of society, will that be an act of violence? We are told through dramatised allegory that an act done without passion falls in the category of inaction."

G.D. next takes up Muslim history to demonstrate that it is possible to proselytize forcibly. "Why not try for unity and love after increasing the strength of the Hindus . . . ever since the Hindu Maha Sabha and the Arya Samajists have exhorted the people to use the sword the saner elements have begun to have second thoughts about launching an attack."

G.D.'s changes of tack and expression of misgivings give way finally to more practical comments on Gandhi's philosophy. "You told me that reforms enforced through brute force are never lasting. But look at the much-hated *suttee* practice, which was put an end to through recourse to law by the British."

He observes that, with regard to the policy of spreading Khadi and boycotting foreign cloth, brute force is merely another name for protective tariff.

G.D. ends

I wish to make it perfectly clear, however, that I do not at all like the cult of violence. On the other hand I like the creed of non-violence. But at the same time I begin to wonder if this love for non-violence is not, after all, due to laziness on my part. Please enlighten me. . . . This I am writing only in order to resolve my own doubts.

The letter is signed, "Yours affectionately, Ghanshyamdas". Gandhi replied on 20 June.

We should remain non-violent and unmindful of whether we succeed or fail in our undertaking. This is the only natural way of explaining the principle of non-violence. . . . Those who were forcibly converted to Islam, say two hundred years ago, cannot be a source of strength. . . . What happens is we are misled by results; in a large society two hundred years are a mere nothing.

G.D. made more detailed critical comments in his next letter, to which, on 20 July, Gandhi replied,

God has given me mentors and I regard you as one of them. They all wish me to become a perfect man.
   You complain about three things: First, my absolving the Swarajya Party from the charge of aspiring to office; second, my granting a testimonial to Suhrawardy; and third, my endeavouring to secure the Congress Presidentship for Sarojini [Naidu].

Having dealt with these matters openly and briskly Gandhi signs off "Keep good health and I will get a lot of work out of you; also give you some. Take milk for at least fifteen days if you like. Take fruit, but not bread. Make it a rule to take butter-milk."

The mixture of homily, discussion of abstract principles and morality in relation to current events, and dietary recommendations runs through the whole correspondence. There is no letter on either side, no matter the degree of conflict expressed within, that does not end with some homely recommendation or expression of affection.

That such a measure of trust and intimacy as even the earliest letters show should have been so rapidly achieved is remarkable. What is plain is that, though each had much to gain from the other, their instinctive liking for each other quickly put the relationship on to a natural and informal footing. If G.D. wrote to Gandhi as to a spiritual father he was none the less determined to get specific answers to specific questions on more mundane matters. There was never any false reverence or solemnity in his address. Gandhi, for his part, found letters a useful way of refining his thoughts on particular problems, and G.D., apart from producing large sums of money on request, provided ample opportunities. Perhaps, more than anything, what kept them close was an informality of nature, a shared quickness of response and a sense of humour.

On the question of G.D.'s reservations about Sarojini Naidu for the Congress Presidentship Gandhi observed, "I do not regard her as an ideal specimen of Indian womanhood, but she certainly proved to be an ideal unofficial ambassador for goodwill work in foreign countries. While saying this I freely admit that I only care for good qualities in people; I prefer to ignore their shortcomings." It was Sarojini Naidu who was to observe later, "It takes all Birla's millions to enable Gandhi to live in poverty."

There were a number of Hindu–Muslim riots that cold weather which a twenty-one-day fast by Gandhi in Delhi scarcely affected. Gandhi, as usual, took up the Muslim case more than was thought politic by other Hindu leaders, at the same time asking G.D. for a donation to help out the Muslim University at Aligarh. The sum mentioned was 50,000 rupees, and it seems that G.D., rather than discuss a joint contribution with his brothers, produced the money himself, anonymously.

The year 1925 produced at least twenty-five letters from Gandhi to G.D. The subjects touched on range from Hindu–Muslim relations to G.D.'s progress in spinning on a special portable *charkha* Gandhi had ordered for him. "Your yarn is quite good. Having started this sacred work never think of giving it up."

G.D.'s second wife, Mahadevi, had been ill for some time and in the same letter Gandhi, who had a facility for switching from one topic to another without preamble, observed:

44

As for your wife, I would suggest your taking a vow that after her passing away you would not marry again. If you have the inner strength to take this vow, I would suggest your doing so in front of your wife. About the matter of Rs 20,000 I shall enquire at Jamnalalji's office.

Shortly after this Mahadevi Birla died, but not without a touching farewell visit from the Mahatma, about whom she had heard so much but never met. Gandhi, passing through Delhi by train, broke his journey on a bitterly cold morning and drove with G.D. to Okhla, a retreat 15 miles away, where Mahadevi had been taken to spend her last days. They arrived at dawn. Gandhi paid his respects to the dying woman, prayed with her, and left immediately to make his connection. Whatever vows G.D. did or did not make he never remarried, though only thirty-two at the time. He confided to a friend in the last year of his life that from the day Mahadeviji died he never gave another woman a thought. Desire ended with the loss of her.

On 13 April, writing from Bombay after another fast, Gandhi rebukes G.D. for not dating his letters, at the same time lauding the benefits of sexual restraint.

How can I forget my own experience? There are means of attaining the state of absolute detachment and the name of Rajaram is one of them. Chanting Ram Nam in the morning and praying to Him to bless one with the state of absolute detachment certainly bring His blessing – to some today and to others tomorrow.

By July the subject had turned to cow protection, Gandhi floating the suggestion that G.D. should take over a moribund tannery with liabilities of 120,000 rupees and run it on idealistic lines, using only the hides of dead animals. In the same letter he asks G.D. to donate "a handsome amount" to the All-India Spinners Association.

In 1925 Gandhi roused in G.D. an interest, later to bear fruit, in the Harijan question. On 3 January 1926, Gandhi acknowledges receipt of 10,000 rupees, "I shall utilise this money in the service of the depressed classes."

During 1926 Gandhi wrote about one letter every two weeks to G.D. The latter was evidently put out by a reference by Gandhi to the business community. "You should not have felt piqued," Gandhi wrote in an undated letter,

> by some such expression as "the Marwari rate of interest". I had made it jocularly. Take my own case. The word "Kathiawari" is used in a derogatory sense, but I swallow it. The description "Kathiawari" generally stands for someone considered an idler. But that does not mean I am one. I would not dream of using the word in a derogatory sense even in a lighter vein. I would like to add for your information that in Gujarat also there is no dearth of incompetent and heartless Shylocks. Whether the Marwaris are good or bad, your only concern should be to be good in body as you are already at heart and to consign the description "Marwari" to the sacred flames of India's sacrificial fire.

In a subsequent letter Gandhi, somewhat unconvincingly, attributed allegedly unfriendly comments by him about Marwaris in the newspapers to inaccurate reporting. "What I require from Marwaris," Gandhi wrote to G.D., "is not only their wealth but their mind also." Be that as it may, G.D. had not been disposed to take over the tannery nor, for once, to make a donation on request. "I never have any expectation from friends that they should agree to my proposals every time," Gandhi concluded meekly.

On 16 April Gandhi returned to the Hindu–Muslim situation, acknowledging at the same time a cheque for 26,000 rupees. In a long confidential letter from his Sabarmati Ashram Gandhi admits regretfully that "my voice does not count with the Hindu public, or at least that section of it which takes part in such disturbances. Therefore, what I say has the opposite effect. Thus my duty lies only in holding my peace."

Nevertheless, after discussing such matters as the banning of religious processions and the employment of Muslims, Gandhi exhorts G.D. to "take a detached view" of apparent govern-

46

ment favouritism towards Muslims. "I was very pleased with the calm, collected manner in which you worked during the riots. Now you should do all that you have to do with the same amount of calmness."

Not surprisingly, G.D. was often puzzled by the conflicting nature of Gandhi's views, urging Hindus to act non-violently one minute, and the next to acquire superior strength for fighting. Similarly, the didactic moralizing tone was not always helpful in answer to requests for advice on specific courses of action. "I was not perturbed by the Calcutta riots," Gandhi wrote.

> I have already said that if the Hindus are bent upon fighting, then, instead of finding fault with it as a symptom of cruelty, we should treat it as a virtue and augment it. This is what seems to have happened in Calcutta. You maintained an attitude of neutrality and the Marwari community saved the lives of nearly three hundred Muslims. That is something for the entire Hindu community to be proud of. Your pledge to wear khaddar deserves my thanks.

In that year G.D. declined a knighthood, an action that earned Gandhi's approval. "This I liked very much indeed. This refusal to accept a title does not mean that we treat the Government as our enemy, nor that titles are bad in themselves, though I for one consider them essentially bad in our present condition." Rabindranath Tagore, knighted in 1915, the year he met Gandhi, had returned his title four years later in protest at General Dyer's actions in Amritsar.

In 1926 G.D. decided to stand as a candidate for the legislature, a step encouraged by Pandit Madan Mohan Malaviya, but not by Gandhi, who was already in conflict with Malaviya over the Harijan question.

Malaviya had meant almost as much to G.D. in his younger days as Gandhi came to mean subsequently. Thirty-three years older than G.D., Malaviya was an orthodox Brahmin who had joined the Indian National Congress in Calcutta in 1886. He had worked successively as a government school teacher in Allahabad and as a newspaper editor. An advocate equally of the Swadeshi movement and of support for the British war effort, Malaviya opposed Gandhi's subsequent non-co-operation movement. On the eve of the 1926 election Malaviya, unable to agree with a resolution moved by Motilal Nehru at the previous session of Congress, formed a breakaway Independent Party.

It was as a member of this Independent Party that G. D. Birla contested and won the election for the Banaras-Gorakhpur constituency, standing against Motilal Nehru's rival candidate.

Gandhi wrote to G.D.:

Whenever there is a difference of opinion between pujya Malaviyaji and myself I find myself on the horns of a dilemma because I respect him so much. But I can say with confidence that it is not for you at least to enter the Council. . . . If you secure a majority of votes, go ahead. It does not look nice to leave the road halfway. Ultimately you will have to leave it. . . . I do not relish the contest you have entered into.

In a letter that got mislaid Gandhi explained to G.D. that Motilal Nehru and the Swarajya Party were "nearer to my way of thinking" than the Independent Party "responsivist" policies advocated by Malaviya and Lala Lajpat Rai, which combined political moderation with uninhibited Hindu communalism.

As early as 1923 Lala Lajpat Rai, an impulsive and short-tempered man, had written to G.D.:

I have been very anxious to meet you ever since I came out of jail. . . . I wish to discuss with you the problem of Hindu Unity and how to reclaim the Hindu untouchables . . . I am of the opinion that the present is the time for quick decisions and prompt action if we want the Hindu community to be saved from ambitious and enterprising enemies.

In the same letter Lajpat Rai observed about their "revered" leader Pandit Madan Mohan Malaviya, "I love him, I respect

The Family. G.D. is on the left of his mother.

1906. G.D. with his younger brother Brijmohan.

In business. G.D. and his brother Rameshwardas.

वंतलाल गांधी
हरिपुरा
१९१४

G.D. aged eighteen. He rode horses and camels with equal pleasure.

Leaving for London and the second Round Table Conference.

The London office.

Walking with Gandhi; early days in India.

1931. Gandhi and G.D. in London.

him, but what I regret in him is his dilatoriness in coming to decisions and in taking action."

In a letter of 28 March 1923 Gandhi had written to G.D., "If I could bring about a rapprochement between the two factions, i.e. Motilalji's and Malaviyaji's, I would spare no pains. But just now this seems beyond my capacity."

Europe and the Death of
Lajpat Rai

In 1927 G.D. decided to spend some months in Europe, encouraging Gandhi to accompany him. Gandhi did not wish to go himself nor did he favour the idea of G.D. going, particularly as a delegate to the International Labour Conference in Geneva.

> About Geneva my opinion is this. I fail to see any great advantage issuing from your visit. If you think it necessary to gain some experience of Europe then go there independently. My inner voice tells me the present is not the moment for it.

As over the question of entering politics G.D. did not heed the Mahatma's inner voice. Nevertheless Gandhi was generous with suggestions once the decision was made. Acknowledging, in a letter dated 16 March 1927, the receipt of a cheque for spinning activities and commenting favourably on Malaviya's growing interest in the *charka* and contributions from G.D.'s brothers Jugal Kishore and Rameshwardas for wells for untouchables, Gandhi continues, "I consider the following rules necessary for maintaining good health while in foreign countries." There follow eleven points of conduct, mostly based on eccentric ideas of English convention. For some unspecified reason Gandhi had the impression that there "people eat six or seven times", even at one o'clock in the night. He counsels G.D. not to take unfamiliar food, to confine himself to three meals a day, and to refrain from eating chocolate and drinking tea between meals. No food is to be taken after eight in the evening, and six miles should be walked every day. European dress was not necessary, the *Gita* and *Ramayana* should be read daily, and mental debauch avoided. "Very few Indians escape this fate . . . for us, it becomes a sort of addiction like wine-bibbing."

Gandhi advised in such detail, he says, "because I have great faith in the goodness of yourself and all your brothers. Rich people like you can be easily counted on one's fingers – you are so gentle, so humble. I want these two virtues to multiply in your case in order to use them for the good of the country."

Gandhi soon began to reconsider the possibility of going to Europe, expressing a wish to meet the French writer, and his own biographer, Romain Rolland. However, he was taken ill on tour in Belgium and the idea was dropped. From Nandi Durg in April he wrote to G.D.,

> You must see the Secretary of State and the Prime Minister with whom you can discuss anything under the sky. You must make a point to visit the jails there, and to acquaint yourself with the living conditions of the lower class people there. . . . Station yourself near the bars in poor as also prosperous localities on Saturday nights for making comparative study.

On 31 May Gandhi wrote again to G.D. from the Nandi Hills. In his letter he discussed matters relating to Malaviya's and his own health, and then turned to G.D.'s.

> I have a suggestion to make for your health. If you have no faith, as indeed you should not, in allopathy, you may go and see the institutions of Louis Kuhne and Just in Germany. The treatment of patients there consists of open air and water. . . . You may also contact the two vegetarian societies at London and Manchester respectively. In these societies there are always some sober, courteous and balanced people; but you will also come across some stupid and vain persons.

G.D.'s first trip outside India was recorded by him in an impressionistic journal, in which his comments show him, in relation to the compulsive and seasoned traveller he was later to become, as something of an innocent. On board ship he puzzled over what made European society appear free, independent and affluent compared to his own backward, ignorant and politically dependent nation.

As the ship approached Europe so did he find the barriers between British and Indians gradually collapsing. He was initially put out by the sight of short-haired women smoking in public, consuming alcohol like water, and dancing till the early hours. "I feel this community is on the verge of destruction." Yet to G.D.'s puzzlement, believing virtue ultimately to prevail, these unvirtuous people had conquered the world and become great. How had they done it?

His conclusion was that, despite their self-indulgence and hedonistic way of life, British men and women were motivated by a patriotic sense that in times of crisis enabled them to sacrifice everything, including their lives, for what they considered noble causes. Indians, on the other hand, disguised cowardliness by calling it forgivingness, were subservient to the powerful and exploited the weak. The comparative analysis of Indian and British characteristics that G.D. had begun in a spirit of superiority had, by the time of his arrival in Marseilles, concluded on a significantly humbler note.

He continued to worry over the incongruity of a nation with so great a philosophical, religious and artistic heritage being reduced to a state of such poverty, dependency and unhappiness. A letter received en route from an "elderly and respected" Indian leader which put the cause of India's distress down to their religion confused him further; "people are enslaved and lead a miserable existence because our preachers have no ambitions or zest for life. Even Gandhiji emphasizes self-sacrifice and renunciation of material things. Sometimes I feel that we must strip away this tendency towards self-sacrifice and ask more of life."

G.D. remained reluctant to abandon his identification with Gandhian principles. In any case, he argued to himself, very few Indians lived religious lives, so it would be wrong to blame these principles for India's decline.

We are alien to the concept of a nation, self-rule, public duty, and public welfare. We hero-worship Shivaji, Rana Pratap and others not because of their struggle for political freedom but because they protected our religion from Muslim invaders. Even now, our people lack any ardent desire for freedom and independence as a nation.

The great cities of Europe – Marseilles, Paris, London – did not immediately impress G.D., but the lush green fields on either side of the train on the way to Geneva, the rich orchards and healthy cattle, the abundance of water, made him think sadly of the Rajasthan peasant and the plight of the poor Indian farmer.

G.D., thinking about Lala Lajpat Rai travelling to Geneva a year earlier for his health, remembers the Punjabi leader saying to him, in reply to G.D.'s view that patriotic self-sacrifice was what India most lacked, "As far as I am concerned there are only two truly good men in India, Mahatma Gandhi and Madan Mohan Malaviyaji."

G.D. admired Geneva, its freshness of air and situation, finding it even better than Darjeeling, his only point of comparison. He felt hungry all the time and was delighted with the pure taste of the milk and water.

His party went by air from Geneva to London, a flight taking eight hours during which time most of them were sick. G.D. chanted Ram Nam to himself and felt nothing worse than "a slight reeling of the brain".

In London he felt the city to be like a huge tree-nest, with strict rules of behaviour. The fact that this smoke-engulfed and foggy city had been at the heart of world domination, both political and economic, made him wary of it. The British appeared to him to be obsessed with their own social activities and totally indifferent to India and its problems. He contrasts the economical way in which government operates in England "because the government is answerable to the people through their representatives in Parliament", with the extravagance of political life in Delhi, where British officers are paid handsome salaries and given palatial houses to live in at the Indian tax-payers' expense.

G.D. ended his European tour with a visit to Berlin, which he found cleaner and more attractive than either London or Paris. He liked the wide, tree-lined roads which curiously he compared with Calcutta's Chowringee. No palace he saw in Europe compared with those of Indian maharajahs, a matter of shame, he felt, for India, because maharajahs lavished money without thought of their subjects, whereas in Europe even kings were answerable to the exchequer.

There is something engagingly vulnerable about G.D.'s comments on this first spreading of his wings. His apparently simplistic comparisons between India and Europe often raise awkward truths. He was only thirty-three and this was almost the first occasion since his months on the run during the Rodda enquiry that he had enough leisure to distance himself from routine problems.

During his stay in Europe G.D. wrote regularly to Gandhi about his experiences. "You have done well in sending me your opinion on different subjects," Gandhi observed in a letter dated 1 October, adding, "It is not true that non-cooperation is responsible for the division of public opinion into two distinct camps. There have always been two camps and what has just taken place is only a difference in form. The Hindu–Muslim question is proving another obstacle in the way."

The letter ends:

My thirst for money is simply unquenchable. I need at least 200,000 rupees for Khadi, untouchability and education. The dairy work makes another 50,000. Then there is the Ashram expenditure. No work remains unfinished for want of funds but God gives after severe trials . . . You can give me as much as you like for whatever work you have faith in.

G.D., now at his father's house in Benares, replied ten days later that he hoped to be able to give between 50,000 and 100,000 rupees during the next year.

Whenever you find any particular kind of work impeded for lack of funds, you have only to write to me. Even as it is I shall be sending money. I can give more, but for the present I have interested myself in several schemes which I consider good for the country. That is the reason for this comparative economy.

In January 1928, G.D. made a donation of 78,000 rupees for general purposes.

I leave the matter entirely to the discretion of the Mahatmaji. If he is not pressed for money I would suggest that preference be given to such schemes as may bring Swaraj nearer. Hindu –Muslim unity and uplift of Untouchables are the two items which I think are at present very essential in the interest of Swaraj.

Such disbursements of funds by a young businessman make an interesting contrast with the reckless personal extravagances of most Indian princes, possessed of fabulous wealth, during the twenties and thirties. The austerity and rigid rules of conduct that obtained in Pilani during G.D.'s childhood ensured that, whatever comforts were available to him, there was never any drive to accumulate money for its own sake or for what it could bring in the way of personal possessions.

In February the Simon Commission, appointed to review progress in constitutional reforms towards self-government in India, arrived to find themselves confronted by strikes, boycotts and mass protests. The fact that no Indian had been invited to participate in the discussions led to agreements between Congress and the Muslims to hold an All Parties Conference to draw up their own constitution. In August, a sub-committee issued what became known as the Nehru Report, advocating Dominion Status as an immediate step, but its recommendations were rejected by the last session of the All Parties Conference in Calcutta in December. The Simon Commission was a fiasco from the outset, but that a real gesture towards Hindu–Muslim unity should have foundered on the rejection of all pleas, especially by Jinnah, the Muslim League leader, for compromise, by the aggressive Hindu Mahasabha leader M. R. Jayakar was a setback. Jinnah later described it as the "parting of the ways". The Delhi University historian, Sumit Sarkar, in his book *Modern India 1885–1947*, commented "Not for the first or last time, Hindu communalism had significantly weakened the national anti-imperialist course at a critical moment."

Oddly, none of these matters – despite the disappointment Gandhi and G.D. must have felt over a wasted opportunity – are referred to in their correspondence. Matters of mutual health, never far beneath the surface, occupied them both. "Nowadays," Gandhi reported to G.D., "my diet consists of 15 tolas of almond milk, 14 tolas of soaked bread, unboiled vegetables and tomatoes, 4 tolas of linseed oil and 2 tolas of wheat paste in the morning. Here I have given up taking fruit. I have gained 1½ lbs in weight in a week."

A fortnight later Gandhi is urging G.D. to fast as a means of curing constipation, but in the end long walks and a changed diet did the trick.

In April G.D. wrote from Benares urging that the boycott of foreign cloth was the most effective retaliation to the Simon Commission. He added, "Please do not feel I am prejudiced in favour of the mills. I will be ready to throw them in the sacrificial fire if ever I feel that by doing so I could help the cause of the country."

As a consequence of disturbances in the wake of the Simon Commission's arrival, Lajpat Rai, the "lion of the Punjab", was struck by a young British officer, and died shortly after as a result.

G.D. was devastated. During the previous summer they had both been in London and Lajpat Rai had written G.D. a long letter.

I want to tell you quite candidly and frankly what I think of you. You see I had never known you so intimately as I have during the time we were together on the steamer and at Geneva. There are qualities in you which I admire immensely but there are some others which I would like to change. You have in you the makings of a great leader and all the qualities of a really generous one provided you

56

change your manners a little. Your present manners give an impression of a little curtness and abruptness which might induce some people who do not know you well to run away with the idea that you are a conceited man.

The best man to learn manners from is Mahatma Gandhi. His manners come very near perfection. . . . Great as he is, greatest of us all, he is very particular in his behaviour towards his friends and co-workers. You are still young and inexperienced; you possess a good intellect and a very ready mind. You must pardon me for saying that as a political leader, which you must develop into in the course of time, you would require a different kind of equipment, both mental and that of manners, from the one which went to make you a successful businessman.

I am in the evening of my life. Gandhi and Malaviya are already dying by inches. Among the intellectuals I place my hopes on Jayakar and among businessmen on you. We want a reliable Hindu leader who would inspire love and confidence among his colleagues to lead the Hindus of North India. I have my hopes in you and that is the reason why I have taken the liberty of writing this letter to you. My love and patriotism have tempted me to do so. Please pardon me if you think I am unnecessarily meddlesome and presumptuous. In that case drop the letter into the waste-paper basket and never think of it again.

G.D., however, knew his own limitations and had no ambition to become a "leader" in Lajpat Rai's sense. He continued, though, to receive reproaches from Lajpat Rai from Paris on his failure to attend a dinner and a reception in London.

You need not have eaten but you should have come. You are a rich man and that is all the more reason for your observing the formal courtesies of life. I wish that people should learn to love you for your virtues other than those connected with your riches. I think you should change a little and follow your two worshipful leaders (Gandhiji, and Malaviyaji) in being considerate even in small matters.

57

From Vichy Lajpat Rai had admonished G.D. for his prolonged stay in Europe the previous summer.

> I am convinced that this is no time for a man of your views
> and patriotism to be absent from India. Every moment is
> vital. Now that you have entered politics you cannot neglect
> political issues. Of course your business interests are very
> important because they supply the sinews of war, but I am
> inclined to think that the next six months are very important
> for India in general and Indian trade and industries in
> particular. The English are drawing some Indians into their
> net and starting a powerful organisation. . . . It is the duty
> of every Indian to counteract such a move and I think you
> are in a position to do a great deal. It is not your money I
> am thinking of but your influence among Indian business-
> men. The more I think of it the more I am convinced that
> you should return to the Assembly and use the Simla Session
> for concerted action.

In subsequent letters Lajpat Rai fiercely attacked religion
and the proliferation of saints as the cause of India's inadequa-
cies. He had no use for Gandhi's advocacy of austerity. Ironi-
cally, since he lost his life as a result of his opposition to the
Simon Commission, he was himself not in favour of a boycott.
His antipathy to Vallabhbhai Patel, Speaker of the Assembly,
led him to write to G.D. from Lahore on his return to India.

> He [Patel] wanted us to announce that we would boycott
> the Royal Commission if it would not have a majority of
> Indians on it. I flatly refused to do so. The Congress Party
> is now divided into several factions. Patel has thus been
> working to destroy our Party. I think I am to blame in this
> matter, also, as I lived so far away from Malaviyaji and
> gave him opportunities to fall into the snares of Patel. This
> is a matter on which I wish to talk to you in detail because
> on this depends the whole of our future political work.

The continual bickerings in the Congress Party made G.D.
even less inclined to commit himself to the political life. Lajpat
Rai wrote again from Lahore, this time attacking Malaviya as

well. "I regret ever having joined him in forming this Party. Patel's conduct during the whole of the session has been very perfidious. While he gave one kind of advice to Srinivasa Iyengar he gave another kind to Malaviyaji."

After Lajpat Rai's death in 1928 G.D. wrote, "He died a martyr's death. His contribution to the struggle for national freedom was great and so was his contribution to social reforms. But with the advent of Gandhism he found it difficult to adjust himself to the changing conditions."

Nevertheless, it was Lajpat Rai, argumentative, moody, passionate, often depressed, who was a valuable modifying influence on G.D. at a time when he was emotionally in thrall to the Mahatma. Lajpat Rai, until finally disillusioned with political manoeuvrings, had been a major force in reshaping the Congress Party on more ambitious lines, his account of the conflict between the old and new leaders forming part of his early autobiographical work, *The Story of My Life*. At the height of tension in the Punjab, which was basically agrarian rather than political in character, Lajpat Rai had been misguidedly deported to Burma. He spent the war years in America, where he worked on his *Indian Revolutionaries in the United States and Japan*, an account of German efforts to foment anti-British activity among exiled Indian, mostly Bengali, revolutionaries.

It was Lajpat Rai's example as an inspired educationist, a tireless social worker and civic administrator – especially in relation to the depressed classes – that set G.D. to think on similar lines. Lajpat Rai failed to interest G.D. in politics as a career and he himself, despite his efforts over the years to reconcile opposing groups within the nationalist movement, had often sickened of the struggle.

The year 1928, during which Gandhi returned briefly to active politics in attending the Calcutta session of the All Parties Conference, saw no slackening off in the requests for money. "I have your loving letter," Gandhi had written to G.D. in July. "As a matter of fact its language will restrain me from stretching for my begging bowl. But a beggar is oblivious of such considerations. Therefore when I have no alternative I shall be at your doorstep."

He soon was, and G.D., as nearly always, did what was asked. It was not an easy time for him, for with increasing Communist infiltration into trade unions, in Bengal most particularly, strikes and labour troubles were causing continual disruption. He was also busy in connection with the Lajpat Rai memorial fund.

Meanwhile Gandhi was experimenting with a diet of almond milk at his ashram. He wrote to G.D. on 30 June 1929:

> Your three letters are before me. I would have no right to remain in the midst of this sublimely beautiful, secluded spot surrounded by snow-clad mountain-peaks, if I had no special work to do here. But this I have. The revision of the translation of the *Gita* had remained unfinished at Wardha. ... So I sit down with the set purpose of completing the half-finished work, postponing all other kinds of activity as long as possible. Now the work on the *Gita* is over.

In the same letter Gandhi discusses Khadi production, his continuing preoccupation with uncooked food and his abandonment – temporary as it turned out – of fasting as a means of protest.

G.D. became seriously worried about Gandhi's health and in August he wrote from Calcutta to Mahadev Desai:

> I feared the crisis long ago and even warned Gandhiji in the very beginning, but as you know he is hopelessly obstinate at times, so impossible to deal with. I have got nothing to say against uncooked food but I maintained that Gandhiji's constitution was the most unsuitable one for any wild experiment. ... I myself was consistently losing weight recently and so I kept for two months on milk according to Mcfadden's system.

Throughout August Gandhi cabled dietetic and health bulletins from his Ahmedabad ashram. On 17 August, "Slight attack dysentery. Certainly very weak but best doctor advising. Shall take goats' milk when becomes imperative.

Uncooked stopped since Thursday." Two days later there followed the brief communiqué: "Commenced curds yesterday. No anxiety."

On 23 August Gandhi returned to the subject at some length in a letter to G.D.

> You need not worry about me. People fall sick even when they take regular diet. I am now taking plenty of curds but I would like to tell you that milk and curds are efficacious only to a limited extent. They are not man's natural items of diet . . . The abatement of carnal desires experienced by so many people while taking raw cereals is not the result of starvation. During the four years when I was on a fruit diet I used to walk forty miles daily and enjoyed the same mental peace. But I have no wish to dilate on this subject.

There is something both comical and endearing about these cranky preoccupations alternating with correspondence on public matters. Three days after this last letter Gandhi fired off a one-line card to G.D., "What have you done about the auditing of the Bengal Congress Committee accounts?"

The answer was nothing, since, as G.D. confirmed from Simla where he was attending a session of the Assembly, he had received no definite instructions on the matter.

In September Gandhi, now in Agra, returned to the matter of the audit. More enthusiastically, he looked forward to a quiet discussion with G.D. on his two favourite topics, health and diet:

> If we two could manage to find time to sit together for some time, as we did during the last rainy season, we could discuss in peace what to eat and what to drink. . . . It is one thing to abstain from ideal food and drink due to physical weakness or just plain incapacity; to grasp its significance is quite another.

In October G.D. wrote Gandhi a long letter of quite a different kind. In it he felt compelled to defend himself against certain charges circulating against him. It was one of the rare occasions when he discussed conditions in his own mills in a

61

letter. After outlining his plans for increased production, a working week of sixty hours, and an 8 per cent wage increase "i.e. more than any other mill in Calcutta", G.D. continues:

As for providing the workers with living quarters I was opposed to the idea from the very beginning on the ground that life in the villages was preferable to barrack life. This was the right approach at the initial stages when the mill was rather small. Now that it has expanded my own thinking too has undergone a change, with the result that at present we are soon to have 700 quarters measuring 12' × 9' each, with a verandah and kitchen each. . . . It is not true that children are employed in violation of the Factory Act. All this is by way of placing the correct situation before you. But I must tell you one thing: it may be that I should fail to act in the best interests of the workers through stupidity or error of judgment, or under bluff, but I don't think I have ever wronged the workers through sheer cussedness. When you again visit Calcutta I intend to take you round my mills.

From Pilani in November G.D. wrote to Gandhi in an attempt to get him to attend the first Round Table Conference in London. This conference, convened largely to undo the harm caused by the exclusion of Indians from the Simon Commission, invited the participation of Indians in the drafting of the Government of India Bill. Gandhi, however, was about to launch his second civil disobedience campaign.
"I firmly believe," G.D. wrote,

that if you do go there it will be all to our own advantage inasmuch as they will think many times before allowing you to return dissatisfied. They might yield everything except Defence. But in case you do not go the situation might take an ugly turn. It is this anxiety that has led me to write this to you. I have never counselled you on political matters but under the present circumstances I have felt it necessary. . . . If they offer Dominion Status you would accept it at once, I know. But I do not think they will offer anything of the kind.

G.D. had recently met the Viceroy at dinner and on the basis of his conversation with him he repeated to Gandhi his impression that, as a preliminary, political prisoners would be released and that after full participation by Indian leaders a formula could be devised that, though falling short of full Dominion Status, would be an advance towards it.

Placed as we are, how can we aspire for more just now? The sum and substance of all this is that it would be decidedly to our advantage for you to meet the British Cabinet. . . . Even if the Conference fails in its purpose we shall stand to gain inasmuch as the left-wingers will come to the fore.

Gandhi, however, was unmoved. At a meeting soon afterwards at Wardha Gandhi expressed distrust of all British intentions. In a letter dated 28 February 1930, he wrote to G.D., "They are only taking advantage of our ignorance and cowardice. The sooner the Assembly is bidden goodbye the better. I have little hope of remaining out of jail till March next."

This was one of several occasions when G.D. and Gandhi, though at one on objectives, opted for different tactics. While G.D., ever the pragmatist, saw the Assembly as an opportunity to acquire experience in the working of parliamentary institutions, Gandhi wanted to wash his hands of it. The Swaraj Party took Gandhi's advice, leaving the Assembly, only to return at the next elections. So it could be said, in this instance anyway, that it was G.D.'s common sense that ultimately proved the better guide to action.

Europe with Gandhi, and the Poona Pact

On 10 April 1930, Gandhi wrote to G.D.:

> I was filled with joy on learning the news of your resignation.
> I am dictating this at 2 in the night. My colleagues have
> brought the news that they are going to take me away today.
> I am sure you will do all you can to promote the cause of
> salt struggle, prohibition, and boycott of foreign cloth. I
> can quite visualise the result of these wholesale arrests.
> Everything is happening according to our expectations.
> What more is there to write?

On 12 March Gandhi had begun his 241-mile salt march
from Sabarmati to Dandi. Accompanied by seventy-eight
members of the ashram he reached Dandi on 6 April, after
twenty-four days on the road. At Dandi he made the gesture
of taking a lump of salt from the beach in defiance of the law,
the manufacturing of salt being a state monopoly. Gandhi was
arrested on 4 May, by which time 100,000 men and women
who had followed him in breaking the law were already in
gaol. It seemed an eccentric cause on which to attach such
symbolic value but by involving the poorest among the people,
and by acting in a peaceful manner, it had an effect far beyond
the immediate issue.

G.D.'s own walk-out from the Assembly had been largely
as a protest against Imperial Preference, and he continued to
attack government policy over the economy. He had written
a long letter from Calcutta to Gandhi on the eve of the latter's
arrest: "It seems I am not destined to see you for quite some
time. But in case you do remain out of prison I will see you
towards the end of May." He went on to discuss the boycott
of foreign cloth and the picketing of mills, differing in both

instances in matters of detail from Gandhi's own ideas on the subject. Gandhi was saying one thing, Malaviya something else, and Motilal Nehru a third, so that the workers, without clear directives, were becoming confused.

Gandhi's next letter was at the end of July, from Poona jail. "It was good that you did not come to Poona. I cannot see anybody. The conditions placed on receiving visitors are unacceptable to me. . . . Incarceration is a kind of moral death, it can mean only that."

Apart from the costiveness of the water, Gandhi was in good health. "My diet consists of milk, curds, raisins, dates and lemons. I take the limejuice with soda or lukewarm water and salt. . . . The entire energy I am left with I am using in spinning and carding."

On 28 October Gandhi wrote again from jail:

In a way I like your spiritual restlessness. True peace will emerge out of it. . . . I can quite understand that you have to devote a great deal of your time to your business, but being lost in it all the time will neither profit the business nor bring you peace of mind.

In December Gandhi wrote twice more from jail, in the first letter recommending Jayaprakash Narayan for a job, and in the second disapproving of speculation.

Speculation means gambling. Now supposing that the market prices will shoot up, I buy 2000 bales of cotton. I do not need any cotton and have also not made any provision for storing it in my warehouse. It is just a paper transaction. I just wait for a rise in the prices and when it does I dispose of much of this quantity. This I call speculation. This kind of business activity has done much harm not only to this country but also to the whole world.

Whatever G.D. thought of this implied censure, he must have reflected that without his family's and his own involvement in such an activity Gandhi's causes would have been a great deal worse off.

In 1929 the Tatas had floated the idea of a joint capitalist organization with European firms as a safeguard against trade union activities, but G.D. and other Marwari businessmen declined to back it. "I have not the least doubt in my mind," G.D. wrote to Purshottamdas Thakurdas, "that a purely capitalist organisation is the last body to put up an effective fight against Communism. What we capitalists can do is to cooperate with those who through constitutional means want to change the government for a national one." It needed to be made clear, Thakurdas wrote to N. N. Majumdar of Tatas, "that they were Indians first and merchants afterwards".

On 29 August 1931, Gandhi sailed for England on the *Rajputana*. He had, after a change of heart that surprised many, been finally persuaded by the new Viceroy, Lord Willingdon, and by friends such as Malaviya and G.D., to attend the second Round Table Conference. Gandhi was nominated as Congress's sole representative. G.D., accepting a government invitation to represent the business community, was on the ship.

A year earlier, after meeting Lord Irwin in Delhi, Gandhi had begun to take a less intransigent attitude towards negotiation. It remains uncertain whether this was primarily due to an instinctive trust in Irwin's good faith and the real possibility of a future conference achieving something more tangible than resolutions, or whether for the first time Gandhi was subjected to commercial pressures he was unable to resist. The conclusion of the so-called Gandhi–Irwin pact, which allowed for the release of political prisoners and the private manufacture of salt in return for the ending of civil disobedience, had disappointed the more radical of the Congress leaders, including Jawaharlal Nehru, but it nevertheless provided a breathing space, however fragile, for a reappraisal of the economy and of the Congress administrative machinery.

G.D. kept a journal, running to fifty foolscap pages, of this second voyage and stay in England. The conference itself, foundering on the familiar obstacles of foreign policy, defence and Hindu–Muslim representation, achieved next to nothing. The princes began to show less enthusiasm for federation than they had done in 1930 and when finally the conference broke

up in December the only positive gain had been the establishment of happy, good-natured relationships between Gandhi
and the people he met, cockneys, unemployed, important
men of affairs, or Lancashire millworkers who had been most
affected by his *swadeshi* policies.

In his shipboard diary G.D. tries to analyse how "this lean
and short man has been able to sway the fortunes of millions
of people almost single-handed". He comes up with no conclusion. Malaviya and Gandhi had made a weird pair on deck,
Malaviya with his own cooking stove and supply of Ganges
water, Gandhi with his spinning wheel and cotton gin. Gandhi
insisted on a place over the stern, even for his evening prayers,
where he was found by most of the Indians on board.

Reflecting on Gandhi's likely reaction to a conference in
which nearly all the hundred delegates, of different political
parties and religious groups, would be nominated by the
government, and tend to toe their line, G.D. wrote:

> I have a feeling Gandhiji would prefer to negotiate with
> Cabinet ministers and at the same time tour the country
> explaining our views in public speeches. If Cabinet Ministers
> are not willing to negotiate Gandhiji will express his opinion
> in the Federal Committee and if that is disregarded he may
> decide to leave.

G.D. was worried at the discrepancy between the attitudes
of the two Indian leaders. Malaviya was anxious for G.D. to
study British policy on currency and other technical matters
while Gandhi was determined to deal with major issues in the
simplest and most general of terms.

Leaving Aden G.D. observed, "The only person Gandhi is
really interested in seeing in London is Winston Churchill
because of his hostile attitude to India. He has no desire at all
to meet people like Bernard Shaw."

By 15 September the Indian party, which had included
Gandhi's youngest son, Devdas, had arrived in London,
Gandhi insisting on installing himself at Kingsley Hall in the
East End, much to the inconvenience of everyone else.
Gandhi's adopted daughter Mirabehn, who had arrived in

India six years earlier from England to devote herself to Gandhi, was also with him, and immediate ill-feeling developed between her and Muriel Lester, who ran Kingsley Hall as a social service centre.

At an early meeting with Sir Samuel Hoare, now Secretary of State for India, Gandhi asked Hoare, "Isn't it worth pondering over why, after being so whole-hearted and ardent an admirer of the British Government, I have turned against it to the extent of asking you to quit India?" Hoare replied that he was proud of what the British had done in the interests of the people of India. "You may be proud," Gandhi said, "although there is no reason to be proud of anything, but you should also be ashamed of the atrocities and injustice your race has imposed on the Indian people."

On 28 September, G.D. recorded, Gandhi addressed the House of Commons, arguing that what India wanted was an equal not a subordinate relationship. "I didn't much appreciate Gandhiji's statement on financial issues," G.D. added, "and I made it known to him. In the evening we discussed the economic issues at great length and finally Gandhiji agreed in future he would not make any statement on them unless he had clarified it with me beforehand."

G.D. himself had apparently come up against personal criticism and confided to his journal, "people don't seem to trust me any more". However he consoled himself with the widening of his experience and the expanding of personal contacts.

Arrangements were made for G.D. to meet Sir Henry Strakosch, the British Government's adviser on Indian financial affairs. On the basis of G.D.'s report on their discussions Gandhi would make up his mind as to whether the exchange rate was beneficial to the Indian people or not. Meanwhile Sir Edward Benthall, a British businessman from Calcutta, had commented to Gandhi, "It appears that Mr Birla, who is a short-tempered man, has influenced you on all economic matters." Gandhi replied curtly, "I am not easily influenced by others."

Gandhi, G.D. recorded, had even less use for Ramsay

MacDonald, now leading a Coalition Government, than for Hoare, and at a meeting between them gave the Prime Minister a thorough dressing down.

A Minority Committee was formed to discuss the communal problem, its members including Gandhi, Malaviya, Sarojini Naidu and G.D. MacDonald addressed them, his speech, G.D. felt, lacking in both sincerity and depth. "Soon after the meeting he came up to Gandhiji with folded hands and expressed his desire to visit his Sabarmati Ashram as an act of expiation."

G.D. had little faith in these committee meetings and asked Gandhi why he was willing to waste his time on them. "I can express my views," Gandhi replied, "and it will be left for others to agree or disagree with me."

On 4 October G.D. referred to a lunch meeting with Benthall in which he began by challenging Benthall about his remark to Gandhi. However, a frank discussion followed in which Benthall accepted that there were those who wished to drag their feet and let the Indian delegation leave empty-handed. "On the other hand there is a more powerful group genuinely interested in arriving at some sort of compromise." What held up any kind of agreement, Benthall insisted, was the boycotting of British goods and Gandhi's announcement of an inquiry into British policy over the years, an inquiry calculated only to increase bitterness.

Further meetings followed between the two, in which they discussed trade and financial matters from their respective viewpoints. At one of these they were joined by Sir Henry Strakosch. G.D.'s pamphlet *Monetary Reform* was the main topic, Strakosch wishing to refute its main contention that the new exchange rate was fixed to serve British, not Indian, business and professional elements. The whole economic as well as political argument of the decade, let alone of the conference, was interpretable according to whose interests were being represented and the degree of concession either party was prepared to make.

About Strakosch G.D. observed in his journal:

He is basically an honest man and knows he can't defend the policy of his own government beyond a certain point. I explained to him, no doubt India is a debtor country but we can repay the debt only by increase of our productivity. In that case, is your policy to develop the indigenous industries or to destroy them? He had no answer.

Although G.D. in his entries admits little progress on any of the main issues he confirms Gandhi's growing popularity. By the end of October "the RTC has lost its importance and the real negotiations are carried out within inner British and Indian circles". More seriously, relations between Hindus and Muslims on the Minority Committee were deteriorating. "Gandhiji is under constant pressure to resolve the problem and doesn't sleep for more than three hours a day. . . . We expected trouble from the Muslims but now the Hindus are becoming impossible to deal with."

G.D. became increasingly disillusioned during the following weeks:

The only person who can do something is Gandhiji but he too seems to have lost hope. How does the British Government expect that Hindus, Muslims, Christians, Sikhs, Parsis and Princes will have a unanimous opinion about separate electorates or the allotment of seats? Are the British people themselves united?

On 5 November G.D. attended a banquet at Buckingham Palace. "Gandhi wrapped a sheet around him and walked in barefooted. I had to go in European dress since I had no Indian clothes with me. . . . For the first time in his life the Emperor was confronted by a half-naked fakir in his royal palace."

Disunity among the Indians was making the conference a painful experience. "Whatever little Gandhiji could have achieved by way of negotiation became impossible because soon after any meeting with the Prime Minister similar meetings followed with communal leaders. As a result we have fully exposed our differences and they have not failed to take advantage."

On 13 November G.D. wrote, "Gandhiji met Hoare yesterday and it became clear that beyond provincial autonomy there is nothing to look forward to."

At a final meeting, when everyone seemed anxious to salvage something from their two months' labours, Gandhi refused to budge over the idea of a separate electorate for schedule castes. "I tried to reason with him, but he was adamant and unwilling to move an inch."

It was one of Gandhi's days for silence so his argument had to be written down. General Smuts began to take an interest in the proceedings, offering to interpret Gandhi's views to the Prime Minister. MacDonald admitted to being impressed by Gandhi's formula but remarked, "Gandhiji is a wonderful person but it is difficult to understand his views."

G.D. observed, "I have my sympathy for MacDonald and said the same to Gandhiji." Gandhi's ability to charm, amuse and at the same time to mystify did not make matters any easier for his own colleagues.

On 4 December G.D. wrote, "The conference is almost over, the delegates are leaving one by one." Gandhi spoke for seventy minutes at the last session, after which G.D. was complimented by Sir Campbell Rhodes for his own contribution. "Mr Birla, if you are ever out of a job, go to Henry Strakosch for a recommendation. You will get a good one."

G.D. made a number of speeches about the necessity of financial safeguards, and the undesirability of the Governor-General having wide powers over every aspect of finance. These were not always well received even by Indian members, G.D.'s astringency and attention to matters of close detail contrasting with the vaguer notions of the Mahatma and others in areas in which they were less experienced.

When the conference broke up Gandhi returned home via Switzerland where he visited Romain Rolland. He was away altogether three months. Within a week of his arrival in Bombay, as a result of an immediate crackdown on so-called subversives by the Viceroy, Lord Willingdon, he was arrested and detained without trial in Yeravda Central Prison, Poona. Jawaharlal Nehru had earlier been arrested on his way to meet Gandhi in Bombay.

G.D. wrote to Gandhi there on 4 January, shortly after his own return, about a name for the English edition of the Hindi paper they were about to launch. It was not an auspicious moment for such a venture, for a new wave of arrests had begun, all Congress organizations being banned and over 100,000 sympathizers put in jail during the next year. By the end of 1932 the civil disobedience movement had lost its main impetus, Gandhi after his months in jail preferring to devote himself to less overtly political causes, such as his work on behalf of Harijans.

G.D.'s speeches in London had borne some fruit, for on 27 January Hoare had written to him from the India Office inviting him to join the Consultative Committee set up to pursue the general policies outlined at the conference. G.D. replied that as an ex-President of the Federation of Indian Chambers of Commerce and Industry, which had not associated itself with the London conference, such an action might seem disloyal to the Federation.

> The best service I can render to my own country as well as to the cause of cooperation is to persuade the Federation to officially offer its cooperation. . . . I came to Delhi to discuss this problem with important members of the Federation and am leaving tomorrow for Calcutta. I shall discuss there with Mr Benthall and others the question of closer cooperation between the two communities interested in trade and commerce.

Hoare, in his reply to G.D., raised the question of the Ottawa Conference on Empire Preference, due to take place in the summer.

> I am aware of course of the past history of the question of inter-Imperial tariff relations so far as India is concerned, but I hope you will realise that the new policy of His Majesty's Government puts this question on a new and

different footing. . . . I will be much disappointed if India is not represented at Ottawa in a spirit which will enable negotiations to take place with a view to the voluntary mutual benefit of the trade and commerce of both countries.

In his lengthy reply, written after consultation with the Federation Committee, G.D. remarked:

It may not be possible at present to have an agreement between a radical India and a most conservative Parliament, but I submit that it is possible to have an agreement between the present Parliament and progressive Indian opinion. . . . I wish you to realise that if a Constitution is introduced without the consent even of progressive people, to say nothing of the Congress Party, its smooth working cannot be guaranteed. . . . I always made a distinction between Gandhiji and the Congress, and I again submit that it is possible for you to give us a Constitution which, though not acceptable to the Congress, may not be rejected by Gandhiji and which can ensure a smooth working in future.

After expressing disappointment over a recent speech by Benthall in Calcutta, the tone of which alienated Indian businessmen, G.D. continued:

But to do constructive work one requires an atmosphere of trust and friendship and this at present is unfortunately lacking in India. Your letters to me, in fact, are a relieving feature of the present unhappy situation. . . . I should therefore like you to know me as I really am. I need hardly say that I am a great admirer of Gandhiji. I have liberally financed his khaddar-producing and untouchability activities. I have never taken part in the Civil Disobedience movement. But I have been a severe critic of the Government and so have never been popular with them. . . . I wish I could convert the authorities to the view that Gandhiji and men of his type are not only friends of India but also friends of Great Britain and that Gandhiji is the greatest force on the side of peace and order. He alone is responsible for keeping the left wing in India in check.

On behalf of the Federation G.D. offered co-operation at the Ottawa Conference with certain reservations.

Shortly afterwards G.D. had a meeting with the Governor of Bengal, Sir John Anderson.

> He speaks very little and seems to understand economic questions very well. I pointed out that 75 per cent of the political troubles were due to bad economics. India was suffering from a low level of prices. . . . In 1921 there was no unrest among cultivators. The political disturbance was confined to the working classes. Why is it that the working classes are so quiet now and the whole agrarian population is so full of discontent?

Anderson seemed uncertain as to the practicality of Gandhi's ideas but G.D. attempted to reassure him.

> About the military I told him that we realised we could not get immediate control but Gandhiji would suggest certain formulae which may be acceptable to all. About finance we were prepared to put ourselves in the position of a factory proprietor who had to deal with the debenture holders. The debenture holder should not poke his nose into our day-to-day affairs so long as we paid him his dues.

In May 1932, G.D. wrote to Lord Lothian, a Parliamentary Under-Secretary at the India Office, recently arrived in India as Chairman of the India Franchise Committee and with whom he had several friendly meetings. After discussing alternative methods of achieving a constitution acceptable to both Gandhi and Congress, G.D. ended his letter:

> I am writing this for your consideration because I very strongly feel that the Government would be making the greatest blunder if, relying on the Mussalmans, the Depressed Classes and the Princes, they introduced a Constitution which would not meet with the approval of nationalist India. . . . The Government should ignore the Congress only if it is their intention that no substantial advance is to be made.

After the Lothian Report was issued G.D. wrote to Lord Lothian in London. "Your remark [in the Report] about the sacrifices of the Congress was simply magnificent. It is impossible to estimate correctly the good effect of such utterances."

Gandhi and many Congress leaders were still in jail, however, and G.D. reported that until they were released there was no chance of the communal question – the same communal question that had plagued the last Round Table Conference – being settled.

He went on, "I am afraid it is not fully realised in England what a serious economic position has been created in India. Unless prices rise substantially we are going to have a lot of trouble in this country some time next year."

The Ottawa Conference, G.D. remarked in the same letter,

has more or less been given a burial from its inception. This time it is again proposed to do something at Ottawa without any regard to the feelings of the Indian mercantile community . . . How much could be achieved by a friendly deal should have been realised by Gandhiji's utterances at Manchester in favour of preference. But in India the Government care very little to do things in a proper spirit. They want to impose things.

Gandhi, still in jail, had begun a fast unto death on the issue of Harijan franchise. G.D. sent telegrams to Sir Samuel Hoare and Lord Lothian among others pleading for Gandhi's release. In due course Gandhi was freed, but on certain conditions. G.D. wrote to Lord Lothian criticizing the gracelessness of the Government's actions.

The Government would have lost nothing had they released him immediately and without any restrictions . . . One cannot understand the logic of the Premier when he wants an agreed solution and yet puts the old man in jail as soon as he arrives in Bombay and then releases him when he is on the verge of death.

Gandhi's fast had, in fact, been directed at the high-caste

75

Hindu establishment rather than the government, though the latter had announced plans to introduce separate electorates for untouchables, a course Gandhi was convinced would simply lead to greater estrangement between Hindus and untouchables.

Alarmed at Gandhi's physical condition Malaviya and other leaders of the caste Hindus and Dr Ambedkar, the Harijan leader, held urgent meetings in Bombay and Poona, the result of which was a pact acceptable to both parties and the government. "I had quite a good hand in getting it concluded," G.D. observed with some satisfaction. Instead of a separate electorate for depressed classes, the Poona Pact allowed for 141 seats in the various provincial legislative councils and 18 per cent of the seats, through general constituencies, in the Central Assembly.

Diet and Decentralization

It is evident from the tone of G.D.'s letters, in which key figures in Anglo–Indian relations are addressed without deference, that G.D. now saw himself not only as a spokesman of the Indian business community but as a responsible mediator. He was still only thirty-eight, a widower for six years, but his association with Gandhi, Lajpat Rai and Malaviya among Indians, his service on Government committees and commissions dealing with fiscal matters and labour relations, his involvement in politics, brief though it was, and Harijan affairs, quite apart from his own immense and growing fortune, had given him a status and independence far above that enjoyed by other comparably rich Indians. He now had another source of influence in the recently acquired *Hindustan Times*, a newspaper of national circulation under the chairmanship of Malaviya. G.D.'s private secretary Parasnath Singh became managing editor, a post subsequently filled by Gandhi's youngest son, Devdas. The *Hindustan Times* was the largest of the provincial newspapers and magazines that G.D. had been picking up over the years.

He had, in addition, encouraged one of the Birla Trusts to contribute generously to the publishing costs of the series *The History and Culture of the Indian People*, edited by the historian R. C. Majumdar. C. V. Raman, the future Nobel scientist, had been helped at a crucial period by G.D., who had written him a cheque for 20,000 rupees to buy the equipment he needed. Rabindranath Tagore and Santiniketan were other recipients of Birla munificence.

G.D. had not neglected Pilani. Middle, high and intermediate schools had been set up at regular intervals between 1921 and 1928 and a year later he set up the Birla Education Trust.

From Yeravda Jail Gandhi continued to write long letters to G.D., mainly on matters of health and diet:

> I take honey and half a lemon in hot water at 4.30 in the morning, followed by one and a half tola of roasted ground almonds and 30 dates in tomato juice at 7 o'clock. At 12 again lemon with honey and lukewarm water. At 4 in the afternoon 15 dates together with one tola of almonds. Before that I used to take 30 dates. . . .

The discontinuing of milk had made Gandhi feel much better.

G.D.'s appetite for details of diet and its effect on health was little less keen than Gandhi's own. On 1 March he wrote to Gandhi:

> My dear Bapu, On the basis of your letter I have prepared a table of your diet showing the total intake of your daily ration converted into calories. . . . You will see from this your daily intake is deficient in protein and fat whereas it is quite rich in all vitamins and also in iron and lime. . . . If you take a pint of milk besides the quantity you are taking it would be wonderfully balanced.

G.D. then goes into details of his own diet, now resulting in a total intake of 150 calories of protein, 500 calories of fat and 1400 calories of carbohydrate. In each case their writing takes on fresh animation when politics can be temporarily relegated to an aside and their respective experiments with food and medicine brought to the fore.

G.D. had made a brief business visit to America in the spring and reported to Gandhi,

> the economic condition was simply worse than what it was in England. . . . In culture they appeared to me to be far inferior to the average Englishman. I did not like the country at all. One thing that impressed me very much was the happy condition of the negroes. They are undoubtedly lynched occasionally in the Southern States but otherwise economically their level is far superior to the middle class Indian and in education there is nothing to complain about . . .

People are very eager to know about you and did not take much interest in India.

Gandhi was not impressed with G.D.'s calorie counting. "I have little faith in calories. At present I am also taking four ounces of toasted bread. The dates have arrived [a present from G.D. from California]. In my view dates from Arabia are better. I am not surprised to read your account of America."

In April Gandhi wrote again from prison. "I like your taking interest in everybody's diet . . . As soon as you discover anything new let me know about it."

In June Gandhi reports a weight of 106½ lbs. "The doctors tell me that I am suffering from tennis elbow as a result of spinning continuously for years; rest is the only cure for it." He continued, "I have made up my mind to study economics as much as I can before I leave this place. I do not hope to be released soon . . . I understand what you say about running the mills all the 24 hours . . . I want to see with my own eyes how the workers fare there."

Gandhi was correct about his release, for he was to remain in gaol for over a year longer, until August 1933. In his absence the civil disobedience movement lapsed, Gandhi himself combining his prison reading in economics with organizing Harijan welfare work, associations and literature. The authorities were happy for him to do this work, a sideline in their eyes – and in the eyes of such as Jawaharlal Nehru – and one which kept him out of mischief.

In June Gandhi wrote to G.D.,

The letter I sent to Gwalior was rather lengthy, but that is all I remember about it. You have to ascertain how the workers view the idea of three shifts and how much they stand to gain from it financially, not ignoring the moral side of the thing. If they benefit financially and lose morally, I would not approve of the idea . . . I am learning Urdu nowadays.

In July Gandhi, having read pamphlets sent to him by G.D. about foreign exchange and currency, observed,

The more I familiarise myself with the science of currency the more convinced I am that what is adumbrated in these books is not the way to solve the problem of the people's poverty. The only way is to devise some method whereby income and expenditure function in close cooperation. That is possible only through a resurrection of cottage industry.

Gandhi was now, on advice, back to taking milk, as well as chapati and vegetables. "But no longer do I notice the cleansing of the bowels that I experienced formerly on a diet of *roti*, almonds and a vegetable."

That same month Lothian was writing to G.D.,

I am sure that you are glad that Lord Irwin has joined the Cabinet. The next hurdle is the communal settlement. Meanwhile I should be very grateful if you would let me know your opinion about conditions in India from time to time and specially about the economic situation.

G.D. did not choose to disagree with Gandhi's simplistic diagnosis of economic distress, merely pointing out that economists were obliged to look at it from other angles. He stressed his own views about the desirability of stabilizing prices at a higher level to reduce the burdens of agriculturalists, and of decentralizing production.

My mind is running somewhat like this. Tariff, Power Plants, the system of Limited Liability Companies and Currency Administration have been much abused and require some conditions to be imposed on them . . . In the first place, tariff protection should be given only to articles which could naturally and not artificially be produced in the country, and secondly, its ultimate object ought to be to divert production to cottages.

G.D. goes on to discuss the application of this to cars, typewriters and sewing machines, to khaddar and gur, banks and insurance companies. "I believe the mill-owners would not object to bearing tax in favour of cottage production provided they were fully protected from outside invasion and were given a sufficient notice about the ultimate goal of the Government."

Distant friends. Jawaharlal Nehru and G.D.

Ethiopia. Guests of the Emperor, G.D. and, behind Haile Selassie, his son Basant Kumar.

Nehru, with G.D. and his three sons, B.K., L.N. and K.K.

Rajendra Prasad, India's first President, G.D. and Nehru.

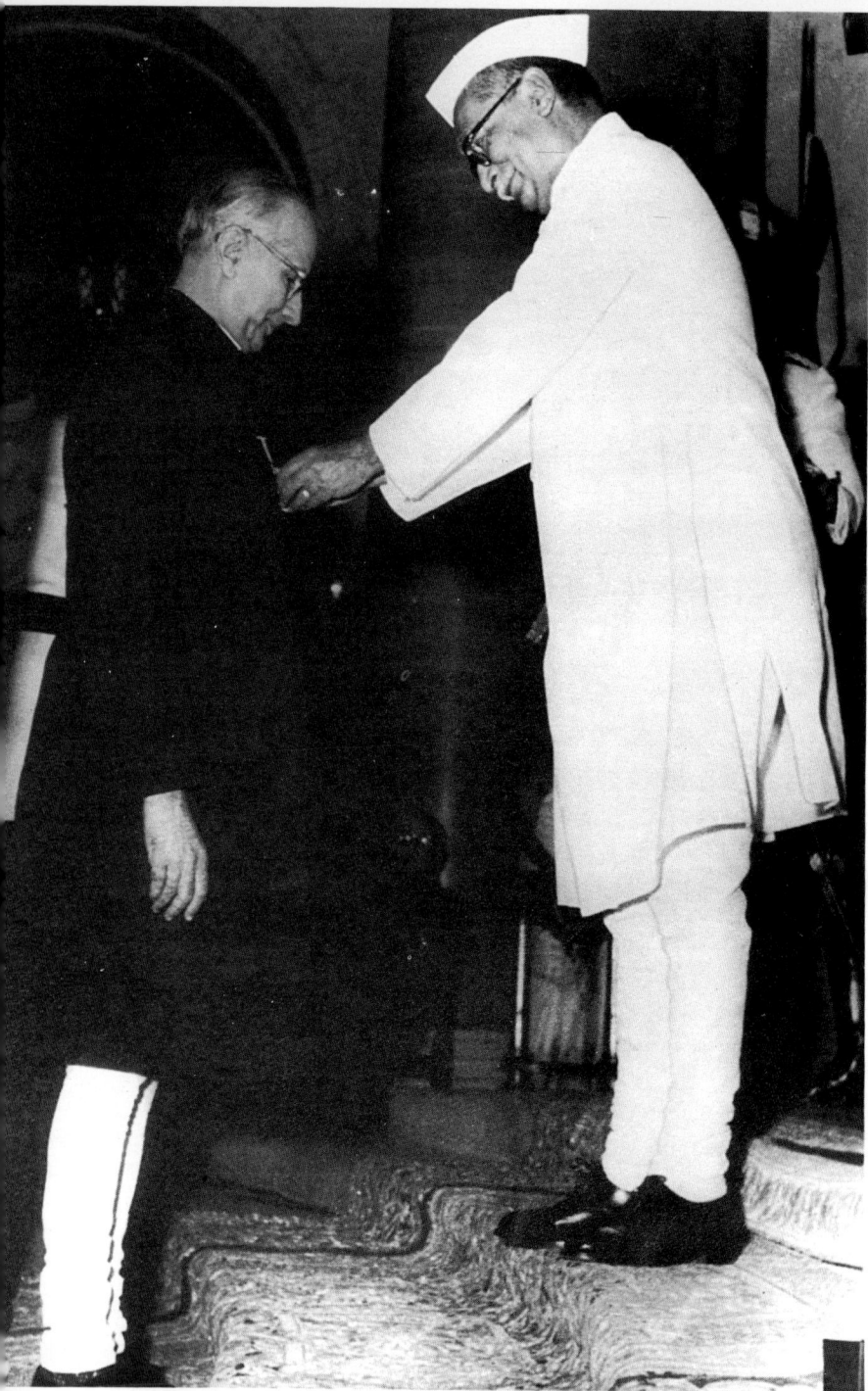

29 October 1957. G.D. receives the Padma Vibhushan, one of India's highest honours, from the President.

How much Gandhi was able to concern himself with protective policies as opposed to the quality of life experienced by workers in Birla factories is not evident. He answered G.D.'s long letter by modestly confessing that although he may not have understood the various books G.D. had sent him they had added to his knowledge. Having demanded copies of the reports of various committees – the Fowler Committee, the Chamberlain Committee, the Hilton Young Committee – he ended,

I fear almonds will not suit you. . . . Wheat, milk, curds, vegetable salad and starch-free fruits like grapes, pomegranate, orange, apple, pineapple and papaya – these are the things that would suit people like you. Almonds can supplant milk only when a vegetable is found equivalent to milk. . . . I am convinced that out of the bewildering variety of vegetables there must be at least one containing that elusive property.

While Gandhi remained in jail G.D. was obliged to write at great length to Sir Samuel Hoare in relation to an invitation to join a special sub-committee to be appointed to discuss financial and commercial safeguards:

We businessmen have got a limited influence; yet it is such an influence as can be of great help, if it is correctly utilised . . . Mere participation in the financial discussion is not the correct use of our influence. After all, what could I or Sir Purshottamdas Thakurdas do in England if we had no backing? . . . The only way for us to render service is that before we participate in the discussion of these safeguards we must be given latitude to use our influence to get Gandhiji to associate himself with the new Constitution, provided of course that we at least are satisfied with it, and I submit that our services could be utilised to create such a circumstance. . . . I am writing this with some confidence as I have known all along that Gandhiji is a man of compromise, and as I believe that you are a great friend of his you are in a position to appreciate him.

G.D., who had been allowed one non-political talk with Gandhi, on Harijan business, after his fast had ended, had recently been appointed President of the All-India Anti-Untouchability League. Since then all correspondence and interviews with Gandhi, even on non-political subjects, had been stopped. G.D. ended his letter to Hoare,

If I am allowed I may discuss matters with Gandhiji without arousing the least speculations or causing any publicity. And I can even come to London to discuss the same with a view to finding ways and means to get his cooperation. But I do not want to pose as one who can deliver the goods when I know I cannot.

Harijans and "*Swadeshi*"

From late 1932 onwards Gandhi and the government had few occasions to clash, Gandhi devoting himself to communal and rural affairs, in the long term indirectly involving all sections of the community in nationalistic ideas. For Gandhi the Harijan cause was essentially humanitarian, a question of freedom to worship and to work, rather than economic. His attitude to the whole caste system fell some way short of that of its more radical critics.

The exchange of letters between Gandhi and G.D. throughout the cold weather of 1932/3 was almost exclusively devoted to Harijan business – the naming of an organization, its financing and general aims, and the founding of the weekly journal, in both Hindi and English, of *Harijan*. Of all G.D.'s early involvements, outside business and Anglo–Indian relations, Harijan affairs took up the most time.

After some discussion the movement, which was conceived as purely social and non-political, was christened All-India Harijan Sevak Sangh. Rajagopalachari immediately raised an objection to the term, "Anti-Untouchability League", wanting the word "Abolition" introduced. Gandhi was converted to his logic – "*Service* to a group of men is not really the object and aim . . . It is really the *doing away* with the evil" and recommended to G.D. they should accept Rajagopalachari's suggestion. G.D. replied, "About the name of the Society I am afraid it would look ridiculous to change it for the third time. Rajaji's letter, although it impressed you so much, did not make an impression on me. But probably it is due to the fact that I look upon all these things with some indifference."

There were other teething troubles. G.D. wrote to Gandhi at Yeravda Jail, "I confess our Secretariat is not as efficient as it ought to be. Poor old Thakkur [Amritlal Thakkurdas, the Secretary] is wandering from place to place."

The *Harijan*, edited by Viyogi Hari, was due to appear in January 1933 but was delayed by minor formalities. Gandhi had sent two articles from prison. He also advised, "I would warn you against issuing the English edition unless it is properly got up, contains readable English material, and translations are all accurate."

The initial resolution of Harijan Sevak Sangh, passed at a meeting held under the Chairmanship of Malaviya, read "The Conference resolves that henceforth it will be the duty of Hindu readers to secure by every legitimate and peaceful means, an early removal of all social disabilities now imposed upon the so-called Untouchables, including the bar in respect of admission to the temples."

This formulation unfortunately led to expectations that could not be fulfilled. G.D. wrote to Gandhi from Gwalior, "Many educated Harijans seem to be under the impression that this Society of ours is going to create a millenium. Any man who is not employed expects employment from us. Any trader in financial difficulty expects us to relieve him of his troubles."

Rumblings now began to develop among caste Hindus in Bengal against the Poona Pact. More seriously the government announced a decision to remain neutral on the Temple Entry Bill, which resulted in its eventual defeat in the Legislative Assembly. "I find neither logic nor fairness in the Government's decision," G.D. wrote to Gandhi.

By late January 1933, Gandhi was enclosing an estimate for the English *Harijan* in a letter to G.D. "I propose to bring out, to start with, 10,000 copies. Then if there is not that demand we might slow down . . . I will give the paper a trial for 3 months, within which it must become self-supporting."

The *Harijan*, Hindi version, eventually got under way and G.D. wrote to Gandhi from Benares, where he was staying with his father in their house overlooking the Ganges,

As regards the Hindi Harijan I have been taking some personal interest in it. As you will notice I have even been contributing articles to it. The defects pointed out by you were already noticed by me and were brought to the notice of Hariji. The second issue, in my opinion, was a decided improvement, yet I think it requires further brightening up.

In March Gandhi was able to report from his prison office, "The English *Harijan* has become self-supporting already. The subscriptions received to date from street sales and annual subscribers leave a balance without the aid of the RS 1044 from the Central Board. Arrangements have been made to issue a Gujarati *Harijan*."

"I am afraid," G.D. was obliged to reply, "the Hindi *Harijan* cannot compete unless you give your special blessings in some of the articles you write in the English *Harijan*."

There were signs now of a rift developing between Malaviya and Gandhi over the Temple Entry Bill and other matters. "There is still a wrongly held notion in official quarters," G.D. wrote to Gandhi, "that the untouchability work is only a political stunt . . . Malaviyaji's attitude, however, has proved at least one thing, that in taking up the untouchability work you have alienated the alliance of some of your best political friends."

After a meeting with Malaviya in Delhi, G.D. wrote to Gandhi,

As regards the ultimate ideal there may be no difference between you and Panditji but in practice you are poles apart. He wants to go slowly and is not prepared to displease anyone . . . Panditji believes that your methods are likely to cause greater delay in getting the untouchables into the temples. In reality, what he wants to do is to avoid a clash with the orthodox.

G.D. was now busy collecting funds for other aspects of Harijan work, such as education, and the improvement of the appalling sewage conditions in the Calcutta *bustees* inhabited by untouchables. "Now the solution for such *bustees* is either their demolition or the making of a proper drainage system," G.D. wrote to Gandhi. Unfortunately "most of the Councillors are interested either directly or indirectly in the *bustees* and when the question of reform comes up they put up opposition".

G.D., in the same letter, expressed disappointment over his efforts to raise money.

I thought people would simply be delighted to pay, at least those who have got money. In Delhi I walked from door to door for two days and I got only 1,500/− after great difficulty. In Bombay, four Marwari firms, after having promised subscriptions, are withholding payment. . . . I myself can pay anything that you want me to pay, but I confess that I cannot bring money from others. . . . I approached some of my Sanatanist friends in Calcutta. But although they talk very politely, they do not pay.

It is a familiar enough story, which Gandhi received without comment. He was more concerned about improving the Hindi *Harijan.* "The only things we find worth reading are your articles," he wrote to G.D. "Your language is both sweet and forceful. But this alone will not satisfy me."

On the question of the *bustees* Gandhi advised,

When you next go to Calcutta I suggest your having an informal meeting of the principal municipal councillors. No matter what vested interests have grown up they should be attacked and the problem dealt with . . . The question behind all the difficulties that arise resolves itself, as a rule, into apathy on the part of those who profess their appreciation of the necessity for reform but are not prepared to sacrifice anything for it.

G.D. underwent an operation to drain the antrum later that year. He wrote to Gandhi from Gwalior.

I am glad that my father paid a visit to you. I do not know how he impressed you with his limited education and way of expression. But he is very good at heart and has got great regard for you. He himself, although a staunch orthodox, appreciates your views and in his own ways carries propaganda in your favour.

86

In the autumn Gandhi was released and at the same time the Sabarmati Ashram near Ahmedabad was abandoned. It was Gandhi's wish that the property should be transferred to the All-India Harijan Organization for the settlement of approved Harijan families, and for the opening of hostels and leather workshops for Harijan and non-Harijan children equally. G.D., as President of the Association, was asked to accept responsibility for its future management. He was glad to do so, and immediately took upon himself the task of raising with Gandhi the problems related to the setting up of a workable constitution. Thus, one further administrative burden was added to the many – commercial, philanthropic and social – already existing.

In April G.D. wrote on successive days to Gandhi, in relation to a malicious personal attack on himself in the *National Call*, and to Lord Halifax, about the failure of the government to come to terms with Gandhi. "The old man is represented sometimes as an impractical and unconstructive visionary and at others as a dishonest, astute and insincere politician. He cannot be both and you know what he is. There is no desire to understand him. There is horror against human contact."

In the same letter G.D. remarked,

To my mind a better mutual understanding more than a better Constitution is the great requirement of the day. A Constitution prepared in an atmosphere of distrust can never succeed . . . Every well-wisher of England and India thus for the time being can only have one mission at heart, that is, of establishing mutual appreciation between leaders in the two countries . . . I know the keen interest you still take in our affairs. But if I am allowed, I may say that India needs your help much more than what you unstintedly gave in the past. You set an example in 1931 but it has not been fully pursued.

Halifax replied appreciatively on 11 May, but in fairly bland fashion. "I have always felt that the present situation is one demanding great patience on all sides, and readiness to see through our present difficulties in the light of the larger hope."

Such language was scarcely indicative of the sense of urgency that Indian politicians, of whatever persuasion, felt to be more appropriate. G.D., more sanguine in these matters, was for the present ready to accept the intention for the deed.

Meanwhile, an article in the *Calcutta Amrita Bazar Patrika*, criticizing an interview G.D. had given on the formation of the Swaraj Party, had roused him to reply privately to the editor, Mrinal Kanti Basu. He wrote on 5 May and again on 7 May, in his second letter observing,

> I think I should explain a little more my reference to the Poona Pact because what I wrote is likely to be misunderstood if not properly explained. Before I left Calcutta for Poona I discussed matters with a prominent Hindu Sabha leader and asked him whether it would be possible for the Hindus in general to make a generous gesture to the Harijans. He thereupon consulted an eminent Bengali leader who is just now opposed to the Poona Pact and he agreed that it was very desirable that such a generous gesture should be made, even to the extent of saying that if it could satisfy the untouchables we should offer them even cent per cent of the seats allocated to caste Hindus.

G.D., conscious of the importance of his own contribution to the Poona Pact and of his responsibility in all Harijan affairs, was determined to see that reporting of his views was accurate to the smallest detail.

Gandhi, in the early summer of 1934, was making a pilgrimage on foot through Bihar and Orissa. Mirabehn wrote to G.D. that Gandhi had been telling the Orissa workers that it was in this way that he could best spread his views on the Harijan question and his advocacy of khadi. G.D. wrote to Gandhi, in Patna, that he agreed "the changing of people's hearts was more important than collection of funds" but he defended a recent speech criticized by Gandhi on account of its vagueness. His letter combines modesty and general deference to Gandhi's moral authority on the one hand, "Please guide me where you think I stand to be corrected", with firm explanations for his actions on the other:

I agree with you that planning in India has to be done with Indian conditions before our eyes. When I was advancing a plea for planning I had never for a moment in my mind the five years' Plan of Russia or anything of the kind. In fact, I see a great danger in over-centralization as they are doing it in other places. Yet there are many good things that can only be done by Government.

Gandhi, much affected by the terrific heat and pestered by insects, still contrived to write lengthy letters to G.D. from halts on his tour. From Chandanpur near Puri he wrote:

I have gone through your prosperity plan. It contains sufficient material for a plan, but the plan itself is not there. A plan should be such as could be immediately taken in hand by the Government as also by the others, no matter if it fails to attract wider notice. . . . I am convinced that in any such plan the charkha should occupy the pivotal point. If you disagree explain why, after dissecting the entire issue. The dismissal of the charkha from the people's daily life has resulted in widespread lethargy, while the absence of scientific animal husbandry is making the animals devour human beings. If we could only blend the charkha with scientific cattle breeding this country of ours would attain to a stage of prosperity denied to the other nations so far.

They resumed their discussions when G.D. joined Gandhi in Orissa for a few days. Back in Calcutta, G.D. wrote to Sir Tej Bahadur Sapru in Allahabad that he had mentioned casually to Gandhi his disagreement with those who found the White Paper Scheme no improvement whatsoever on the Montagu–Chelmsford reforms. Gandhi had reacted in astonishment and asked G.D. to prepare a note comparing the two constitutions. G.D. was now asking Sir Tej, as the authority on the White Paper, to do this, with Gandhi's agreement.

Sir Tej replied,

I do not think any useful purpose will be served by my writing any memorandum on the subject as the Congress has already taken a decided line and I cannot flatter myself that anything coming from me can have the least chance of persuading them to alter their viewpoint. I have all along held that the White Paper falls short of our expectations . . . but with all its defects I have been of the opinion that in certain respects it will make our position distinctly better.

It was only to help Gandhi to make up his mind that G.D. had written for a confidential assessment of the relative propositions, not for a public statement, as G.D. explained in a subsequent letter to Sir Tej.

For some time now the workers had been uncertain as to what exactly Gandhi meant by "Swadeshi". Gandhi's own statement that Swadeshi was its own definition scarcely helped, so that at a meeting in Bombay of the All-India Swadeshi League Gandhi attempted to clarify his views. He ended:

I have no doubt that true swadeshi consists in encouraging and reviving home industries. That alone can help the dumb millions. It also provides an outlet for the creative faculties and resourcefulness of the people. . . . I do not want any of those who are engaged in more remunerative occupations to leave them and take to the inner industries. Just as I did with the spinning wheel I would ask only those who suffer from unemployment and penury to take to some of these industries and add a little to their slender resources.

There was nothing in this with which G.D., as industrialist and mill-owner, had reason to disagree. Nor did he. "I have read Gandhiji's definition of swadeshi very carefully," he wrote to Chandrashankar Shukla, one of Gandhi's entourage at Cawnpore, "I had heard his views in Orissa and I entirely agree with them."

By August Gandhi was sufficiently out of sympathy with Congress in its various manifestations to contemplate leaving the Party. "The growing corruption and untruth are becoming unbearable," he wrote in a message to Rajagopalachari as he passed through Wardha on the Grand Trunk Express. Gandhi was anxious to go to the Frontier to see for himself whether the Front Red Shirts were guilty as alleged of violence and he also wanted to visit Bengal "to wean the terrorists" there from murders. For the present, however, he remained at Wardha, recovering from the effects of a fast.

Commenting on Gandhi's possible departure from Congress, G.D. observed in a letter to Mahadev Desai:

> Roughly speaking, those who like Bapu's retirement from the Congress and those who dislike it have got their own motives. Moderates like his retirement because that will lower the prestige of Congress. Socialists like it because they hope to have a free hand. The Parliamentary Board dislikes it because they fear it may harm them. But in spite of all this there is a common feeling and that is this, that Bapu is hopeless. I think everyone has begun to realise that he is too big to be properly understood.

That was one way of reacting to Gandhi's unpredictability. Mahadev's own feelings were not dissimilar, though more charitably expressed. "He soars high up in the skies but his feet are always on the ground. That is why we never miss the human touch about him and yet always know that we can never soar where he soars."

In late November Gandhi received a polite refusal from the Viceroy's secretary to his request to visit the North-West Frontier; "it is not desirable at the present time". G.D. in Calcutta had his tonsils out. "They kept me under chloroform for forty minutes. It was a peculiar sensation. When I awoke I thought I was in a pocket edition of death." While this was happening Jawaharlal Nehru, in an interview to *The Pioneer*, observed, "I am convinced that the days of capitalism and the privileged classes are over and that a new structure of society is inevitable . . . not necessarily on the Russian model but on the general lines of the Russian conception. The alternative is fascism."

Elsewhere he remarked,

> The truth about the English in India is that they are prey to their own fears. . . . Every Englishman, whether soldier

or civilian, sees himself as an army of occupation in a conquered country which is ready to rise at the first opportunity. I can understand, even if I cannot excuse, the conduct of General Dyer at Amritsar. It was the product of the fear complex which is the cause of half the troubles of the world.

G.D. would not probably have argued about Nehru's view on the English, but their disagreement about the way in which Indian society should evolve, economically if not politically, was central to policy-making discussions in the years leading up to Independence.

To G.D., more than to Nehru, the series of Communist-led strikes in textile and other industries throughout 1934, culminating in a Bombay general strike, and the general increase of militancy in the unions, were symptoms that needed to be dealt with. The communists had picked up many new recruits from among those ex-*habitués* of the detention camps who had once either been revolutionary terrorists or supporters of Gandhi, but who, after the abandonment of civil disobedience, found the options too tame. What to Nehru and others on the left of the national movement was something in the nature of an interesting conflict in ideologies, a subject for abstract debate, was a matter of practical urgency for those, like G.D., who had to deal with large workforces every day of their lives. The dreamers and diehard Marxists had little if any experience of industry or labour relations, still less any understanding of economics. As it happened, the confrontation between left and right in Congress, between socialist planning and Indian business interests, took a strange turn. While Nehru's presidential addresses at Lucknow and Faizpur seemed, in the words of the historian Sumit Sarkar,

> to embody virtually all the radical aspirations and programmes of the Left . . . the Right within the Congress was able to skilfully and effectively ride and indeed utilize the storm, and by the summer of 1937 Congress ministries were being formed to work a significant part of the Constitution which everyone had been denouncing for years.

Nehru had in fact alienated many Indian businessmen by his speeches, to the extent that a manifesto was issued by twenty-one of them in May 1936, denouncing socialism as being a threat to all property, religion and personal liberty. G.D. had no part in it. On 20 April, from Birla House, New Delhi, he wrote to Sir Purshottamdas Thakurdas, with whom he had been instrumental in founding the Federation of Indian Chambers of Commerce and Industry and with whom he had often talked at 2 Ridge Road in Bombay, that he was perfectly satisfied with what had taken place in Lucknow:

Mahatmaji kept his promise and without his uttering a word he saw that no new commitments were made. Jawaharlalji's speech in a way was thrown into the waste paper basket because all the resolutions that were passed were against the spirit of his speech. I understand that he was in a very small minority . . . Rajendra Babu spoke very strongly, and some people attacked Jawaharlalji's ideology openly. It must be said, however, to the credit of Jawaharlalji that he fully realised his position and did not abuse his powers. The Working Committee which he had constituted contains an overwhelming majority of the "Mahatmaji Group". He could have caused a split by resigning but he did not. I am told that official circles, when they read his speech, were overwhelmed with joy because they saw in it a source of split in the Congress, but Jawaharlalji avoided it.

About Nehru G.D. observed in the same letter:

He seems to be like a typical English democrat who takes defeat in a sporting spirit. He seems to be out for giving expression to his ideology but he realises that action is impossible and so does not press for it. He confessed in his speech that tall talk was a bad habit in India and that there was no chance of any direct action in the near future. It could be said therefore that things are moving in the right direction.

Confident that his analysis of the situation was correct G.D.

wrote from Calcutta to one of the nationalist co-signatories of the manifesto, Walchand Hirachand:

> Do you think you were right in signing that manifesto against Jawaharlal? If its merit is to be judged by the results then I must say that you have been instrumental in creating further opposition to capitalism. You have rendered no service to your castemen. It is curious how we businessmen are so short-sighted. We all are against socialism and yet nothing is being done to carry the argumentative propaganda and even people like Vallabhai and Bhulabhai who are fighting against socialism are not being helped. It looks very crude for a man with property to say that he is opposed to expropriation in the wider interest of the country. It goes without saying that anyone holding property will oppose expropriation. . . . Apart from this, our duty does not end in simply opposing socialism. Businessmen have to do something positive to ameliorate the condition of the masses. I feel that your manifesto, far from helping, has done positive harm to the capitalistic system.

While business was sorting out its various positions in relation to Congress policy, important developments crucial to the future of England and India were taking place. The Government of India Act, which had its origins in the abortive Simon Commission of 1927, was finally passed in August 1935. Much of G.D.'s correspondence at the time, both to Gandhi and to influential members of the government, was devoted to points of detail in it and to Indian reaction towards it.

While the Bill was still being prepared G.D. had written to the Secretary of State, Sir Samuel Hoare:

> I am writing this after reading the Joint Select Committee report very carefully and after the splendid speech that you delivered in the House of Commons . . . I have nothing to say about the report. You have rightly stated in Parliament that in India it has satisfied few. On the other hand, your words spoken to me during my last interview with you "howsoever radical a Secretary of State may be with the

present Parliament", it is impossible to go beyond a certain stage are still ringing in my ears. . . . But I am looking upon the situation entirely from a different angle.

The substance of G.D.'s letter was one that was to become increasingly familiar with the passage of time, simply that without personal contact and trust any recommendations would be badly received. "May I submit that it is the method of advance, rather than its measure, which will always count. Montagu–Chelmsford reforms were introduced in an unfortunate atmosphere and I hope the mistake will not be repeated." About the JSC report G.D. had written to Mahadev Desai, "Its recommendations are nothing more than a provision of granting of powers of attorney by a master to his employee which could be cancelled at will."

Since the Bill fell short of complete Independence, had a number of safeguards written into it, and was framed largely without Indian participation, it was natural for many Congressmen to oppose it. It was equally opposed by diehards within the Conservative Party. Nevertheless, G.D. was anxious to arrange a meeting between Gandhi and government representatives, not to negotiate on constitutional matters but simply to establish an understanding. "I think if they do this," G.D. observed to Desai, "the rest will look after itself."

Sir Samuel Hoare had replied politely but non-committally to G.D.'s letter:

I am afraid we are not in agreement on the constitutional question . . . It is evidently the safeguards that occupy the prominent position in your mind. To us here the impressive fact is that there is to be so large an extension of self-government . . . The general feeling here is one of prudence. You would probably call it caution. But certainly it is not one of illiberality.

G.D. wrote back:

I may accept what you say, that the scheme reflects an act of prudence and not one of illiberality. But don't you think you would like the best in India to share your views and get

95

up and say "The Constitution is not what we want but we will work it honestly for constructive purposes because what it is lacking in letter is to be made up in spirit" . . . When I say this, I am not talking as people generally do with vague ideas but as a practical businessman who believes that given goodwill such a position is possible to be achieved and that it must be achieved . . . You can always count on my service for any step that you take to create a cordiality which is at present lacking in the Indian atmosphere and which is so necessary in the interest of both the countries who by destiny are bound together.

Hoare replied on 30 January 1935. He ended his letter,

I tried in a recent speech at Oxford to give a sketch of the new constitution as I imagine it working, and send you a copy in case it interests you to read it. You will see that I developed there some of the ideas expressed in my last letter to you. I have to maintain what you call the human touch with more than one school of thought.

G.D. had meetings in early February with the Viceroy, the Home Member Sir Henry Craik, and the Governor of Bengal, on all of which he reported at some length in letters to Gandhi. His main concern was to prevent Gandhi from taking the hard Congress line about the proposed Bill:

I am still sticking to my views and the more I talk with my friends the more I get confirmed in it, that it is not correct to say that the proposed constitution is worse than the Montagu reforms. Of course this could be made worse, even tyranical, but this could as well be made better and far better than the existing position and I would, therefore, ask you to keep an open mind.

The Government of India Bill was not the only thing on G.D.'s mind, though it took him to London in the summer to try and effect a working relationship between the British Government and Gandhi and other Congress leaders. Both Gandhi and the Governor of Bengal approved of the idea and sent him letters of introduction.

More immediately G.D., aware that unresolved Muslim–Hindu differences had effectively scuppered both the Round Table Conferences, wrote a series of letters on the subject of joint electorates to Gandhi. As long as Jinnah remained the leader of his community, G.D. was to observe later, all proposals and negotiations for a settlement other than Partition were doomed to failure. Nevertheless, G.D., in consultation with friends such as Bhulabhai Desai and Sardar Patel, made every effort to get some kind of Congress–Muslim League settlement so that a united front could be presented before the final framing of the Act. But there was no co-operation from Jinnah and no support from the Sikhs or from East Bengal. "It is a great tragedy," G.D. wrote to Mahadev Desai,

and we can draw a moral from it. First, there is not even one Bengalee to support us boldly. This may be a condemnation of Bengal, but Congress is no less responsible for it. We never backed anyone in Bengal and so not one advocate of our viewpoint is to be found. The communal question remains unsolved, and by our failure we stand before the world thoroughly humiliated.

Intermediary

In London G.D. wasted no time in contacting influential people. He had remarked, at a meeting lasting over an hour with the Governor of Bengal shortly before he left, that it was only by making a *rapprochement* with Gandhi, despite talk of retirement still a powerful figure, that the government could prevent the left wing of the Congress from taking control. It was with this objective in mind, the establishing of sympathetic relations between the government and the followers of Gandhi during the months before the Act could come into operation, that G.D. met Sir Findlater Stewart, Chief of the Secretariat for the India Office, and R. A. Butler, then Under-Secretary of State. "To me," G.D. observed, "it was already evident that the English in London sincerely believed that a great step forward towards India's self-government was about to be taken as soon as the Bill became law, whereas in India there was an equally genuine feeling that it would be a great step backwards."

As usual, G.D. reported back fully to Gandhi on what had taken place. In his meeting with Stewart G.D. had insisted that what was required was Dominion Status in action, and that the defeat of Gandhism, through government suspicion of Gandhi's motives, would simply lead to Communism. For various reasons elaborated by G.D., it was only with Congress that the government could deal, the Muslims being content with the Constitution as it was, the Communists being against agreement on any conditions, and the Liberals all talking with different voices. On being asked whether Gandhi could deliver the goods, G.D. replied yes, but that he was getting old and after he died there would be no one acceptable left with whom to negotiate.

Butler, G.D. reported, was intelligent, charming but demoralized. G.D. explained to him that though Congress was represented in the Assembly the government took no notice of their views and there was no personal contact. Butler, accepting that the atmosphere was bad, observed sadly, "We feel disheartened when we think that this Bill, for which we sacrificed our health, our friends and our time, is supposed to be a retrograde step." When Butler asked if Communism was on the increase G.D. replied that it was and the reason was the rejection of Gandhism by the government.

G.D. met Sir George Schuster, involved in preparations for the next Empire Economic Conference, the same day. Schuster, a former economic adviser to the Colonial Office and Finance Member of the Executive Council of the Viceroy, was friendly but said that with 20 per cent of the population in England undernourished and two million out of work nobody could take much interest in India. He advised G.D. to avoid Simon as being "useless and not straight" and to try and see Baldwin, even if only for fifteen minutes.

On 26 June G.D. had constructive meetings with Stewart and Lothian. Stewart, having confessed that they did not like Gandhi to be on the other side of the fence, observed that one of the troubles was that although Gandhi was revered by nine-tenths of the population he had no constitutional position.

Lord Lothian, in a talk lasting forty-five minutes, came straight out with his view on the Bill:

I agree with the diehards that it has been a surrender. You who are not used to any constitution cannot realise what great power you are going to wield. If you look at the constitution it looks as if all the powers are vested in the Governor-General and the Governor. But is not every power here vested in the King? Everything is done in the name of the King but does the King ever interfere? Once the power passes into the hands of the legislature, the Governor or the Governor-General is never going to interfere. . . . The Civil Service will be helpful. You too will realise this. Once a policy is laid down they will carry it out loyally and faithfully.

Lothian, agreeing with G.D. that there would have to be an accelerated degree of Indianization, concluded that military control would be the only real threat. "You have got every other thing." He explained, in relation to the apparent gracelessness of the Bill's presentation,

> We could not help it. We had to fight the diehards here. You could not realise what great courage has been shown by Mr. Baldwin and Sir Samuel Hoare. We did not want to spare the diehards as we had to talk in a different language. Besides this, the other difficulty was Lord Willingdon. He has great distrust of the Mahatma and he is not a very brainy man.

These various meetings – and in due course G.D., before his return in September, met virtually everyone of importance in Anglo-Indian affairs – confirmed G.D.'s original opinion that the differences between the two countries were largely psychological, the same proposals open to diametrically opposed interpretations. He had not, probably, taken in before his visit how considerable, in the eyes of British conservatives, the concessions had been. It was not his function to argue over them, however, merely to work towards a way in which the Bill could be sympathetically received to mutual advantage.

If nothing else, successive conversations made clear to G.D. that the agents of the Bill had at least as heavy odds against them at home as they had in India.

On 29 June, in a letter of over 5000 words, G.D. reported to Gandhi on developments so far. It is hard to overestimate the value of his work as an intermediary, for no one else, in either an official or non-official capacity, was taking it upon themselves to attempt any kind of reconciliation between entrenched opponents. After G.D.'s four months in London there could at least be no excuse for either side being unaware of the other's position.

In his first few weeks in London G.D. talked, in addition to those already mentioned, with Lord Zetland, Secretary of State for India and a former Governor of Bengal, with Halifax, Linlithgow and MacDonald. He became friendly with Lord

Derby, lunched in the House of Commons and had meetings with important men in the City, such as Sir Thomas Catto, and with leading Labour politicians. Even so, he complained about the slowness of his progress, since people are "booked for weeks ahead. . . . Hoare is so busy with Germany, Italy and China that he has asked me to wait and remind him again and again about our interview."

G.D.'s persistence ensured that the problem of India, at one of the most crucial moments in her history, with a new Viceroy due to be appointed and the Government of India Act to be put into operation, would not be ignored.

To Gandhi G.D. reiterated his view that the Bill would depend for its success on the spirit in which it was worked. If the Governor-General used his powers, then it would be pure autocracy, but if, as argued by each person G.D. had talked to, it was intended that he should have no more power than a constitutional monarch, "then the Bill could bring in a very good regime". G.D. contrasted the goodwill and sympathy expressed in London with the oppressive atmosphere in India. He ended,

> When men like Zetland, Butler, Lothian and Sir Findlater Stewart talk in such a manner, assuring me that the safe-guards are not meant for meddling with the affairs of the Ministers, I cannot help feeling they are talking with sincerity. . . . Mere sweet words have never deceived me in my business dealings and I would be very surprised if I am carried away in this respect by their excellent behaviour and eloquence. . . . I hope it will not all end in smoke.

What G.D. tried to make plain in his various interviews was that Congress would not be attracted simply to run a government machine. If they were to be involved whole-heartedly they would want to concern themselves with education, social projects, taxation, banking, employment and such other matters as they would eventually have to deal with on the attainment of self-government.

It was along these lines that G.D. reported the general drift of his discussions to Gandhi. He also gave the Mahatma brief impressions of those with whom he came into contact. About Butler he wrote, "He has no tinge of racial bias or superiority. He is very distressed at the way in which we suspect their motives," and about Lord Derby, "The most charming personality I have come across. He is very rich and influential and stands on no ceremony. He has told me to ring him up whenever I need his help and he will either come to me, or send for me."

G.D. was anxious for confirmation from Gandhi that he was working on the right lines:

> I hope I am representing you correctly and faithfully. I have to work hard against genuine misunderstanding. When I got Mahadevbhai's letter from Quetta [about the recent earthquake] my heart simply broke. What a contrast between the atmosphere prevailing there and the one prevailing here. I did not imagine the difference between the two in India.

G.D.'s next meeting was with Ramsay MacDonald, to whom he repeated the familiar complaint, "Whenever we offer co-operation it is refused and we are snubbed. Mr. Gandhi is treated as an outlaw and yet you want us to appreciate the reforms." MacDonald observed about the Viceroy and Gandhi that they were like "two pieces of good music. They are both good if separately sung but if sung together there is no harmony. That is the trouble." MacDonald's main theme was that if Congress contributed to working the Constitution, the safeguards – the discretionary powers of the Governors – would never need to be used, but if they set about wrecking it they would be playing into the hands of the diehards.

Not untypically, G.D. ended the meeting by suggesting a change of diet for MacDonald's insomnia. MacDonald replied, "I want a doctor friend, otherwise I do not believe in doctors. I breakfast with Horder every morning and that helps me a lot." He talked of old days, G.D. reported, when he had been to India and had a lot of shooting.

By the end of his first month in London G.D. cannot have had any doubts about the affection responsible Englishmen felt for India nor indeed, despite the distraction of urgent matters nearer home, their willingness to make time for him. Gandhi was not in office and G.D., as his confidential emissary, was on a self-imposed mission. Yet reservations were never expressed about the value of exchanges of view on this level, rather an optimism that by thoroughly understanding the atmosphere in both countries, the respective leaders could more confidently take the next step.

G.D. got little joy out of his dinner with the Labour leaders – Attlee, Rhys Davies, Morgan Jones among others – at the House. "Almost all of them unintelligent and dull," he reported to Gandhi. "Attlee somewhat reactionary." Attlee had grown increasingly irritated as the evening wore on, drawing attention to Gandhi's inconsistency and political cunning, and the corruption in Congress. However, after a series of acrimonious exchanges, they parted as friends. "I do not think it was a waste of time," G.D. concluded.

On 2 July G.D. met Lord Linlithgow, and later in the week Lord Halifax, Lord Salisbury and Sir Samuel Hoare, the latter for only eight minutes. The Bill was still at the Committee stage in the House of Lords, but Hoare assured G.D. that everyone was determined to make the reforms a success, Churchill excepted.

In mid-July G.D., largely to clarify his own views, sent accounts of his discussions and his own recommendations to Halifax, Linlithgow and Stewart. To Gandhi he observed about Salisbury, "Old deaf man, not much grit or wit, but feels his responsibility." Salisbury expressed admiration for Gandhi's saintliness, character and good intentions but added patronizingly, "the great mistake you Indians make is that you confuse great qualities with experience. England has got the experience of 1000 years behind her. You have none." When G.D. retorted that India's background and culture were both more creditable and ancient than England's, Salisbury continued, "I do not want to under-value your great civilisation and philosophy but your country is not a democracy. You have yet to learn." G.D.'s conclusion was that Salisbury was "a nice man" but not of much use.

To Dawson, the editor of *The Times*, G.D. wrote, after a brief meeting, to congratulate him on an article emphasizing the need for the personal touch,

> As I pointed out to you, Lord Halifax put 60,000 men in gaol and yet he could command confidence. Sir John Anderson has put 2500 men in gaol without trial without making himself unpopular. It is because he has made his critics – by his personal touch – see that the job is as unpleasant to him as to his critics.

On 13 July Gandhi wrote from Wardha assuring G.D. that he found nothing amiss in his reports.

> But what I most fear is that when it comes to making conditions the result will be nil. The question of the release of the political prisoners and the detenus, the closing down of the Andamans as a penal settlement, and the restoration of land to the civil resisters is quite likely to remain unsolved. I would not like you to raise such issues on your own initiative but if they are raised by the other party discuss them by all means. In the present climate little can be hoped for by way of understanding. This does not mean, however, that you should stop trying. You must continue to exert yourself as you have been doing already.

G.D.'s most important meeting was a twenty-minute interview with Baldwin. To Baldwin, who confessed ignorance of the nature of G.D.'s mission, G.D. ran through his estimate of the three essential conditions for the success of the reforms, none of which was in existence. These he outlined as a realization by the Civil Service that they were servants, not masters or politicians, and that they should not favour any political party; a realization by Congress that they could achieve political freedom through working the proposed reforms; the appointment of highly qualified governors who would work like constitutional monarchs and not meddle with the affairs of ministers. Specifically, what G.D. advocated were new moves towards improving relations before, not after, the appointment of a new Viceroy.

Baldwin appeared sympathetic and gave assurances that only the very best men would be appointed. He added, "In the past Congress had been anti-Government. Anti-Government meant anti-British, but they should realise that now to be anti-Government would mean being anti-Indian."

Baldwin agreed that it was a pity Irwin had been recalled so soon after concluding the Gandhi–Irwin pact and remarked that if he had been younger he would have liked to have gone out to India himself. "There could be no two opinions," G.D. noted, "about the fact that he is an honest, straightforward and simple man, and he impressed me as a student of politics. He has got a peculiar habit of enjoying a hearty laugh without any special reason, and he does it at an interval of every two minutes."

G.D. saw Baldwin in the morning. In the afternoon he was taking tea with the Archbishop of Canterbury and explaining Gandhi's policies of non-violence. "His creed is to change the heart of his opponents by persuasion; if not through argument, through self-suffering." G.D. made clear to the Archbishop that though Gandhi had retired from Congress he was still the sole leader, a dictator without force of arms. "He is thus a living symbol of India." Every time he sought a meeting with the Viceroy the door was slammed in his face. The Archbishop promised to do what he could and counselled patience meanwhile.

The next letter from the Gandhi camp expressed further satisfaction at G.D.'s efforts but made mention of "a few paragraphs about you [in the Indian newspapers] in very bad taste and verging on base ingratitude".

On 22 July G.D. lunched with Lord Linlithgow, who, it was already rumoured, was to be the next Viceroy. Linlithgow began:

May I sum up the position? We have been talking amongst ourselves and I must admit we are all very much impressed with your views. We have discussed many ideas, including those supplied by you, but I cannot say we have been able to pick up any one of them. The future Viceroy cannot go to India or the Secretary of State and it would be unfair for Mr Gandhi to be invited without giving him some reasonable promise of success. The present Viceroy cannot break the ice because he complains he has been boycotted. That is the position. But you can have the satisfaction of feeling that even if you have not achieved anything substantial you have largely succeeded in impressing us with the strength of your case. We fully realise that if the Reforms are to work effectively there must be an agreement about the future between the right, left and centre.

G.D. put the idea to Linlithgow that a political conference attended by governors, political leaders and Gandhi could be summoned by the present Viceroy, at which future developments could be discussed in a friendly atmosphere.

Linlithgow agreed to go into the possibility. Over lunch the talk ranged from the breeding of bulls to experiments in education in Pilani, from problems in milk transportation to the effects of the car on village life. After G.D. had expressed the view that while he was in favour of extensive primary and middle education he was against unrestricted higher education, Linlithgow said that Sweden regulated its supply of graduates so as not to cause a glut but only an Indian minister could do it without being misunderstood.

As they were parting Linlithgow asked about Gandhi's age and health. G.D. replied, "I have never seen a healthier man in my life. He works hard, sleeps little and eats little, and yet is most cheerful."

On 29 July G.D. received a note from Lord Lothian suggesting a meeting.

There are clearly going to be difficulties in the way of carrying out the kind of proposals which you originally had in view. On the other hand your visit here is undoubtedly awakening people to the very real problem which I do not think they had fully understood before and will, I think, bear fruit in other ways. I heard a great deal of appreciation expressed about your initiative.

G.D. was anxious not to leave London without some specific proposals to report. But if these were not immediately forthcoming he had at least the consolation of knowing he had not wasted his time. He confided as much to Gandhi.

There were still contacts to be pursued. He lunched with the directors of Lloyds Bank and told them that within ten years India would be exporting cloth to Lancashire, a forecast that upset them. There was a lunch with Wilson Harris of the *Spectator*, at which G.D. discussed the problem of Indian lascars in the East End who had English families which they could not support. G.D. offered to take fifty children to India but the parents would not part with them.

On 30 July, his round of visits almost over, G.D. wrote to Gandhi,

> The more I have watched things the more I have come to the conclusion that there are two distinct atmospheres, one in London, the creation of the politicians and statesmen, the other in India, the creation of the Viceroy and officials. . . . How to improve the atmosphere in India is a problem and it depends entirely upon personalities.

G.D. was, in his own words, "determined to pull every possible string on Gandhiji's behalf". His biggest coup, in his own eyes, was an invitation to lunch at Chartwell from Churchill, arch-opponent of every concession towards Indian self-government.

This was fixed for 9 August, by which date G.D. had managed final meetings with Zetland and Lothian before they departed to Scotland for their summer holidays, Lothian inviting G.D. to visit him before sailing for India.

"Curiously enough," G.D. wrote, "meeting Mr Churchill was one of my most pleasant experiences." When G.D. arrived Churchill was in the garden. "He wore a workman's apron which he did not change at lunch and went out again into the garden wearing a huge hat with a big feather in it."

Churchill did 75 per cent of the talking.

It was never boring but he is badly informed about India.

He has peculiar notions. Villages, he thinks, are entirely cut off in India from towns. I corrected this. No townsman is a pure townsman in India. Everyone maintains touch with his village. Twenty-five thousand men that I employ in my mills went to their villages more than once a year. Therefore on the roll there were more than 50,000.

Churchill said, "I do not like the Bill but it is now in the Statute. I am not going to bother any more. You have got immense powers so make it a success." What, G.D. inquired, was his test of success. Churchill replied:

My test is improvement in the lot of the masses, morally as well as materially. I do not care if you are more or less loyal to Great Britain. I do not care about more education but give the masses more butter. As the French King said "fowl in the pot". Tell Mr Gandhi to use the powers that are offered and make the thing a success. I did not meet Mr Gandhi when he was in England, it was then rather awkward, but I should like to meet him now. I would love to go to India before I die. If I went there I would stay for six months.

Churchill asked G.D. if Gandhi wanted to wreck the Constitution, to which G.D. replied, "Mr Gandhi is indifferent. He believes that political liberty will come through our own efforts and that our political progress will depend entirely upon us."

Churchill, having expressed genuine sympathy and affection for India, said,

I have real fears about the future. India is a burden on us. We have to maintain an army and for the sake of India we have to maintain Singapore and Near East strength. If India could look after herself we would be delighted. I have all along felt there are fifty Indias. But you have got the thing now; make it a success and if you do I will advocate your getting much more.

Before leaving England G.D. sent a summary of his impressions to Lord Halifax under the title "Some Points about the Political Situation in India". It began,

The Irwin–Gandhi pact was a great step binding India and Great Britain together. This created a precedent. It struck at the roots of the method of securing political advance by means of disorder and substituted the method of mutual discussion and confidence. Its implications, however, were realised by few except the two authors.

In his exposition G.D. runs through the main events of the succeeding years: the rapid burial of the pact by Congress and government for different reasons, the failure of civil resisters to adopt Gandhism in its pure form, its exploitation by radicals in pursuit of political freedom but without faith in the philosophy, the subsequent reaction against Gandhism.

After the "fast unto death" and the Untouchable crusade the radicals drifted towards the left and Gandhi, resigned to the fact that violence and "the Parliamentary mentality" had crept into Congress attitudes, under the guise of non-violence, withdrew civil resistance and set himself the task of reforming Congress thinking by concentrating on the eradication of social, religious and economic evils, especially in relation to Harijans and the villages. Unable to influence Congress in practical matters except by enforcing his views Gandhi had retired from active membership.

Further points G.D. touched on were the failure of Congress members of the Assembly to sign the Viceroy's book, a source of much distress to Lord Willingdon, the plight of Congress moderates engaged in simultaneous battles against the socialists and the government, the attitudes of Muslims and civil servants in the present situation, and the unfortunate decision of the government to refuse permission to trusted Indian leaders to visit Quetta after the recent earthquake.

Halifax sent a copy of G.D.'s potted history, seen from an Indian viewpoint, to Linlithgow. G.D. sent a further note raising the problems of political prisoners still in gaol, the return of confiscated land, and terrorism.

While the Congress should not exclude punishment from their *modus operandi*, the Government, in my opinion, should not exclude the method of reconciliation. The release of

Sarate Chundra Bose is a step in the right direction and I think his brother Mr Subhas Bose, too, could be handled properly. It would not be beyond the ingenuity of Sir John Anderson to find a formula.

G.D. ended his accompanying note, "I am writing all these things for your consideration, because some day you will have to give serious attention to these matters and you may like to think ahead."

G.D. left England with high hopes, much cheered by a note from Lord Lothian assuring him that the new Viceroy, Lord Linlithgow, would arrive in India "with a definite mission to establish personal contact with the national leaders".

The New Viceroy

G.D. arrived back in India on 12 September. He found rulers
and ruled as full of mutual distrust as when he had left Bombay
four months earlier. Nevertheless, he wrote to Lord Lothian,
he was hopeful that Lord Linlithgow's personality would
change the whole atmosphere. More significantly, on a visit
to Wardha he had gained an assurance from Gandhi, which
he was invited to pass on to the incoming Viceroy – namely,
that Gandhi would use all his influence to dissuade Congress
from making any further commitments about the reforms
before the new Viceroy arrived.

Lothian was delighted, and replied at length.

> I believe the whole future of India now turns upon whether
> or not her young men and women throw themselves into the
> elections in order that they may assume responsibility for
> government, first in the provinces and then at the Centre.
> It is only in this practical work that they will develop their
> political muscles and the kind of character and ability that
> will enable them to deal with the fundamental problems
> which confront India, whatever constitution she has –
> communalism, poverty, minorities, the princes, the power
> of property and so on.

If the Constitution was found lacking after experience in
trying to work it, then, Lothian continued, there would be a
case for demanding revisions, or if that were denied, for taking
more direct action.

> But if they now go in either for civil disobedience and
> non-cooperation or for violent revolutionary methods, they
> will fail to learn how to govern in a liberal and constitutional
> way and get confirmed in those rigid and dictatorial methods

which are wrecking Europe by destroying individual liberty, replacing individual thinking by mass organisation, and leading the world back to war, and which will certainly divide and lay India in ruins.

Immediately after his return G.D. had gone to see Gandhi at Wardha to fill in the details of his London summer. A general election had taken place in England in the autumn, the government being returned with an increased majority. G.D. meanwhile was faced by a strike in one of his mills, the workers being under the impression that there were to be dismissals and wage cuts. A telegram was sent to Gandhi that read "Birla Mills Labourers strike six days. Heavy wage cuts. Authorities unyielding. Police and Goondas employed. Read National Call." To this Gandhi replied, "Intervention improper without full knowledge. Circumstances suggest impartial arbitration subject men's return work and both parties accepting award as final and binding."

The strike, for a variety of reasons, lasted a fortnight. G.D., in a letter to Gandhi, admitted to tactlessness on the part of the management, but he denied any reduction in wages, despite the fact that the mill had been running at a loss for the last twelve months. The mill was closed down briefly but after a series of meetings, order and good relations were restored. G.D. however was not entirely happy, both sides having lost out in the dispute, which in the end proved to have been provoked by rumour without any real substance in fact. Gandhi's secretary wrote to G.D.,

> We are all so deeply thankful that the strike is over. The beauty of this whole business is that Krishna Nair's and Brijkrishna's version of the dispute tallies entirely with your own. Krishna Nair gratefully mentions the graceful way in which you received the workers' representatives and discussed everything. In view of all this, may it not be well that this storm *did* break out?

The same letter contained less encouraging news. "Bapu has had a fairly bad breakdown and he realises it himself." A change of diet from soya beans to fruit and milk and a week's rest resulted in a general improvement and a reduction in blood pressure, but G.D. remained worried. He advised a stay in Birla House, Delhi, which would guarantee complete rest, if he could manage the journey.

To Lord Linlithgow G.D. wrote on 21 December,

The communal situation is getting worse from day to day without any signs of improvement. For the situation to calm down the Hindus in Mohammedan provinces, and vice versa, have to realise that majority rule must prevail. Being a Hindu myself, I add with some hesitation that there is a general impression throughout the country that the British in India, as well as abroad, will always stand by the Mohammedans however unreasonable their actions or attitude may be. At Karachi and at Lahore this impression received a shock, but it is there all the same.

Sir Samuel Hoare resigned shortly before Christmas, a matter of some sadness to G.D., who was involved in altercation on another front. On 19 December G.D. had written to the Governor of Bengal's secretary complaining of gross injustice in respect of the Harijan Sevak Sangh, of which he was President, in the recently published Report on the Administration of Bengal 1933–34.

This Sangh is a purely humanitarian body having nothing to do with politics. Pandit Jawaharlal Nehru was never authorised to collect funds for the Harijan Sevak Sangh, nor to my knowledge did he ever make an attempt to do so. I do not agree with Pandit Jawaharlal's political views, but I cannot convince myself of his collecting money under the guise of Harijan work. He is not irresponsible and dishonest. I fear the Government has been misinformed with the object of discrediting the Harijan Sevak Sangh.

The Governor's secretary replied:

I am to make it clear that the statement in the Administration Report was not in any way intended as a reflection on the activities of that body or on the Harijan movement itself, but was concerned only with the possibilities of that movement being exploited for subversive purpose. If you study the speech of Pandit Nehru, delivered at the Albert Hall on the 18th January, 1934, you will see that he has emphasised his point of view that the conflict with the Government would become inevitable if the Harijan movement was started with great force. You will perhaps agree that it was not unreasonable to interpret that speech as meaning that the Pandit himself regarded the movement as one possessing real potentialities as a factor in furthering the revolutionary policy which his speech was devoted to advocating. His Excellency fully accepts what you say regarding the activities of the Harijan Sevak Sangh for which you are responsible and it is perhaps hardly necessary to assure you that the movement for improving the condition of the depressed classes is one with which, in itself, Government has every sympathy.

That, more of less, was the end of the matter.

Early in 1936 G.D., his children now growing or grown up and seen only at intervals, busied himself in setting down points that should be the criteria for responsible self-government. His six main contentions were that Indians should "foster, promote and protect" their own industries, shipping, banking and insurance; that they should be able to use credit and currency in the best national interest; that they should run the railways, Indianizing the services; that the military should be brought under Indian control and extravagance in administration curtailed; and that they should have power to lay down a recovery programme, with a view to adjusting taxation, redistributing wealth and improving education.

G.D., as usual flitting from city to city in his restless way, was anxious to reconcile the two positions between the government and Congress, whereby the former was concerned with making the reforms work, regarding the safeguards merely as insurance, and Congress was concentrating exclusively on the safeguards.

Reception of the Act in India was initially hostile, both Jinnah and Congress regarding it as showing few advances over propositions formulated as early as 1919. Governors would retain discretionary powers over the summoning of legislatures, the giving of assent to bills, and the administration of certain mainly tribal areas. Federation would depend on the formal agreement of over 50 per cent of the princes, an agreement that in fact was never forthcoming.

The main gains from an Indian point of view were the increase in the electorate from six to thirty millions and responsible government replacing provincial diarchy. Financial control, too, was to be transferred from London to Delhi, though nominally still in the hands of the Viceroy.

Curiously, no mention was made of Dominion Status. Lord Linlithgow, in a private letter to Zetland several years later, confided, "It is no part of our policy, I take it, gratuitously to hurry the handing over of controls to Indian hands at any pace faster than that which we regard as best calculated, on a long view, to hold India to the Empire." Such a concept of the British Government's priorities scarcely seems in accord with the sentiments expressed at all levels to G.D. in England during the summer of 1935, let alone with the Irwin offers of 1929.

In early 1936 Gandhi again became ill, high blood pressure being checked by the removal of most of his teeth. "His absolutely toothless smile is even richer than ever," Mahadev reported to G.D. In London Nehru was making speeches to the effect that Russia was India's best friend and Japan a weakening power. "I don't know about Russia," G.D. commented in a letter to Gandhi, "but I know definitely that Japan is not a weakening power."

In April Lord Linlithgow arrived to take up his duties. On the 19th G.D. was obliged to write to him,

I would not have written immediately on your arrival but there is a matter which owes an explanation from me. I am the virtual proprietor of the *Hindustan Times*, a daily paper printed in Delhi which was responsible for that canard about Lord Halifax arranging an interview between Your Excellency and Mr Gandhi. . . . Immediately I read the story at Gwalior I phoned to the Managing Director who himself was shocked at the publication. He was asked to contradict the story which was immediately done. I write this to express my sincerest regret and to say how unhappy I felt over this episode.

The *Hindustan Times* was causing G.D. much concern. So reckless were some of its pronouncements and so inaccurate certain anecdotes that Gandhi took it upon himself to write to his son Devdas, then editor, "In my opinion, the *Hindustan Times* has become an altogether useless paper. It does not publish a single correct report, whatever reports are published are harmful. If you are not able to improve its standard you should wash your hands of it."

Early that spring Jayaprakash Narayan's book *Why Socialism* had been published, Mahadev Desai recommending it to G.D. and asking for his reaction. Narayan, briefly in G.D.'s employ, was later to become Indira Gandhi's sternest critic, especially during the Emergency period. G.D.'s attitude was not favourable:

I am for the equal distribution of wealth but I do not think it can ever be achieved through ways and means Jayaprakash Narayan has suggested. If all wealth was nationalised and equally distributed it would increase income per capita only very slightly. More production not socialism is the first necessity.

I find that Jawaharlalji and others swear by Russia. It is funny how they do this and abuse Germany and Italy. I bracket them together. Their success in production is due largely to dictatorship. Hitler has 97% of the people behind him. This is a fact whether we like his philosophy or not. If 97% of the people reject Russian theory, who is Jawaharlalji to say this is good but bad for the people in Germany. Why should our socialists feel shy of the ballot box with adult franchise?

In early May G.D. began a lengthy correspondence with the Viceroy, now in Simla, on the breeding of cattle, and freight charges, subjects close to Linlithgow's farmer's heart and about which he wrote with undisguised enthusiasm. This involved the kind of technical detail, which could be put to practical use, that was equally dear to G.D. In the letters between Gandhi and G.D. discussions of diet and medical treatment alternated with reports on Congress and Harijan activities; in correspondence with the Viceroy conditions in city byres and the regulating of return fares for cattle provided welcome relief from graver affairs of state.

Despite the non-controversial nature of these exchanges there were underlying hostilities in the air, about which G.D. wrote to Lothian in June. Unless Linlithgow could break them down the Congress would probably refuse office and adopt wrecking tactics, leading to the imposition of special powers. "It is exactly what Jawaharlal wants." If the battle between capitalism and socialism was conducted in the legislature there would be an open conflict between Nehru and the Congress right wing. "The other side of the picture that I can imagine is Jawaharlal in jail and youngsters developing from socialism into communism and the Government into fascism. I fear the latter is the more likely possibility."

On 5 August G.D. saw the Viceroy in Delhi, his first meeting with him since his arrival. They talked unproductively for nearly an hour, with Linlithgow inquiring about the relationship between Gandhi and Nehru and expressing his fears that Congress did not really want office for fear that the necessary steps they would have to take might lead to unpopularity. Would Gandhi, under any circumstances, agree to accept office, Linlithgow asked. G.D. gave his assurance that if there was the possibility of doing constructive work for the masses Gandhi would not hesitate. The talk turned happily to cattle and they parted cordially, the Viceroy confiding that until the elections were over it was difficult for him to make a move for fear of suggesting partiality. G.D. was disappointed.

With the elections approaching G.D. begged Gandhi not to appear indifferent towards them. "I have begun to realise their importance more and more." Gandhi was reluctant to make promises. "What can I do during an election?" he wrote to G.D. from Sevagram. "The only thing I shall try to do is to prevent discussions within the Congress, and this I am already doing." Mahadev Desai wrote to G.D. from Wardha,

> Bapu is getting more and more absorbed in his village work and feels no inclination to give any time to correspondence or to writing . . . The fact is that he is turning his mind off from Congress and all other outside activities and rivetting it entirely on the village and its problems. Perhaps when you are here you will be able to gain a proper insight into his present mood.

G.D. was due to spend several days with Gandhi in September at his Sevagram ashram. Gandhi developed malaria and instead G.D. prepared to spend two weeks in Simla as an official adviser to the Indo–British Trade Conference.

On 20 April G.D. had written to Thakurdas, "The election which will take place will be controlled by the Vallabhai Group and if Lord Linlithgow handles the situation properly there is every likelihood of the Congress coming into office."

It was an accurate forecast. Congress won 711 out of 1585 provincial assembly seats, with absolute majorities in five out of the eleven provinces. According to Sumit Sarkar in his *Modern India* G.D. contributed five lakhs of rupees to the Congress Central Parliamentary Board headed by Sardar Patel.

Shortly after the elections were over G.D. had a second meeting with the Viceroy, from which he emerged rather more hopeful. The Viceroy, after an initial query about the entry of Birla Brothers into the motor business, expressed pleasure at the Congress majority. "I am not at all surprised. I knew it. But my men did not know it." The Viceroy assured G.D. that he was not going to allow any Governor to use his power and that although he could see no urgent necessity for a meeting between him and Gandhi there was no difference in their attitudes to the Constitution.

G.D. now found it necessary to write at length to Gandhi,

Gandhi having contributed an article to the *Harijan* on a minimum wage for mill-workers. It is hard to believe that G.D.'s intricate calculations can have meant a great deal to Gandhi, whose simple attitude to human issues and economics was not conducive to detailed argument. G.D. was nevertheless at pains to justify the working conditions and wage structure in his own mills. He accepted that there was much more to be done in terms of social welfare, but "in my opinion the textile industry in India has been a great success. It has replaced Lancashire by providing cheap cloth. It has not been a failure from the investors' point of view, nor could it be said that the wages were maintained at a lower level as compared with Japan." The average wage in the Birla Mills, for 2700 men, was 26 rupees, the highest paid receiving 100 rupees a month and the lowest, the doffing boys, 12 rupees. Gandhi's requirement of a minimum wage of 26 rupees would, according to G.D., mean a reduction in wage for as many as would have an increase, if the mills were to remain viable.

On 12 March G.D. wrote to Lord Halifax that only a meeting between the Viceroy and Gandhi could give the Service "an assurance that the Congress is a friend and not a foe". It appeared to G.D. that Linlithgow was being affected by the unhelpful attitude of his own high officials and the reactionary views of European businessmen. In Calcutta the latter had been incensed at the Viceroy preferring an invitation to dine at the Calcutta Club, with its mixed Indian and British membership, rather than at the exclusive Bengal Club, which did not admit Indians as members. These factors, together with the legacy of Willingdon's distrust of Gandhi, the effect of which spread right down through the Civil Service and business, and the effects of the terrorist campaigns of recent years on local opinion, were gnawing away at the goodwill and sympathy with which Linlithgow had arrived in India.

The gist of G.D.'s disquiet was, not for the first time, the essential unco-operativeness of the administration. How much this was in fact the case, rather than an impression, remains debatable.

In any case G.D. was able only a few days later to write to the Viceroy, via the latter's private secretary J. G. Laithwaite, that the conditional acceptance of Gandhi's formula by the Working Committee of Congress for the taking of office "was a great triumph for the right wing of Congress".

The condition related to the use by the Governor of his special powers, but though the Viceroy declined to make any public assurances on the subject, the Working Committee had sanctioned office-acceptance on the grounds that it would not be easy for governors to use these powers. Congress ministries were soon installed in Bihar, Bombay, Madras, Orissa and U.P. "So over the major part of the country," Sumit Sarkar observed, "the persecuted had become ministers, the new assemblies met to the strains of the *Bande Mataram*, and the national flag for which so many had faced *lathis* and bullets flew over public buildings."

Yet, as Sarkar points out, there were anomalies: despite an enormous increase in Congress membership, the rise of labour movements and the installation of popular ministries, there was the curious spectacle of a party committed to Purna Swaraj working within the framework of the derided 1935 Constitution and through a Civil Service and Police Force with whom it had hitherto had only unpleasant relations.

It is an indication of the trust G.D. had in Gandhi's judgement of moral issues that as soon as an unofficial strike broke out in the Kesoram Cotton Mill, he wrote explaining the situation and asking for advice. There had been intimidation of returning workers and the management had put up a notice requesting those who did not wish to work to make way for replacements. "I have tried the method of persuasion and have failed," G.D. wrote. "Even the labour leaders have failed. Now, either I import workers from other places under police protection and thus break the strike or I must surrender on the question of increment of wages." "The dictates of morality," Gandhi replied,

> would require you to tell the workers quite plainly that so long as they fail to pursue the path of justice the mills would

remain idle; no new hands would be recruited. In case, however, they leave their quarters peacefully without creating a situation, you should feel free to get new men instead. This would be morally right as well as economically feasible. If you feel my answer fails to cover the situation you may write to me again.

G.D. appeared content with his answer, though its practical value seems questionable.

In the event, despite Kesoram being as G.D. described to Gandhi, full of "notorious Muslim goondas", the workers drifted back. "I asked them to form a Union which with great hesitation they have done. I have invariably found that every strike is due to lack of personal touch between the workers and the management."

Such an admission in relation to his own mill must have seemed ironic to one who had been unceasingly preaching the importance of the "personal touch" to British officials during the last year. The truth of the matter would seem to be that it was only when labour relations deteriorated to the point of production being impaired that G.D. found the time or the necessity to involve himself in local issues. At Kesoram G.D. recognized that at least part of the reason for the strike was the offhand manner of his manager.

Early in May 1937 Gandhi took time off from his village preoccupations to give a series of interviews, the purpose of which was to facilitate working relations between the Congress ministers and the government. Reassuring and conciliatory speeches by Zetland, the Secretary of State, did much to improve the general atmosphere, but curiously, when mutual distrust seemed to be melting, Gandhi himself began to niggle over details. His reactions to Zetland's speeches, as telegraphed to Reuters, Bombay, and *The Times* in London, concentrated on the difference between ministers being sacked and asked to resign.

Surely it is no strain upon the Constitution Act for Governors to give the assurance that whenever a situation is created which to them appears intolerable they will take upon their shoulders the responsibility of dismissing the ministers which they have the right to do instead of expecting them to resign or submit to Governors' wishes.

G.D. was dismayed by what appeared to him and to many others as unnecessary quibbling on Gandhi's part and he used all his powers of persuasion to get Gandhi to accept government assurances for what they were worth. He wrote to Mahadev Desai:

> I do not share the opinion that the Government have no desire to see the Congress accept office . . . But there is an impression in Government circles that the Congress have no desire to accept office and are putting forward all sorts of excuses. I therefore still hold the same opinion that it will be a great mistake to break after Lord Zetland's speeches which in my opinion meet the point. I do not remember in the past having entertained any doubt about Bapu's decisions but on this point I do entertain doubt and so I write this. I am not a Congressman and therefore have no status in this matter but I think it my duty to say this because perhaps Bapu may reconsider the situation.

In June 1937, G.D. was in Europe taking part in negotiating the Indo–British Trade Pact. In Venice he read an interview which Gandhi had given to the *News Chronicle*. "It has removed all misunderstanding about the position," G.D. wrote to Mahadev Desai.

> As I had pointed out at Tithal people did feel as if he was demanding something new. . . . I am satisfied to note that I too had forwarded Bapu's views to the Viceroy on exactly the lines of his interview to the *News Chronicle*. I had put a great emphasis on the point that Bapu was anxious that Congress should accept office and after putting this emphasis I had a little fear in my mind whether in doing so I had correctly represented him. . . . Where I feel hesitation in agreeing with Bapu's point is this: Is it worth while now after all these talks to break? Please tell Bapu that whatever be my personal views on this point I will put his views

strongly and correctly before the highest authority in London whenever and wherever I get an opportunity.

A week later G.D. felt constrained to emphasize to Gandhi that "the people here are most anxious to get the Congress into office . . . The atmosphere is quite different from what it was in 1935." It was Gandhi and Congress, G.D. felt, who were now hanging back and splitting hairs over a formula. In an effort to break the deadlock G.D. himself drafted a formula dealing with the solitary remaining obstacle, the Governor's powers in relation to the dismissal or resignation of ministers.

Towards the end of June G.D., now based in Grosvenor House, saw Halifax, Lothian, Sir Findlater Stewart and Zetland in quick succession. None of them felt that in actual practice Congress's demands for dismissals rather than resignations would be any the more effective.

In retrospect the distinction between resigning and being asked to go seems absurdly trivial as the basis for Congress decling to accept office. G.D., having felt it to be so at the time and having urged both sides in turn to yield, felt depressed at his failure. He wrote to Gandhi that "if I have not succeeded at least I have impressed". He urged Gandhi yet again to do everything to work the Constitution.

In 1922 and 1930 there may have been good reasons for openly opposing British policy but now perhaps it could be possible for us to achieve what we desire through friendship with Great Britain. As long as we are in opposition mutual distrust will always prevail . . . We need experience in administration. The work of construction should now be undertaken. That is how I feel.

G.D.'s efforts to act as honest broker were not wasted. He wrote to Desai from Grosvenor House on 7 July:

Reuters has just now telephoned me that at the insistence of Bapu the Working Committee has decided to accept office in the six provinces and I was simply overwhelmed with joy to hear this news. I have no doubt in my mind that Bapu

123

has taken the correct decision and no one but Bapu alone could have done this.

G.D. went on to say that he was having further meetings with Halifax, Stewart, Zetland and Lothian. "I am going to impress upon them that if it was difficult to get the Congress in it would be still more difficult to keep them in" unless the spirit of the agreements were adhered to.

After the meeting with Halifax G.D. wrote again to Desai that he had made clear that Congress was not just coming in to work the Constitution but to advance towards their goal of complete Independence. "They could either do it through the Constitution or through direct action."

G.D. ended,

I find everyone here sympathetic and they assure me that British public opinion will fully support the Congress in advancing towards their goal, which, of course, they interpret to be Dominion Status. If Independence means severing the connection with the Empire, then they are totally against it. In Dominion Status we have the right to secede, and that is quite enough.

Desai had suggested a visit to Lourdes on G.D.'s way home but he replied that all he wanted now was to get back to India as soon as possible. On 17 July he wrote again,

Bapu is the most popular person just now here. They talk of his commonsense, judgment and all other virtues, and his stocks have gone up very high. But what pleases me most is that everyone says that if Congress could manage the provinces for five years in good order Independence will come within a tenth of the time that we have estimated.

G.D., however, felt some apprehensions about the Congress side of the bargain. "Uncorrupted administration and solidarity amongst ourselves is the main thing that is needed. I fear more communal troubles and embarrassment from our own men."

On 18 July Gandhi wrote to G.D. from Sevagram, "I read all your letters with great care. Now we know what has happened. Whatever Jawahar did or said in the Working Committee was simply marvellous . . . the beauty is that we still disagree. What you have been doing is good."

Gandhi meanwhile had written an article for *Harijan* by way of a Congress manifesto and on what he called his "conception of office acceptance". In this Gandhi makes unequivocally clear that Congress's working of the Government of India Act, "wholly unsatisfactory for achieving India's freedom", was to be regarded as merely a flexing of muscles. He advocates prohibition, free salt and use of Khadi cloth in all Congress provinces. Ministers should dress and live simply, not ape the British. Attention should now be concentrated on villages and the peasantry, not on the cities. Most important, Congress ministers "will show their Muslim colleagues that they know no distinction between Hindu, Muslim, Christian, Sikh or Parsi".

Gandhi ended his article,

If the Englishmen or anglicised Indians can but see the Indian, which is the Congress, viewpoint, the battle won by the Congress and complete Independence will come to us without shedding a drop of blood. In the prosecution by the Congress of its goal of complete Independence it [office-acceptance] is a serious attempt on the one hand to avoid a bloody revolution and on the other to avoid mass civil disobedience on a scale not hitherto attempted. May God bless it.

The calls to economy and simplicity may not have been to every future minister's liking, but Gandhi, having exerted the major influence on the Congress decision to accept office, was intent to leave his own mark on ministerial conduct.

Gandhi submitted two further articles to *Harijan*, one on ministerial pay, the other on "the fundamental difference" between the old and new orders, in both cases arguing against high salaries, whether for officials, teachers or doctors, and on behalf of co-operative endeavour, what Gandhi called "modified socialism". All the chief ministers objected to the articles and they were never printed.

Towards the end of July G.D. lunched with Churchill at his house. "As usual he was very cordial and charming, but very ill-informed about India." G.D. encouraged Churchill to go to India and see things for himself. He was in favour of accepting an invitation from Linlithgow but wanted an assurance that Gandhi would welcome his visit. "Give your leader my greetings and tell him that I wish him all success. Don't feel shy of fighting socialism. Accumulation of wealth is a good thing because it creates initiative but of course capitalists have to be servants not masters." Churchill gave it as his opinion that war was unlikely to be staved off for more than a year. "Italy is dreaming of an Empire . . . Russia and Germany are finding common ground." He himself would agitate for rearmament in England.

In India the Viceroy invited Gandhi to call on him at his house in New Delhi. "I have no particular business of a public nature with which to trouble you. But it will be a real pleasure to meet you and I gratefully hope that you may find it possible to come.'

On 4 August Desai wrote to G.D. from Viceregal Lodge. "A strange place for me to write from, is it not?" The discussion between Gandhi and the Viceroy, which lasted ninety minutes, had gone off amiably. Gandhi was granted his request to visit the Frontier after which the subjects discussed were "rural uplift, cows, handmade paper, reed pens and so on".

In a subsequent letter from Wardha, Desai passed on Gandhi's view that personal contacts were of limited value and that he would not personally wish to invite Churchill or Baldwin or other friends to come to India and "talk all kinds of imperialistic nonsense . . ."

This bleak response to one of G.D.'s most ardently held tenets, the importance of personal contact at the highest levels, must have been a disappointment. G.D., in a series of talks with Lord Lothian, as well as in his letters to Gandhi, had stressed the need for reciprocal visits between British and Indian leaders.

Gandhi, it seemed, wanted none of it, on either a public or

a personal level. He himself achieved a signal success later that month is settling the hunger strike of the Andaman prisoners, a tangible indication of what G.D. meant when he tried to persuade Lothian that if in Europe the conflicts were between communism and fascism, India could and would demonstrate the efficacy of non-violent civil disobedience.

The British Government had shut down in August for its leading lights to go fishing and shooting. It was from the opulent Hotel Baur au Lac, Zurich, that G.D. next wrote to Gandhi, this time an immensely long and detailed letter outlining the proposed terms of the Ottawa Pact. These, as suggested by G.D. and Sir Purshottamdas Thakurdas, the leaders of the Indian delegation, argued for continuation of all Indian preferences in operation, and in exchange for no limitations on Indian trade in jute, carpets and leather and an increased import of Indian cotton by the United Kingdom, India would offer a further reduction of 5 per cent on Lanca-shire cloth.

G.D. was anxious for Gandhi's approval before they put their signatures to any document, but Gandhi as usual was reluctant to endorse anything that came into the sphere of collective Congress responsibility. Desai wrote to G.D., now in a Zurich hospital convalescing from an operation on the antrum, that "the securest position for you to take is that no agreement is final unless it has received the imprimatur of Congress". Gandhi himself wrote a few days later counselling G.D. to consider the merits or demerits of the proposed agree-ment "quite independently of its relevance to the political issues".

Gandhi's health was not, at that time, good. Much that happened in the Working Committee irritated him, he was constantly being visited by ministers asking for advice, a valued member of his staff had committed suicide on the premises, and he was still writing his weekly article for *Harijan*, now concentrating on the case for prohibition.

G.D. had long been at him to organize his secretariat efficiently. Now Desai requested help. G.D. replied, "I have been quarrelling with Bapu for the last seven years about your

Secretariat, but in vain. Every bit of letter he must write himself, sometimes with his right hand; sometimes with the left. Your typists are a collection for a museum."

Desai was writing several times a week to keep G.D. in touch with what was happening in India. G.D., for his part, felt amply compensated for his absence by what he called "the very interesting task" of representing Gandhi to the English and vice versa.

G.D., on his return from Switzerland to London, was much involved in devising a formula for the release of political prisoners in Bengal, the detention of whom, as he tried to impress on British ministers, was the source of continual local unrest. Unfortunately the situation was complicated by irresponsible non-Congress leaders advocating violence, Bengal politics, as a result, degenerating into a series of feuds, despite there being a coalition government.

On 7 October G.D. sailed for India, arriving in Bombay on the 19th. In December he had a long discussion with the Viceroy and a fortnight later with the Governor of Bengal, Lord Brabourne, the principal topics being the gradual release of political prisoners, Federation and its drawbacks, and the responsibility of provincial ministries for dealing with communal clashes and unrest in their areas. "The exaggerated expectations that have been raised are just now at the root of all these troubles," G.D. wrote to Gandhi, "unless the Congress tells the peasants clearly that their position could be improved ultimately through their own hard work alone and not by any stroke of a wand, I don't think this discontent will subside."

Of the various problems facing both the Government and the Congress in their early months, the communal disturbances were the most grave. Federation having been rejected by the leading princes in turn, and never enthusiastically pushed by the Viceroy (or indeed for that matter by Gandhi), the Muslim League, in the initial stages on reasonably friendly terms with the provincial ministries, became increasingly bitter over what appeared to them anti-Muslim attitudes and policies in Congress. While Jinnah began speaking of "Congress Fascism", as for instance at the Patna Session of the League in 1938, he himself was being denounced by Congress speakers in such terms as an "out-of-date politician making a fetish of constitutionalism" and the League described as "a coterie of a few knights, Khan Bahadurs, and Nawabs".

In both cases the charges appear to have been made for political purposes rather than with real justification. It nevertheless remained true that unrest during the twenty-seven months of Congress pre-war provincial rule was less a matter of economics than of Hindu–Muslim enmity. There was never, however, serious threat to Congress as the majority party during this period. Although aware of Muslim disillusionment they had other priorities, such as educational reform and a trade and industrial policy. In the process, despite Gandhi's and G.D.'s own ceaseless advocacy on their behalf, Harijans found themselves neglected.

A House Divided Against Itself

G.D. continued to keep in touch with the Viceroy throughout 1938 and whenever trouble arose over points of procedure, political detainees or the performance of Congress ministers he was quick to act as the voice of the Gandhian conscience and to interpret as well as he could the views of the one to the other.

G.D. was not only fully involved in his own business activities – by this time the Birlas owned five sugar mills, four textile mills and a jute mill – but also in continuing negotiations for an Indo–British trade pact. These in fact broke down temporarily in June, by which time Gandhi was under constant abuse in certain sections of the press. He was also undergoing a painful self-examination about his long-held views on celibacy, veering from one extreme to the other and determined to air his conflicts publicly, much to the dismay of his friends. Mahadev Desai wrote to G.D. from Wardha on 8 August,

> Never did I curse Bapu's stay in Maharashtra more than now. As a people they are a most vindictive and quarrelsome lot, and already one of the scurrilous Marathi papers has been asking for someone to finish Bapu off. Well, it was Poona which had the rare honour of throwing a bomb on Bapu and I should not be surprised if something nasty happened here too. There is no filthier Press in the world, I think, than Marathi . . . Bapu is keeping well and of course he flourishes on abuse.

Gandhi wrote twice to G.D. in August on money matters before setting off on a tour of the Frontier with Ghaffar Khan, the handsome Pathan known as "the Frontier Gandhi". Gandhi enjoyed the adventure and put on weight, but felt there was nothing practical he could achieve in political terms. On his return G.D. visited him at Wardha where Gandhi rested for a few weeks before embarking on a month's tour of Gujarat.

Gujarat was Gandhi's native state and it was here that he involved himself personally in local activities directed against the much-disliked and autocratic Dewan of Rajkot, who had disposed of his advisory elected council. Although the princes had failed to agree on most matters to do with Federation, many princely states, under pressure from popular movements, had undergone striking changes in administration. Gandhi, agitating for civil liberties, independent courts and a reduction in privy purses, chose Jaipur, where there was widespread famine and discontent among the peasants, and Gujarat for mass *satyagrahas*. G.D., drawn into discussions over tactics, was against such action. He wrote to Gandhi:

> I am not ignorant about the situation in Jaipur and while I know that hundreds are very eager to start satyagraha there I do not think there are even half a dozen persons who have imbibed the spirit of satyagraha. They are very eager to break the law just now because they think that the situation just now is most favourable for starting a campaign of "no rent". Even without anybody doing anything there may be trouble. But if there was someone to incite them trouble becomes a certainty.

The Viceroy had intimated to G.D. that while he sympathized with Gandhi over the need for democratization in the states, Gandhi's involvement was not making the situation any easier. In February, G.D. wrote to Gandhi's secretary,

> Recently, after reading Bapu's articles about the Indian States I have felt as if they were written in a very irritated mood. Two sentences I distinctly disliked. One was where he said that "military was making merry at the expense of innocent men and women". The other was about "organised goondaism." ... It is very difficult to explain the position from here, but I don't agree with Bapu.

On 4 February Gandhi's secretary, Pyarelal, wrote back to
G.D., attempting to explain Gandhi's mood and language.

It is the immorality of an agent of the British Government
compelling an Indian ruler to break his plighted word to his
people and the unblushing falsehood with which it has been
sought to bolster up that action that has set him ablaze. . . .
With regard to the Viceroy, his profession of sympathy
would not carry us very far.

G.D. could not accept this. "I again disagree with Bapu
about words like 'organised goondaism' and 'barbarous' used
about what Young [the Police Commissioner] did . . . Jamnalalji admitted that the police were very polite to him. Let Bapu
take rest and let God look after Rajkot and Jaipur."

Gandhi, despite concern over his blood pressure, decided to
go to Rajkot himself. He began a fast there on 3 March, a
gesture that was widely assumed to be the start of a country-
wide agitation. Once Gandhi became aware of this interpreta-
tion he immediately called off his fast. From Rajkot he went
to Delhi where he had a series of talks with the Viceroy and
visited prisoners on hunger strike.

Subhas Chandra Bose had meanwhile been re-elected President of Congress and in April Gandhi wrote to him at great
length explaining the incompatibility of their views.

Taking all things into consideration, I am of the opinion
that you should at once form your own cabinet, formulate
your programme definitely and put it before the forthcoming
A.I.C.C. If the Committee accepts the programme all will
be plain-sailing. . . . If on the other hand your programme
is not accepted you should resign and let the Committee
choose its President.

Bose resigned, forming his own Forward Bloc with the
intention of uniting the leftish elements of the Congress under
his leadership. Bose's influence, however, except in Bengal,
diminished rather than increased and in August he was de-
barred from holding any Congress office for three years, a
disciplinary measure taken after Bose had defied Congress

regulations in calling for a country-wide protest day against an AICC resolution.

In May Mahadev Desai wrote to G.D. from Rajkot:

It is our great misfortune that Bapu often resents our reaction to his steps but later comes to the same conclusion as we and then expresses it with a vehemence that embarrasses us all . . . The more I meet these people [government officials] the more I am convinced that the whole of our agitation was a picture of our impatience.

Throughout the summer of 1939 the Rajkot affair dragged on, Gandhi's increasing querulousness and changes of tactics involving him and his friends in unnecessary meetings, journeys and correspondence. With events in Europe occupying everyone's minds, Congress's internal problems and divisions began to seem equally remote. On 29 August G.D. wrote to Mahadev Desai, enclosing a draft manifesto prepared by the Federation of Indian Chambers of Commerce. Since the contents expressed views likely to be incompatible with the attitude of Congress, G.D. asked for Bapu's reaction. The main gist of the manifesto was a plea that the question of "complete and fully responsible government at the centre, including control of foreign policy and defence" be taken up immediately as a condition of India's voluntary co-operation in any war against the Axis powers. Mahadev cabled back, "Congress apart Bapu dislikes. Statement requires vital changes. No immediate necessity for it."

On 3 September, without consultation with either the provincial ministries or the Congress leadership, the Viceroy unilaterally associated India with Britain's declaration of war on Germany, though technically India was automatically at war as soon as His Majesty was. Nevertheless, Linlithgow's surprisingly insensitive act alienated many Indians and the goodwill that initially existed towards Britain's war efforts rapidly melted away. At the end of October all the Congress ministers resigned.

It is doubtful whether a Congress decision to declare war on the basis of preliminary consultations with the Viceroy would have made any practical difference, but it would certainly have been conducive of a healthier atmosphere.

The Working Committee of Congress had earlier issued a Resolution Regarding War, a nebulous document that affirmed "Congress can take no sides . . . the Congress must dissociate itself from all war preparations going on in the country" and commending "the method of non-violence to the nations of the earth".

Justifiably, G.D. expressed his disappointment over what he called "a rambling document". To him it was clear Gandhi had little hand in it – "the language sounds more like Jawaharlal".

G.D., it turned out, was right. "The Working Committee," Desai wrote, "had not the gumption to take the line suggested by Bapu while Jawahar had the courage of his convictions. We have neither assimilated Bapu's non-violence nor have we evolved our own policy."

On 17 October the Viceroy made a statement almost as vague and noncommittal in terms of India's future as the Congress Working Committee's resolution had been in terms of their own attitude. About it G.D. wrote to Desai that "it is rather disappointing. But I feel we deserved it. We are a house divided against ourselves and in such a mess the Viceroy could not have given us any other reply than what he has given."

On 30 November G.D. wrote again, conveying his own analysis of the general position and suggesting that the Viceroy was anxious to get Congress back in office but that the Muslim League was demanding from Congress equal recognition.

After Christmas, the war still appearing a remote prospect from India, Calcutta was "humming with all the big guns" as G.D. described it to Mahadev Desai. His impression was that Dominion Status was assured and that the Viceroy's Cabinet could be enlarged to include leading Indians. "Don't you think," he wrote to Desai, "that in the picture I have drawn we get all we need and can digest . . . and don't you think that independence is more or less assured of realisation through this process?"

Others were less convinced. Gandhi began a long amicable

correspondence with the Viceroy about the distinction between Dominion Status and Independence, but their meeting in February, from which much was hoped, had little immediate result. Gandhi concluded from it that the Viceroy's hands were tied and that he would have to continue to "educate the world as to what we stand for". Now it was no longer a question of Dominion Status but of an Independence

determined by ourselves, meaning the elected representatives of the nation, call such an assembly what you will. Unless British statesmen definitely concede this they do not mean to part with power. Neither the question of defence nor that of the minorities nor of the princes nor European interests need come in the way of her making the clear declaration.

Gandhi was not blind to the fact that communal tension and the problem of minorities were serious obstacles to the British Government making any such declaration. As for civil resistance, meanwhile, Gandhi observed,

it is not a panacea for all our ills, internal and external. It is a specific and sovereign remedy for extraordinary situations . . . I say with a full sense of my responsibility that we are not ready and that even if we were ready the time for it is not ripe.

The Viceroy, for his part, felt let down by Gandhi's uncompromising attitude. "Myself and Devdas both share the feeling of the Viceroy," G.D. wrote to Desai, "because we also feel that Bapu was unresponsive and unhelpful."

Nevertheless Desai felt able to observe that "Bapu alone is capable of holding back the tide of the civil disobedience movement and this he is already doing and will continue to do so till the very last."

Gandhi wrote several articles for *Harijan* in the early part of the year. Not all of them met with G.D.'s approval. On 8 March he wrote to Desai:

You know I hate civil disobedience. In the name of non-violence it has encouraged violence. In the name of construction it has destroyed many things. Yet it brought about a wonderful awakening in the country. But if this psychology continues any Government, even our own, would become an impossibility.

Gandhi, G.D. felt, was simply being exploited by Congress, in whose ranks he was a misfit.

He is being exploited because the leaders know that he alone can lead the country to a successful mass civil disobedience movement. By identifying himself too much with the Congress he has effaced the distinction between himself and the leftists. Non-violence and violence have become, in a way, synonymous. I think this is the most anomalous position and I feel disgusted at times. If you so desire you may show my letter to Bapu.

G.D. was anxious to press home on Gandhi that "in my opinion we are going the wrong way and as the position is very critical he should reconsider the position in the light of the views held by some of us".

In the same letter G.D. refers to the rise in anti-British feeling "which must in the end result in violence". He complained in a further letter to Desai – almost all future letters for Gandhi's eyes were addressed for convenience sake to his secretary – that "we have pitched our demands so high that we have made it impossible for Englishmen to come to an honourable settlement".

Gandhi himself answered this time.

I share your distress but it is my firm belief that we cannot possibly accept anything less than what we are asking for . . . If they are not agreeable that will only go to show that they are not inclined to give India the whip hand. The manner in which the princes have been desporting themselves is proving increasingly obnoxious. Who told you that I am disinclined to come into contact with the princes? All I need is a faint gesture coming from the other side.

With the Germans overrunning Europe G.D. became increasingly concerned over India's attitude.

Of what avail is our non-violence to Norway, Sweden and Denmark? Doubts assail me again and again as to whether our position is morally sound . . . I feel we ought to have made a better contribution. I don't think Bapu will agree but, he too, I find, changes and perhaps in this matter too he may.

Gandhi tried to answer these objections in an article in *Harijan*. It was not altogether convincing. Having clarified the differences in his attitude between the 1914–18 war, when he campaigned vigorously for recruits, and the present one, Gandhi observes, "I shall grieve if Britain goes down. But the moral influence of the Congress cannot be available to Britain unless she washes her hands clean of India."
He concluded by rehearsing old grievances:

In spite of the unanimous support that Britain got during the [1914–18] war from India, the British attitude was translated into the Rowlatt Act and the like. The Congress accepted non-violent non-cooperation to meet the British menace. There is the memory of the Jallianwalla Bagh, the Simon Commission, the Round Table Conference, the emasculation of Bengal for the sake of the misdeeds of a few. The Congress having accepted non-violence I do not need to go to the people to give recruits. Through the Congress I can give something infinitely better than a few such recruits. Of that evidently Britain has no need. I am willing but helpless.

The gulf between Gandhi and G.D. at this stage was considerable. On 15 May, after the Dutch surrender, Desai wrote to G.D., "Hitler's stocks are steadily rising in [Bapu's] eyes. I said, 'That is all right so long as you do not say so publicly.'" Desai, not for the only time, showed more sense than his master.
Gandhi himself next wrote to G.D., "Europe is going through the holocaust of internecine carnage . . . Be that as it may, my heart is hardened in this respect." Gandhi had now taken to using phrases such as "Hitler is not that bad" and

unrealistically offering to go to Germany as a mediator.

In England the replacement of Chamberlain by Churchill merely resulted, as far as India was concerned, in less generous offers than those envisaged by Amery, the new Secretary of State, and by Linlithgow in an effort to gain Indian support. Churchill had already made his attitude plain in a private letter written to G.D. as early as April 1937:

> You should seriously consider the present state of the world. If Great Britain were forced or persuaded for any cause, Indian or European, to withdraw her protection from India, it would continuously become the prey of Fascist dictator nations, Italy, Germany or Japan, and then indeed with the modern facilities there would be a severity of Government even worse than any experienced in bygone ages. The duty of the Indian electorate and of Congress is to take up the great task that has been offered them . . . and at the same time do everything they can to win the confidence of Great Britain, and offer to her gratitude and loyalty for being the guardian of Parliamentary government and Indian peace.

In November 1942 he would declare, "I have not become the King's First Minister in order to preside over the liquidation of the British Empire."

Not much, it became clear, was to be expected from that quarter, particularly in the light of Gandhi's tame reaction to what was happening in Europe.

In July 1940 G.D. sent a telegram to Gandhi's HQ at Wardha suggesting that, as Britain was planning to evacuate children to the Dominions, India as a "good humanitarian gesture" should invite a few thousand children. He also warned Gandhi against rejecting the Viceroy's offer of unobtrusive police protection, the German radio having broadcast British intentions to assassinate him and the Viceroy fearing that this might be set up by German agents to create anti-British propaganda. Gandhi declined, explaining that "no assassin can curtail anybody's life or a friend protect it" except by God's will.

In October *Harijan* ceased publication, Gandhi having declined to operate under censorship of any kind. He telegraphed the Viceroy to this effect, affirming that his criticisms of the government were friendly despite being fearless, even to the point of advocating civil disobedience.

Relations between Linlithgow and Gandhi now deteriorated, and Gandhi, against what he termed a "wholly unnecessary Gagging Ordinance", threatened a fast. G.D. did his best to dissuade him, pointing out that, in the first instance, suspension of *Harijan* had been unnecessary and that if Gandhi's intentions towards the government were indeed friendly then a fast would merely be coercion of a kind of which Gandhi himself disapproved.

In November Mahadev Desai, in his capacity as editor of *Harijan*, made a lengthy and impressive speech at a press conference held in Delhi shortly after the arrest of Jawaharlal Nehru. Nehru had been sentenced to four years' imprisonment for anti-war speeches, though the latter were no more provocative than the resolutions made by the Congress Working Committee on the outbreak of hostilities. Desai, having advocated "the right to propagate non-violence as an effective substitute for war" concluded with a plea for liberty that is "no greater than was being enjoyed in Great Britain and South Africa". Quoting the words of a British judge in a case brought against the *Daily Worker*, "The expression of views, no matter how unpopular, how fantastic, or how wrong-headed they may appear to the majority, is a right, and a right which I, among others, am paid to see preserved." Desai continued,

> Let me tell you that it is a libel to say we are hindering the war effort. We do not go near recruiting depots, we do not surround munition factories and, as Gandhiji has declared, we have no intention to do so. We do not want to stop anyone who voluntarily wants to help the war. What we do want to stop is the exaction that is going on by means of coercion, intimidation, and torture, and we want to tell the people of India that if they will win swaraj through non-violent means, they may not cooperate militarily with the British in the prosecution of this war.

There is no doubt that both Gandhi and Nehru, however eloquent their anti-war speeches, held back from advocating real damage to British interests. It is equally true that many British, both civilian and serving soldiers, were dismayed by the curtailment of liberty in India.

Gandhi now replaced his idea of a fast with the intention of extending civil disobedience to "qualified persons selected from particular groups", among them various Congress bodies. He communicated his plans to the Viceroy accordingly, repeating his view that while he and Nehru never had the slightest intention of "paralysing" the government's war effort, as had been recently alleged, what would help Hitler and the enemies of Britain was "the present utterly irresponsible and repressive policy of the Government including the wholly unwarranted arrests and imprisonments".

Unrealistically Gandhi continued to hold the conviction that while British methods would never defeat Hitlerism, his own, "if any at all", could, as he wrote to Sir Reginald Maxwell, the Home Member. Maxwell replied, "I am glad to know that you are only seemingly in the opposite camp and that your end is the same as ours. Although I regret that there should be difference about the method of attaining it I see that I must leave you to work things out in your own way."

That would seem to have been a fair and courteous enough exposition of the views on both sides. Gandhi, however, was determined to carry out further acts of *satyagraha*, being scrupulous throughout in keeping the Viceroy informed. On 24 December Gandhi wrote an "Open Letter to Herr Hitler" in which, having addressed the Führer as "Dear Friend", he continued:

We have no doubt about your bravery or devotion to the Fatherland, nor do we believe that you are the monster described by your opponents. But your own writings and pronouncements leave no room for doubt that many of your acts are monstrous and unbecoming of human dignity. . . . Hence we cannot possibly wish success to your aims.

Gandhi went on "But ours is a unique position. We resist British Imperialism no less than Nazism. If there is a difference it is in degree." Gandhi concluded by making a generalized plea for peace, aware that the appeal for non-violent resistance which he had earlier made to all Britons would be likely to fall on deaf ears. There is, hardly surprisingly, no record of the letter ever having been replied to or received.

G.D. spent two days with Gandhi at Wardha just before Christmas. Gandhi was involved in a time-consuming correspondence with people seeking permission to offer *satyagraha*. In a note on his visit made after he had returned to Calcutta, G.D. recorded his impression that Gandhi wanted to minimize any embarrassment caused by his movement, instructing *satyagraha* to be suspended on all Sundays, before 9 a.m., and during Christmas. "There is not only no trace of bitterness in him but, on the contrary, there is a definite cordiality towards H.E. and his other British friends."

It was, G.D. believed, a wise move to confine *satyagraha* to the single issue of freedom of speech, rather than to the constitutional issue, since it was a matter easier of solution. About the Open Letter to Hitler G.D. remarked, "One not knowing him may think that he has no proper sense of values. But this could only be said by one who does not know him."

"It is unfortunate," G.D. wrote,

> that the rulers and politicians know little of each other as men. I have been in close contact with Viceroys and Governors during the last twenty years. Some of them have been exceedingly kind and nice to me. But every time I met a Viceroy or Governor we only discussed politics. . . . It is a great disadvantage that we rarely know the rulers as men.

At Wardha G.D. suggested to Gandhi that the immediate expansion of the Viceroy's Council to include men of repute who belonged neither to Congress nor to the Muslim League might help to end the present impasse. "Gandhiji's reaction was not unsatisfactory. . . . He realised the difficulty of getting independent men from outside the two parties, but I gave him a few names and he thought they may not be a bad selection."

G.D.'s assumption was that no such executive council would keep political leaders in gaol nor attempt to muzzle them. "I pointed out that such a Cabinet may also be able to build a bridge between Hindus and Muslims and also could do the spade work for constitution-making after the war." Gandhi confined himself to the observation, "Yes, perhaps."

On his return to Calcutta G.D. was disturbed to find the Viceroy no longer felt able to see him. He had requested a meeting in which to put to him the ideas he had discussed with Gandhi at Wardha.

It transpired, from an interview with the Viceroy's secretary, that G.D.'s money was believed to be behind "the movement", i.e. Congress, and that in the present conditions of hostility between the government and Congress personal friendship should be put aside. To the question, "but surely you are a Congressman?" G.D. replied, as he reported in a letter to Desai,

> No, I am not a Congressman. But I am a Gandhi-man. To me Gandhiji is more like a father. I am deeply interested in all his philanthropic subjects like khadi and Harijans. Gandhiji has never asked me to join the political war. The Viceroy should have, by this time, known that no man among Indians has worked harder to help him or stood more loyally by him than myself.

G.D. was not to be soothed subsequently and he wrote to Desai that he had informed the secretary that this was the last chapter of their talks. "In any case, this brings to an end my relations with the Viceroy."

War and Cripps

In March Mahadev Desai, on behalf of Gandhi, proposed a formula on the basis of what G.D. had suggested at Wardha. After observations that Gandhi would not be satisfied with anything less than "unfettered" freedom of expression and that, as regards the constitutional question, Gandhi could have no interest in the formation of a Cabinet to carry on the war, the draft concluded,

> Government can themselves declare that they cannot obviously expect the Congress with its policy of non-violence to join a Cabinet formed to prosecute the war militarily and that therefore they must choose representatives even from other parties who have not the conscientious objection that the Congressmen have. Either the present Council can announce the grant of unfettered freedom of expression – which would be more graceful – or the new Cabinet to be formed can make the announcement.

This was followed two days later by the issuing of a "Note on the Repressive Policy of Government", by which it was sought to crush a "moral revolt" by means of a policy of indiscriminate imprisonments and detentions.

Later that month Desai wrote to Desmond Young of the Home Department that it seemed possible to restart *Harijan*. "But before we do so," he wrote,

> I owe it to you to tell you again that both Gandhiji and I are completely identified with the satyagraha movement, and our editing of *Harijan* cannot but bear the colour and impress of that identification. . . . If you feel therefore that we had better not restart the paper you have but to send

me a wire. I will not misunderstand it and say nothing in public about it.

In the event, after a cautionary note about the Defence of India Rules from Sir Richard Tottenham, which he concluded by saying, "I am however glad to infer from your correspondence that should Mr Gandhi in fact decide to resume publication it will be in the hope of assisting rather than of causing embarrassment to Government". Gandhi changed his mind. "Under the circumstances we cannot restart. And even if we did so I am sure we should come to grief in a month or so."

In May Gandhi wrote in his own hand to G.D. "I have just finished reading your article dealing with the economic condition of India and I like it very much indeed. Earnest efforts should be made to secure justice and fair play for our country. There is a pressing need for many more of such writings."

If there was some measure of agreement now between the advocate of cottage industries and the industrialist about India's commercial future, there was a certain gulf between them on details of daily life. In May G.D. had written to Gandhi from Calcutta about information he had received concerning a Muslim conspiracy in Bombay. Three hundred men had collected in a mosque and were proposing "to cut all Hindus in Sinhi Gali". The police had proved unconcerned and G.D., passing on a request from his informant that he consult Gandhi, had done just that. Gandhi had replied airily, "We need not bother with such things. Only those who are cowardly allow themselves to be frightened. My own advice to you in the present context is to fear nothing and to tell others to do likewise. Acts of hooliganism will continue unless the Hindus use their own guts."

G.D. was disappointed in Gandhi's reply. "I had taken it for granted that you would take up the matter and write about it. . . . Is it because you consider it a waste of time and energy to deal with anything that does not spur you to give a clarion call to do our duty in respect of our higher obligations?"

He went on to say that the Hindus, including the Marwaris,

Waiting in the wings. G.D. with Indira Gandhi.

Margaret Thatcher received by G.D. on her visit to India in 1981.

Better relations. G.D. and President Eisenhower.

1964. G.D. with the West German Chancellor, Ludwig Erhard.

President Tito, an expansive host.

With Khrushchev in Moscow.

Prime Minister Lal Bahadur Shastri, the "little big man", with G.D.

G.D. in London. Attlee is on his right, and Aneurin Bevan on Atlee's right.

in Calcutta were far from scared but that "the Khaksars have been parading the streets, duly armed with spades. This they are doing in broad daylight, though the law forbidding such activity is equally applicable to both Hindus and Muslims."

Gandhi replied patiently. "The reason why I remained unimpressed was that there was nothing in that letter of which I had had no experience before."

G.D. had been working for some time on a memoir of Gandhi which he called *Bapu*. Gandhi wrote to him, "*Bapu* still contains a couple of factual inaccuracies. I have marked the relevant portions." He found that "the language is sweet, the style easy-flowing. Here and there one comes across a repetition of the same argument . . . but this defect will escape detection from the readers."

In September G.D. wrote to Gandhi from Mussoorie outlining an ambitious new plan which he wished to place before the next meeting of the Harijan Sevak Sangh. "I feel that it should be possible to give a greater spurt to the Harijan work." What he had in mind was the setting up of six ashrams with accommodation for 200 students in each. There would be training in crafts up to matriculation standard. "The sites for such Ashrams should be far removed from the cities, somewhere in the woods, and on the banks of one river or another." G.D. proposed that half the students should be caste-Hindus, paying full tuition and boarding charges of thirteen rupees a month, while the Harijans should be educated and maintained free.

Gandhi approved. "I like your scheme very much indeed." He was planning a tour to raise money for the Deen Bandhu Andrews Memorial and suggested he might call in at Pilani. G.D., delighted at the prospect, was anxious about arrangements for those who would want to meet the Mahatma. "The crowd may be 50,000 strong. . . . Those who will come will use the camel-back as their means of transport. Will these remaining 15 days suffice me to make adequate arrangements for water and ablution for this multitude? I am rather sceptical."

The visit never came off, Gandhi's and Desai's health and

general changes of mood taking them instead to Birla House in Juhu, on the beach outside Bombay, for treatment.

G.D.'s private fortunes had inevitably benefited during two years of war. By early 1942, however, the war that had scarcely seemed more than a distant rumour, bringing with it nevertheless greatly increased production, employment and profits, was on India's doorstep. Singapore fell to the Japanese in February, Rangoon on 8 March and the Andaman Islands a fortnight later. There was a feeling in the air among nationalists of all parties, their opportunism whipped up by Subhas Chandra Bose, that Britain was on her last legs and that there would never be a better moment for India to exploit her weakness. The communists alone, pledged to support the Soviet Union in their struggle against the German invaders, were obliged to ally themselves with Britain, if only morally. Not since the disastrous retreat from Kabul a century earlier had British fortunes in Asia been so low.

G.D.'s reactions to the situation, which might at any time before the breaking-off of relations with the Viceroy have been predictable in their concern, were now less clear. Cripps had arrived in March with a draft declaration for discussion with the various Indian leaders. The main points of the document were post-war Dominion Status with the right to secession, and immediate and effective participation by Indian leaders "in the counsels of their country", though Britain would retain control of the defence of the country for the length of the war.

A compromise formula was on the point of being agreed when Churchill, persuaded by Linlithgow and the then C-in-C, Wavell, that Cripps was going beyond his brief, halted negotiations. Cripps was obliged overnight to talk in completely different terms, withdrawing earlier promises of a national cabinet with joint responsibility.

Gandhi had taken little interest in any of these proceedings, but Nehru, only too aware of the precarious situation of the Allies in an anti-Fascist war, had done all he could to meet Cripps more than halfway. He more than anyone had a right to be aggrieved by Cripps's *volte-face*, a situation not helped by Cripps's denials of his initial position. No one else appeared put out, the British mainly because they felt they had made a gesture, the other Congress leaders mainly because they had set little store by Cripps's mission anyway. "Cripps' visit to India was a bit late," G.D. wrote laconically to Gandhi.

On 16 May Gandhi stirred himself to announce in a press interview "this orderly disciplined anarchy should go and if as a result there is complete lawlessness I would risk it". In June he was writing to G.D., "My mind is made up; my plans for the coming struggle are nearing completion. I am only waiting for the Working Committee meeting. I have made my preparations."

G.D. was reading Louis Fischer's *Men and Politics*, while Fischer himself in his journalistic capacity was spending several days with Gandhi at Sevagram. Fischer, an authority on Stalin's Russia and a copious writer on, as well as future biographer of, the Mahatma, had recently had a long talk with the Viceroy whom he reported as saying to him:

> Gandhi has been very good to me all these years. And that is to say a good deal. If he had remained the saint that he was in South Africa he would have done a tremendous amount of good to humanity. But unfortunately politics absorbed him here and made him vain and egotistical. But it is nonsense to say . . . that he is a spent force and may be ignored. He has a tremendous influence, sees the masses as no one else does, and only next to him comes Jawaharlal. The rest in the Congress are all paid for the work. It is a businessman's organisation. They finance it and keep it going.

About Gandhi's next move the Viceroy observed: "He is planning to instigate the people in U.P. and Bengal. I am not going to be precipitate but if his activities affect the war effort I shall have to put him under control."

In July food shortages and profiteering were widespread. "The remedy lies in certain steps," G.D. wrote to Desai, "first of all, fixing such prices of controlled articles that would have a reasonable relation to the price of replacement." He proposed a network of shops organized to sell grain without profit and

147

for transport to ensure deliveries of salt and sugar. "Partly the problem has arisen by consumers hoarding larger stocks than usual."

By now the principle of separation was coming into sharper focus, though the Congress professed to be unclear as to what the League meant by Pakistan. Gandhi in *Harijan* repeatedly asked for an authoritative definition, saying that he and Congress were willing to be converted. "Nehru, on the other hand," G.D. wrote to Desai, "does not even want to talk of Pakistan. . . . I think the two statements are contradictory to each other."

In the same letter to Desai G.D. observed, "You know my views about Pakistan. I am in favour of separation and I do not think it is impracticable, or against the interest of Hindus or of India. As long as we will quarrel there is no salvation for India. We should not forget that the Muslims – every one of them – now want it. Even the Congress Muslims are no longer an exception."

It was G.D.'s opinion, expressed in more than one letter to Desai, that recent Congress politics had confused everyone and that though the whole country had become anti-British there was little enthusiasm for a bitter struggle.

In Calcutta Gandhi was photographed at Birla House in conversation with General and Madame Chiang Kai Shek. "Jawaharlal," Desai wrote to G.D., "has allowed himself to be made a complete ass of, or he is participant in the game with the Generalissimo – I hope and pray not the latter."

Gandhi, Desai confided, was anxious lest G.D. had committed himself publicly in his views about Pakistan. More importantly, he added, Bapu was determined on a last throw, "When he said on the last day to the Working Committee that he would give a notice to Government that they must not think of keeping him in prison alive, they all sat silent and stunned."

This last throw, which entertained the odd notion that if the British withdrew Japan would "reconsider her plans", led up to the Quit India resolution – opposed only by communist members – passed in Birla House, Bombay by the Congress

Working Committee on 8 August 1942. At some time in their talks at Wardha Fischer had asked Gandhi whether it was really true that the Congress Party was in the hands of big business and that he himself was supported by Bombay mill-owners. "Unfortunately, it is true," Gandhi replied, and to the further question, "Doesn't it create a moral obligation?" he answered, "It creates a silent debt but it does not pervert our policy." Fischer went on, "Isn't one of the results that there is a concentration on nationalism almost to the exclusion of social and economic problems?" Gandhi disagreed. "Congress has from time to time, especially under the influence of Pandit Nehru, adopted advanced social programmes and schemes for economic planning."

Fischer left Wardha, convinced of Gandhi's friendliness, charm and uniqueness of personality. He also came to understand his characteristic intellectual method: "He enunciated a principle, defended it, then admitted with a laugh that it was unworkable. In negotiation, this faculty could be extremely irritating and time-wasting. In personal conversation it was attractive and even exciting."

By the time Fischer said goodbye he knew Gandhi was determined on a mass civil disobedience campaign, and that nothing – the consequences neither for India in the war with Japan nor for himself – would deter him. Gandhi was less concerned than he ever had been with the future. For the present, all that mattered was that the British should go.

It was Fischer's impression, "in the light of subsequent events", that the best time for India to have been granted independence would have been between the summer of 1942 and late 1944. British and Allied troops would still have been in the country as security and an Indian government representative of all interests could have been installed on a provisional basis. Now with Cripps having departed empty-handed and Indo–British relations at a low ebb, with the Japanese slipping into Burma and the Indians themselves deprived of any voice in their affairs, there was total apathy.

Gandhi gave his views regularly in *Harijan* throughout June, July and August. They were both uncompromising and ambiguous, in the familiar Gandhi pattern. He argued for negotiations between a National Government and the Allies for a treaty that would link the defence of India with the defence of China. He emphasized that while India would welcome Allied armies on Indian soil he himself, unrealistic though he knew it to be, would argue for the disbandment of the Indian Army. "After the formation of the National Government," he admitted however, "my voice may be a voice in the wilderness and nationalist India may go war-mad."

This was far from Nehru's attitude; what he wanted was "a people's war, a people's army and increased production". In this view he was joined by Maulana Abul Kalam Azad, the leading figure among Congress Muslims. But there was to be no further move towards a National Government, and both Gandhi and Nehru in their different ways seethed with frustration.

It had been two years since Gandhi had even spoken to the Viceroy. In the course of an interview with the *New York Herald Tribune* he remarked,

> If anybody could convince me that in the midst of war the British Government cannot declare India free without jeopardising the war effort, I should like to hear the argument. . . . My complaint is that all these good people talk *at* me, swear *at* me, but never condescend to talk *to* me.

At the AICC meeting of 7 and 8 August a resolution was passed declaring that India would resist aggression with armed as well as non-violent forces and that if the Congress leaders were arrested the vows of non-violence should still be regarded as sacrosanct. In the meantime, while Congress demands were being discussed, Indians should consider themselves as already free and no longer under the heel of imperialism.

Before dawn of the day after the meeting the police swooped, arresting the most important delegates, Gandhi, from Birla House, and Nehru among them. Gandhi's destination was to be the Aga Khan's palace outside Poona. Mahadev Desai, amongst others, was in his party and his wife was allowed to join him.

Fischer, calling on the Viceroy after leaving Wardha with a plea from Gandhi for a meeting, found his message indifferently received. "1942 was Churchill's first opportunity in office to cope with a civil disobedience movement in India," Fischer was to write later. "The British Government preferred suppression to discussion."

It was not quite as simple as that, for, accurately or not, rumours were put about in government circles that the Japanese might now conceivably be welcomed as liberators, if not by Gandhi's supporters then certainly by the large and vocal following of Subhas Chandra Bose. Gandhi may have proclaimed privately the view that Bose would have to be resisted, but he had also written a draft for the Allahabad Working Committee session in April which had stated that India bore no enmity to Japan and that if India were freed "her first step would probably be to negotiate with Japan".

Nehru wisely insisted on the suppression of these views but he also admitted that "It is Gandhiji's feeling that Japan and Germany will win. This feeling unconsciously governs his decision."

Since the passionate anti-fascism of Nehru found him in a minority among nationalists with an eye to a future under the Axis powers, the reluctance of Britain to accede – at the bleakest moment of the war and with the Germans advancing relentlessly on Stalingrad – to Congress demands is at least comprehensible.

Within ten days of the arrest of the Congress leaders the back of the rebellion they had advocated – or had seemed to do so in a fairly vague document permitting various acts of petty sabotage – had been broken. But the popular uprising that took place apparently spontaneously at the imprisonment of the Congress leaders led to a situation that was, while it lasted, in the words of Linlithgow in a telegram to Churchill, "by far the most serious rebellion since that of 1857, the gravity and extent of which we have so far concealed from the world for reasons of military security".

Wholesale violence and destruction took place, particularly in the eastern part of the United Provinces and Bihar, during which roads, railway lines and telegraph wires were cut, buildings set on fire and looted, and British officials and police killed.

As soon as armed police and troops entered the fray the most wanton of the rioters were rounded up or dispersed. But with outposts of independent disaffection lingering on, an almost mortal blow had been dealt to the confidence and goodwill which, despite political differences, British and Indians had habitually displayed towards one another.

The question that remains is whether there was any real justification, in the light of the Congress resolution of 7 August, for the arrest of the leaders. The decision was apparently taken by the Viceroy on his own initiative, Wavell, the C.-in-C., being out of the country and neither of the generals commanding the Presidency Division in Calcutta and the Eastern Division at Ranchi being aware, let alone consulted, of his intention.

G.D., quoting Gandhi's recorded answers to questions put to him in internment, was adamant that arrests were totally unjustified by any allegations of potential resorts to violence. Gandhi, under interrogation, disclaimed all responsibility for the sabotage that followed his arrest, denying particularly that Congress had issued secret instructions encouraging it. To further questions about Congress opportunism at a time of Allied crisis and his own pacifism he replied:

If the National Government is formed and takes power on the basis of giving military help to the Allied Nations I obviously cannot obstruct and will not obstruct. I cannot directly participate in any act of violence. But Congress is not pacifist in the same manner as I am. And I naturally would not do anything to obstruct the execution of the Congress intention.

Gandhi's replies exonerate him of deviousness, but they do not take into consideration such confidential circulars as that put out by the Andhra Pradesh CC a week before the AICC meeting, which included, among suggestions for boycott and picketing, the arranging of labour strikes, the stopping of trains and the cutting of telegraph wires. Even this document, however, was non-operational without the Mahatma's consent.

Alarmed at the prospect of a twenty-one day fast threatened by Gandhi unless he and the Congress was cleared of all charges, G.D., in conjunction with K. M. Munshi, Governor of the United Provinces, decided to summon as representative a conference as possible to urge Gandhi's release.

Telegrams were dispatched to assorted dignitaries, representatives of the Hindu, Muslim, Sikh, Parsi and English communities, and in due course a meeting was held in a marquee put up in the Federation of Indian Chambers of Commerce compound. Various resolutions were passed, all of them confined to humanitarian rather than political or constitutional issues. They were to no avail. Gandhi remained in his princely prison, initially without access to newspapers.

By the end of the year anti-British demonstrations and activities, which had spread sporadically from the cities to the country, had more or less fizzled out. Gandhi, having languished in gaol for several months, now began writing to the Viceroy more in sorrow than in anger but nevertheless threatening a fast unless the wrong done to the Congress leaders was ended. Linlithgow's reply expressed disappointment that Gandhi had failed at any stage to condemn the crimes and violence of the preceding months or even to dissociate himself from them.

What Gandhi described as "growls" and "counter-growls" continued, each blaming the other for the scenes that had developed following the August arrests. "I regard the use of a fast for political purposes," the Viceroy wrote, "as a form of political blackmail for which there is no moral justification and understood from your own previous writings that this was also your view."

The fast went ahead, despite an offer from the Viceroy of release for as long as it lasted. Gandhi declined the offer. Within a week his condition had deteriorated to an extent that there were grave fears for his life.

He survived, none the less, induced finally to drink orange

juice and goats' milk. Once he was out of danger there was general agitation for his release, not least by non-Congress leaders on the Viceroy's Council. Linlithgow would have none of it, nor would he allow him even such a non-controversial visitor as Roosevelt's personal envoy in India.

The Government, in almost every way, came badly out of Gandhi's imprisonment; it was not simply the injustice of it, which was what hurt Gandhi himself most, his lack of opportunity to exonerate himself from charges that were never substantiated, but the demoralizing and debilitating effect his isolation had on Indians and sensitive opinion generally.

For Gandhi, his time in the Aga Khan palace was one of intense sadness. Mahadev Desai, his secretary and companion from the earliest days after his return from South Africa and perhaps closer to Gandhi than anyone, died of a heart-attack soon after their internment there. In February 1944 Gandhi's wife Kasturbai also died, of bronchitis, Gandhi refusing her pencillin. Their long-estranged eldest son, Harilal, brought to the deathbed by his mother's wish, arrived drunk and had to be turned away.

On 6 May 1944, Gandhi, suffering from anaemia and various intestinal ailments, was released. After some weeks by the sea at Birla House, Juhu, he returned to his old ashram near Wardha.

During Gandhi's removal from Indian affairs and the arrest of the Congress leadership the Muslim League, not surprisingly, increased in power and prestige. By the time Gandhi was free, Jinnah, in his early days both a member of Congress senior to Gandhi and Nehru and a passionate advocate of Hindu–Muslim unity, had made the concept of Pakistan desirable for almost every category of Muslim. Subhas Chandra Bose, too, had not been idle, moving between Berlin and Japanese-occupied Singapore in his attempts to get backing for his non-communal Indian National Army, composed substantially of Indian POWs from Japanese internment camps.

Bose's Forward Bloc movement in India and his army were, however, little more than irritants, opposed equally by members of Congress and the communists. When Bose himself mysteriously disappeared his army suffered the indignity of being taken prisoner a second time, this time by the British.

Gandhi's feeling of helplessness in his remote palace while Jinnah and Bose travelled and spoke freely was bad enough; worse for him, perhaps, was his inability to help during the terrible Bengal famine of 1943–4. There were various causes of this – inflation, shortage of rice and transport, hoarding – but the most serious was lack of organization and the absence of any kind of rationing.

No letters were allowed between Gandhi and G.D. from his arrest in August 1942 to his release in May 1944. G.D. was anxious to pick up the threads again but reluctant to add to Gandhi's heavy burden of correspondence at a time when his health was precarious. He therefore addressed his letters at first to Pyarelal Nayar, who had replaced Mahadev Desai as secretary.

Gandhi, though free, suspected, wrongly as it turned out, that he might be rearrested at any moment. He was planning to spend some days at Birla House, but wrote to G.D.'s brother Rameshwardas, who was in Bombay, that he was under pressure not to stay at any Birla residence. He was inclined to disregard objections, unless requested by himself or G.D. not to.

Gandhi's first act, once he felt strong enough to take up the cudgels again, was to try and establish better relations with Jinnah. After a brisk exchange of letters they met in Jinnah's Bombay house almost daily for several hours between 9 and 15 September, every evening resuming their dialogue in detailed letters to each other. It was to no avail. Jinnah was intent on partition at any price and he wanted it decided before any question of independence. Independence could wait.

Gandhi had been meeting with opposition from Hindus in his own party about his plans to come to terms with Jinnah and the League. He was picketed in his ashram and threatened with violence if he attempted to leave. Pyarelal wrote to G.D. from Birla House, on the morning of Gandhi's and Jinnah's first meeting, that the leader of the pickets "appeared to be very highly strung, fanatical and of a neurotic type" and that when arrested he was found to be carrying a dagger.

When the Police Officer who arrested him banteringly remarked that at any rate he had the satisfaction of becoming a martyr, quick came the reply, "No, that will be when someone assassinates Gandhiji." "Why not leave it to leaders to settle it among themselves; for instance, Savarkar might come and do the job," jocularly remarked the Police Officer in question. The reply was, "That will be too great an honour for Gandhiji. A jamadar will be quite enough for the purpose."

Gandhi's letters to G.D. after the breakdown of the Jinnah talks were back to the familiar themes of raising money, this time for a memorial to Mahadev Desai. In November Gandhi received a complaint from the Joint Secretary of the Delhi Textile Mazoor Sabha about conditions in the Birla Mill, comparing them unfavourably with those in the only other big textile mill in Delhi. "The workers look towards you to intervene in the matter."

The letter was forwarded to G.D. by Pyarelal. G.D. explained the situation as simply as he could, a long and detailed account of the circumstances – shift work, wages, benefits, housing – following from the mill-manager. Gandhi's friendship with G.D. left him open to numerous requests for intervention of this kind and G.D. was scrupulous in investigating and producing satisfactory answers in each case. Gandhi, for his part, had no scruples about his association with rich industrialists and no amount of censure deflected him from such friendships, the benefits of which, however undeniable to both parties, were incidental. If G.D. was able on occasions to lean on Gandhi, so did Gandhi on him; the depth of their mutual regard was never in doubt.

It was already clear now that Gandhi's health – he was seventy-five – made it essential that he be freed from all parochial anxieties and administrative worries over the ashram. G.D. urged rest and a change of climate for him. Pyarelal wrote to G.D., "In spite of all the detachment that Bapu has cultivated he is very human and the presence near him of someone from among his Old Guard cannot be over-estimated. There is something frightening in his utter spiritual isolation."

In June Nehru, Azad, now President of Congress, and other leaders were released on the orders of Wavell, the new Viceroy. They had been in gaol for two months short of three years. Wavell immediately invited leaders of all parties to Simla to discuss proposals for a new plan for India. Jinnah and Gandhi both attended, as well as representatives of the Sikhs and Harijans and former provincial prime ministers. The idea was to set up a new Executive Council in which the only non-Indians would be the Viceroy and the Commander-in-Chief. Unfortunately, Congress demands on the one hand for representation in relation to their numerical superiority, including Harijans, rather than on the basis of equal proportions of Muslims and caste Hindus, and Jinnah's insistence on the right to choose all the Muslim members of the Council himself, led to an impasse. Since the Congress had many Muslim members, including its President, and had always insisted on being a national not a Hindu organization, this was an insulting demand. Nevertheless, of the two main negotiating parties it was the Congress, guided by Gandhi, who showed themselves the more willing for compromise.

No sooner had the Delhi Mill matter been sorted out to everyone's satisfaction than Gandhi received another complaint. Pyarelal wrote to G.D., "Some people have been writing to Bapu about a Birla mill that is proposed to be erected in Gwalior. There is dissatisfaction over the acquisition of the land. I hope you will look into the matter . . . The situation is being exploited by a group of local Communists."

Gandhi, in an effort to recuperate and restore his strength, was maintaining long periods of silence. He was also having a naturopathic treatment for bronchitis. It was to Pyarelal, therefore, that G.D. replied, explaining that land acquired was merely leased to the mills and that compensation to the cultivators whose land had been acquired was paid by the state. In G.D.'s opinion the amount of compensation was too low and he was in the process of persuading the state to raise it when communist abuse of both the state and himself made matters worse. Pyarelal replied:

> Bapu was relieved to find that you were doing your best in the matter. The mere fact that some irresponsible people are exploiting the situation should not allow the just and legitimate interests of the poor to be jeopardised. If the Durbar does not pay heed to your advice it may be best to put your project in cold storage or drop it altogether.

G.D. took up the matter of the Nagda agriculturists with the Revenue Minister, who found the Birla proposals "extravagant" but promised to look into them.

During March G.D. and Gandhi exchanged numerous letters and telegrams on their favourite subject, their health. Each showed enthusiastic concern about the other. On 19 March G.D. cabled, "Fever left but cough still persisting. Am taking toast vegetable and milk no butter. Would you suggest any change in diet." Gandhi telegraphed back by return, "Report incomplete unclear. If you take milk state vegetables. Any case advise half ounce butter direct from milk with toast and salad well chewed. Drink hot water honey soda. Practise regulated deep breathing on empty stomach. Report. Love, Bapu."

Such affectionate advice and queries must have been a welcome change from the criticism they were both undergoing in their respective spheres. G.D. was depressed at the amount of malice and envy evident in both political and private life. "Muslims are abusing Hindus and Bapu the most," he wrote, "Hindu Sabha is abusing Congress and the League. The Congress sees nothing good in its opponents . . . I frankly see a gloomy future for us. In spite of all the abuse hurled at me I believe (this may be a false belief) that I have always taken a right and just view of things."

In May relations became ruffled when G.D., due to go to London with leading industrialists such as Tata and Kasturbhai, read a United Press report that Gandhi had expressed the opinion that any deals negotiated would be likely to be "shameful". He sent off a pained wire explaining that the industrial delegation was a non-official body paying its own expenses and with the simple aim of making contacts and studying new production methods.

Gandhi replied in typically equivocal and vague fashion: "My statement was necessary, it deals with hypothetical case. No hasty opinion. Statement expresses view which I have always held. You have nothing to regret since you, Tata, Kasturbhai proceeding wholly unofficially. You have my blessings and prayer in terms of famishing and naked India."

The real nature of Gandhi's objection emerged in his next letter to G.D., sent on the eve of G.D.'s departure. It was that while any political prisoners continued to rot in gaol "we should not be expected to place orders with British firms for capital goods".

G.D. wrote from Karachi, his plane having been delayed.

How did the idea of our placing any orders happen to enter your mind? I myself do not know. Besides it would be a superfluous effort on the part of any one of us to go all the way to England for the purpose of placing orders when the hotels here are packed to capacity with those who are here to book our orders. In order to meet the challenge of the present shortages it is absolutely necessary for us to add to our existing capacity to produce more . . . Rest assured I am going to give Tata a good dressing down since some of his utterances have earned my disapprobation.

Under Labour

Labour's landslide victory in the July 1945 election had surprisingly little effect on British policy in India. G.D. had not taken to the Labour leaders when he met them in London before the war and he had no confidence that a socialist government, however apparently liberal in its leanings, would be any more sympathetic to Indian aspirations. In a sense he was right. Attlee and Bevin were tough negotiators, without Churchill's imperial bluster but with a proper sense of Britain's traditional holdings and prestige.

Nevertheless, soon after the surrender of Japan in August, Wavell was summoned to London for discussions with the new Secretary of State, Pethick-Lawrence. After a series of Cabinet committees it was decided that the original Cripps proposal of 1942, allowing for the formation of an Indian constitution-making body after the holding of elections, should be implemented. This, Wavell warned the committee, would not in his opinion now be acceptable to Hindu or Muslim opinion, but he was over-ruled by Cripps whose advice, given to him by G.D., B. Shiva Rao and others, was that the Hindus at any rate would be agreeable.

Wavell became increasingly unhappy about any proposals made without further consultations with Indians. He told the Secretary of State, "It was perfectly easy to draft something that would get past the Committee, but that if it promised something we could not fulfil it would be dishonest, and if it was completely unacceptable to one of the two principal communities, it would be highly dangerous."

Wavell dissociated himself from the revived Cripps proposal, commenting in his journal, "Birla, and Shiva Rao and other Congress propagandists are, I know, seeing Cripps and Attlee, and they are taking all they say as gospel."

Despite his misgivings, Wavell's views were disregarded and he returned to India in September with authority to promise early realization of full self-government, the setting up of an Executive Council which had the support of the main Indian parties, and the formation of a constitution-making body.

The winter of 1945–6 was notable, apart from the run-up to the elections, for the decision to try token members of the Indian National Army, of whom some 20,000 were prisoners. A Hindu, a Muslim and a Sikh were the first to be tried in the Red Fort in November, Nehru himself acting as one of the counsels for the defence. The trial united every category of Indian in opposition and the sentences passed were soon remitted.

Shortly afterwards a naval mutiny broke out in Bombay, mainly over demands for increased pay for British and Indian sailors, but also as a protest over bad food, the trial of INA prisoners and the use of Indian Army troops abroad. The mutiny, which involved a hunger strike, lasted only a week but provoked wide public demonstrations of sympathy and support. Gun battles took place, during which over 200 civilians were killed and 1000 injured.

Curiously, Gandhi was violently against the mutiny, as were Sardar Patel, Jinnah and Nehru, for different reasons, while the communists applauded it, calling for a general strike. The Naval Strike Committee, in its last message, observed, "Our strike has been a historic event in the life of our nation. For the first time the blood of men in the Services and in the streets flowed together in a common cause."

It was in this uneasy climate, aggravated by the use of Indian troops in Indonesia, that the elections were contested, Nehru being the main Congress speaker and Patel handling the administrative details. Many people were disturbed by the apparent extremism of the Congress electioneering speeches, Nehru's in particular.

Sir Stafford Cripps, writing to G.D. in red ink on Board of Trade paper, remarked,

I do hope that your Congress friends will give us some help by not being purely negative in their outlook. The statements made by Congress were not very helpful to those of us here who are trying to push this matter through and tend to add enormous weight to the arguments of those opposing.

G.D. replied:

You will hear rather intemperate speeches at election time. But they should be discounted. Unfortunately the Indonesian trouble is agitating the mind of the public a great deal. I am hoping that H.M.G. will make a helpful move towards the solution of this question too. Democracy and self-government for Indonesians are no less necessary than for other nations.

In November Wavell wrote to Pethick-Lawrence, "I have evidence that G. D. Birla is alarmed at the violence of Congress speeches and has told the editor of the *Hindustan Times* which he owns to lower its tone." Pethick-Lawrence, expressing satisfaction at this news, replied, "It rather looks as if the richer supporters of Congress may be beginning to wonder where the caravan is going."

G.D. was nevertheless more optimistic than usual: "I definitely see a bright and friendly future. Much will depend on how both sides act, which will again depend on the proper approach and personal contacts."

His optimism was short-lived. A Cabinet Mission, consisting of Pethick-Lawrence, Cripps and Alexander, arrived in March 1946 with a plan, in G.D.'s words, "expressly designed to avoid partition" but one which immediately aroused Congress's suspicion. The members of the Mission, together with Wavell and Indian leaders, spent the best part of three months in attempts to frame a new Constitution. While they were working strikes broke out all over India, making administration sufficiently difficult for Wavell to call for the speedy installation of an interim government, in which Congress would have the responsibility of dealing with all labour problems.

This, in the end, was what resulted, Nehru heading a

caretaker government at the very moment at which communal riots of the utmost violence broke out in Calcutta, spreading to Bombay, Bihar and the United Provinces. Voting in the elections had been on predictable communal lines, with the communists giving Congress close fights in certain provinces, and the League winning almost every seat available to it. Congress captured 57 out of 102 seats in the Central Assembly and over 90 per cent of non-Muslim votes.

The League remained adamant about Partition. G.D. was not perturbed. "I somehow or other not only believed in the inevitability of Partition but always considered it a good way out of difficulties."

Jinnah had recently made a speech in Bombay in which he declared,

> We could settle the Indian problem in ten minutes. If Mr Gandhi would say, "I agree that there should be Pakistan; I agree that one-fourth of India, composed of six provinces – Sind, Baluchistan, the Punjab, the North-West Frontier Province, Bengal and Assam, with their present boundaries, constitute the Pakistan state."

Such words would have stuck in Gandhi's throat, though had he co-operated in the proposed reforms of 1919 instead of, as Philip Mason has it in *The Men Who Ruled India*, "appealing to the religious emotions of the Hindu peasantry", there might have been unity and no need for such a declaration.

The cold weather was coming to an end. Gandhi wrote typically to G.D., "I keenly feel the urge to put up in areas inhabited by scavengers wherever I decide to go." G.D. was worried about Cripps's fatigued appearance in the increasing heat. "Tell Sir Stafford I can doctor him without fees," Gandhi remarked, delighted at an opportunity to pass on medical advice and dietary recommendations. Sir Stafford duly added sour milk to his menu.

The Interim Government, reluctantly joined by the Muslim League under Jinnah, was so uneasy and at odds in its functioning that even the most resolute opponents of Partition began to change their minds.

In December of that year G.D. had written at length to Major Henderson, MP, having read the news that a parliamentary delegation under the auspices of the Empire Parliamentary Association would be visiting India.

I still feel that if what I suggested to you in London had been adopted both the parties would have known where they stood. In other words, the only solution is to concede self-determination to both the communities. I would do something like this. First of all, I would take a joint plebiscite (Hindus, Muslims and Sikhs) of the border districts of the Punjab and Bengal asking for their vote whether, in case India was to be separated, they would like their districts to be in the Pakistan or the Hindustan area. On the strength of this plebiscite we shall have a new alignment of the provinces. After that I would give the fullest autonomy to each newly constituted province, including the right to secede. If the people of these provinces, Hindus, Muslims and others decide to separate from India, they can. This is the only solution.

Henderson passed the letter on to the India and Burma Committee of the Cabinet.

In India G.D. had a long lunch with F. F. Turnbull, Private Secretary to the Secretary of State, the gist of what passed between them being referred to the Viceroy. The main subjects were the constitution and function of the Interim Government, economics and the risk of civil war if Jinnah declined to come into the executive. Turnbull ended his account of the meeting,

Mr Birla mentioned several times with particular reverence Sardar Patel. I suspect it is Patel who is running this parity question [Jinnah had asked for parity for the Muslim League with Congress in the Interim Executive, a request G.D. had said Congress would find unacceptable] and that he is using Birla to inject alarm into the Cabinet Delegation.

The failure of the Cabinet Mission to get Congress and the League to work in harness and the subsequent riots in Calcutta led G.D. to write to Henderson, with a copy to Cripps,

I am writing this when things are quietening down. According to moderate estimates nearly 6,000 persons have been killed and an equal number injured. . . . I had seen the riots of 1926 which were very serious. But the present one has no parallel in the history of India. Cruelty and fury were let loose without restraint. It is reported that the night before the riot started motor lorries belonging to the Government of Bengal paraded the streets occupied by Muslim Leaguers for directing the mob.

G.D. added, "The Ministry of Bengal [a Muslim League one] has completely lost the confidence not only of the Hindus but of a large section of Muslims."

Shortly before the formation of the Interim Government, but after the announcement of its members, G.D. had written to Cripps a letter highly critical of the Viceroy who had been touring Calcutta in the wake of the riots. Wavell had not only shown little inclination to take a strong line against the League leaders who had incited the trouble but hinted that he might have to drop altogether the idea of a Constituent Assembly.

If a settlement between the two political parties is to be achieved the only way is to leave it to the Congress as the authorised Government to handle the situation. They are themselves most anxious to secure the cooperation of the League. . . . But the method proposed to be adopted by the Viceroy will lose the League and the Congress both. The Viceroy must either trust his Government and give them his support or recall them. This wavering policy will be most disastrous for India.

Wavell, meanwhile, had become steadily less hopeful of accord between the leaders in the Interim Government, a view shared by the Governor of the United Provinces, Sir Francis Verner, who, according to Wavell,

was pessimistic about the future of India, said that the Congress leaders were quite incapable of running the country . . . and that there was a complete lack of harmony and discipline in the Congress High Command. Patel, with

Birla's backing, was trying to break Nehru, and they were all frightened of the left wing.

Both Nehru and Gandhi did all they could in Bengal and Bihar to soothe relations between Hindus and Muslims. Cripps wrote to G.D., "I think Gandhi's contribution to pacification has been very marked and I am most grateful to him for all he has done."

Gandhi's help was being sought in another matter, a group of villagers from Sambalpur in Orissa requesting his intervention with G.D. over alleged discharges from the Birla-owned Orient Paper Mill into the Ib river at Brajrajnagar. As was customary, Pyarelal passed the letter on to G.D. "If there is anything you want me to tell Bapu, do please let me know." G.D. looked into the matter and reported back the result of his enquiry. Just as G.D. was used as an intermediary by both Gandhi and British officials in their dealings with each other, so was Gandhi approached by those seeking redress for real or imaginary grievances against the Birlas.

The public and the private were never far apart in their relationship. Pyarelal next wrote from Dattapara,

Bapu is determined not to leave East Bengal till there is peace between Hindus and Muslims. He would stay in the midst of the Muslims and eat what they give him. There are suggestions that there should be big settlements of Hindus in East Bengal. Bapu does not like the idea. The trouble is not communal. It is political and the solution can only be found by the political leaders of both the communities.

Gandhi himself wrote from Srirampur to G.D. about his journeys on foot through the mainly Muslim villages.

Goodbye to Delhi, to Sevagram, to Uruli, to Panchgani – my only desire is to do or die. This will also put my non-violence to the test. I am determined to emerge victorious from this ordeal. If you feel like seeing me you will have to come here. I am not going to take part in the Constituent Assembly. ... In case it is possible to hold it in an atmosphere of peace laws may be framed for the provinces which actually participate in its sittings. What part the military and the police will play in the future will also have to be decided. What will the Muslim provinces do? What will happen to the provinces where the Muslims are in a minority? What will be the rôle of the British Government? Also, how will the princes desport themselves?

Let my friends also bear in mind that what I am doing here is not being done in the name of the Congress, nor have I ever entertained any such idea.

A month later Gandhi wrote again.

I have only this much to say in this regard that one should not match barbarity with counter-barbarity. What took place in Bihar was sheer savagery. In such cases stories from the Mahabharata and the Ramayana can only tempt one to take the wrong path. Our public conduct should be characterised by self-restraint; it should also find sanction in our age-old tradition. I am entirely working in that direction.

Gandhi was set on solving the "communal-political problem" at village level, making individual Hindus and Muslims stand surety for the lives and property of returning refugees. The trouble-makers, many identifiably guilty of murder and looting, were, however, still at large and the government was showing no signs of taking action.

"I cannot envisage how Bapu's mission can end," Pyarelal wrote to G.D., "I am afraid he is being driven unknown to himself into a fit – the final resort of non-violence against hatred and unreason. Unless there is a move from above I see grave danger ahead."

G.D. had meanwhile written again to Cripps emphasizing "that it is essential to make a declaration fixing the final date when under all circumstances power will finally be transferred to Indian hands. As long as this uncertainty continues no agreement is possible."

"The prolonged marooning of Gandhi in East Bengal," as

G.D. described it, was testing not only his own powers of non-violence but the endurance of his various helpers, scattered in isolated villages in what one of them referred to as "ratholes". Many of these Noakhali villages, barely above ground in the delta between the Ganges and the Brahmaputra, could only be reached by boat and bullock cart. The political life of India, in one of its most crucial periods, was having to get on without its most influential and, at this time, moderating figure.

Gandhi's unworldliness was being further demonstrated at that time by various experiments he was conducting by lying with nubile and naked young girls – family members and children of his entourage – as tests of his own chastity. When these became known Gandhi, to the distress of his friends, wished to make a public statement. Sardar Patel and Gandhi's son, Devdas, in particular wrote pleading with him to keep his private life private. Gandhi wrote to G.D. from Raipur in February, the fourth month of his Bengal pilgrimage,

> All I wish today to write is that you should give up your attitude of neutrality . . . The link between you and me is your faith that my life is pure, spotless and wholly dedicated to the performance of *dharma*. If that is not so, very little else remains. If I am conducting myself sinfully it becomes the duty of all my friends to oppose me vehemently. I can commit mistakes, I have committed mistakes; for aught one knows this may prove to be my biggest at the fag-end of my life. When I take M. in my lap do I do so as a pure-hearted father or as a father who has strayed from the path of virtue? What I am doing is nothing new to me; in thought I have done it for the last 50 years; in action, in varying degrees, over quite a number of years. Even if you sever all connection with me I would not shed a tear.

Gandhi, in his next paragraph, goes on unconcernedly to lament the plight of local Hindu weavers. His friends, however, prevailed upon him, though not without difficulty, to abandon both his practices and his innocent proclamation of them.

In March, Gandhi, having tramped hundreds of miles and

held hundreds of meetings, left Bengal for Bihar. He had not solved the communal problem but by his example of humility, patience and compassion he had made both Hindus and Muslims more tolerant of each other and paved the way for the return of Hindus to their ancestral villages. Nowhere more than in East Bengal during these winter months was Gandhi's determination for sense to triumph over prejudice better demonstrated.

While Gandhi had been in East Bengal Attlee, summoning the Congress and League leadership to London, had done everything that he could to persuade Jinnah to join the Constituent Assembly. He was unsuccessful. Nehru, on his return, tracked Gandhi down in the village of Srirampur and sought his advice.

Gandhi was not prepared at any time to consider proposals that would lead to the division of India. Nor instinctively was Nehru, but he could not, in the light of League intransigence, carry his party with him. Congress agreed to proposals that would divide India into three federated states. Gandhi would have no part of it.

On 20 February 1947 it was announced from Downing Street that it was intended to effect the transfer of power to responsible Indian hands not later than June 1948. A week later came the news that Wavell was to be replaced by Mountbatten as the last Viceroy.

G.D. had written to Pyarelal in January that "Hindu–Muslim unity will come, if it comes at all, in the Constituent Assembly." Hopes of this, since the failure of the Nehru–Jinnah meeting in London, were already receding. "There are strikes everywhere," G.D. wrote.

There is a coal shortage and many factories are likely to close down. Teachers in Delhi are on strike. Everyone wants higher wages and less work. I am told that in place of 5000 clerks in the Delhi secretariat the number has gone up to nearly 50,000. The whole economic structure seems to be collapsing.

I am sure of one thing. All our statesmen and politicians

are giving greater weight to politics than economics. But I feel that economics will be the real test of the efficiency of our own Government. The country needs freedom, no doubt, but along with it it also needs more education, more cloth, more food, better sanitation, better health and better houses. Nothing is happening in this direction so one cannot help being a bit pessimistic.

In Bihar Gandhi continued the village touring he had done in Bengal on behalf of the Muslims. He would not leave, he said, until his presence was no longer needed.

It was an invitation from Mountbatten, less than a week after his arrival in India, that succeeded in interrupting his work. After his talk with the new Viceroy, the first of six that were to take place within a fortnight, Gandhi delivered an address to the Asian Relations Conference in Delhi. "The real truth is in the villages and in the untouchable homes of the villages. If you want to give a message to the West it must be the message of love and the message of truth."

The spirit of the talks between Mountbatten and Gandhi was informal and friendly. In between his meetings with Gandhi, Mountbatten saw Jinnah. Jinnah insisted on Pakistan. Gandhi, speaking again on behalf of the Congress, rather than for himself, said they would have preferred a united India but if there was to be no prospect of that, then rather than massacre and counter-massacre, Congress would probably agree provisionally to some form of partition. Jinnah, after a struggle, accepted that both Punjab and Bengal would have to be divided. It was on this understanding that the talks ended, Gandhi ultimately dissociating himself from their conclusions.

For two weeks Gandhi, basing himself in the Harijan area on Kingsway, held public prayer meetings, at which he not only urged Hindu–Muslim unity but asked leave to read from the Koran.

As soon as he could he returned to Bihar, intending to stay there. Nehru, however, sent for him after two weeks to attend the crucial Working Committee meeting on 1 May.

His presence turned out to be an irrelevance. Faced with

the bleak alternatives put to them, the Congress, aware that refusal on their part to accept Pakistan would compromise the whole notion of independence and, if Jinnah's threats were to be realized, lead to civil war, gave in. Gandhi, almost alone, held out.

He went back to Bengal and to Bihar, hoping that by some miracle his efforts at the humblest levels might achieve what meetings between leaders had failed to do.

But the violence continued. Mountbatten returned to London and on 3 June Attlee announced what came to be called the Mountbatten Plan. Jinnah had got what he wanted, though the Plan left it open "for further negotiations between communities for a united India". If the Muslim League was satisfied no one else was, neither the British Government, nor the Viceroy, nor the Congress Party, nor the princes, nor representatives of other minority parties.

There was no will in Britain to stay in India, certainly not to continue to accept responsibilities there after a long, exhausting and economically demoralizing war.

Assassination and the End of a Friendship

Many, even among the Congress leaders, felt the moral rightness of Gandhi's view, even as they could not accept its practicability. Gandhi took no part in the complicated processes and decision-makings that preceded Independence and when the time came he could not find it in his heart to celebrate. Instead, he spent Independence Day, 15 August 1947, in Calcutta, making calm where all round there had been appalling hostility and aggression. He had not given up, but henceforth he would be more of a private citizen than he had ever been.

On 26 August Mountbatten wrote to Gandhi:

> In the Punjab we have 55,000 soldiers and large-scale rioting on our hands. In Bengal our forces consist of one man and there is no rioting. As a serving officer as well as an administrator, may I be allowed to pay my tribute to the One Man Boundary Force?

The magical peace that had descended on Bengal lasted two weeks, then the hatred returned with renewed force. Bitterly disappointed, Gandhi announced that he would begin a fast that would only end "when sanity returns to Calcutta". He gave a statement to the press in which he said, "What my word in person cannot do, my fast may."

This time Gandhi demanded a written pledge signed by representatives of every community in the city. After three days it was delivered to him and he broke his fast.

Gandhi was anxious that there should be no feeling of oppression.

> If a single step is taken under pressure of the fasts, not from conviction, it would cause oppression, but there should be

172

no oppression if there is complete cooperation between the head and the heart. The function of my fast is to purify, to release our energies.

The day after he had begun to take food again Gandhi announced that he would leave for the Punjab, hopeful that he could accomplish there what he had achieved in Bengal. Wherever else killing and looting took place during the following months complete harmony survived in Calcutta and Noakhali.

There were to be no further exchanges of letters between Gandhi and G.D., for Gandhi broke his prospective journey to the Punjab in Delhi and there he stayed, in Birla House, until his assassination five months later. There was time enough now for talk and no need for correspondence.

Delhi, Gandhi said, resembled a "city of the dead". Hindu refugees had poured in from Muslim Punjab and the Muslims in Delhi had to bear the consequences of their ill-treatment. A steady stream of visitors came to Birla House with tales of murder and robbery. Every evening, as in Bengal, Gandhi held prayer meetings in the garden, at which he pleaded for mutual tolerance. During the day he visited the refugee camps that had sprung up all round Delhi. As before he begged that Muslims should be allowed to live on in safety and Hindus and Sikhs feel able to return to their homes in Pakistan.

Gandhi had with him an even larger entourage than usual, both men and women. "Frankly speaking," G.D. said in a broadcast after Gandhi's death, "some of his guests I did not like, nor were they liked by Bapu's associates."

Gandhi's pleas fell on less receptive ears in Delhi than they had in Bengal. While Calcutta was peaceful, in Delhi mosques were desecrated and Muslims harassed and killed. Gandhi was not only dismayed by the violence in the city. He was upset by signs that Congress and the government were on the way to becoming synonymous, a situation that could rapidly lead to a one-party system. When, after the resignation of the party president J. P. Kripalani, voting for a successor took place in the Working Committee, Gandhi nominated the Socialist leader, Narendra Dev. Although Nehru was agreeable, Dev was defeated. Next Rajendra Prasad, like Kripalani an old colleague of Gandhi's from Champaran thirty years earlier, was put forward by Nehru and Patel as a candidate.

Gandhi was not consulted, except by Prasad himself. Prasad accepted Gandhi's opposition to the idea but was later persuaded to stand. He became President and Gandhi's hopes of a critical presence in the Congress hierarchy faded.

On 13 January 1948 Gandhi began a final fast in an effort to bring India to its senses. As had happened in Calcutta, the political and religious leaders, shamed into action, held urgent meetings. After five days they came to Birla House with solemn pledges. Gandhi broke his fast.

On 20 January the evening prayer meeting was interrupted by an amateurish bomb, aimed at Gandhi but exploding harmlessly some way off. Gandhi brushed aside all requests from his friends for extra protection.

Ten days later, in similar circumstances, three shots from a pistol fired at point-blank range by a militant Hindu killed him almost instantaneously.

G.D., among many other of Gandhi's friends, had tried to dissuade him from the last fast but he was not to be moved. While he was still fasting G.D. left on business for Bombay, anxious about the outcome. Once Gandhi had started to eat again he quickly recovered his usual high spirits. At first he was too weak to walk to the evening prayer meeting and had to be carried in a chair.

On the day of his assassination Gandhi had a meeting in Birla House with Patel, the Home Minister and Deputy Prime Minister. The relationship between Nehru and Patel, on whose co-operation the success of the government rested, had shown signs of strain. Gandhi enjoined Patel, as he had earlier Nehru, to mend their friendship. It was his final act of pacification.

At the moment of Gandhi's death G.D. was in his home village of Pilani, where he had gone for the day. On his return he found his house overflowing with people. Gandhi was lying on the floor, some reciting the Koran at his side, some the Bhagavad Gita, some the Granth Sahib. "I found dear old Bapu," G.D. was later to write, "lying in his eternal sleep as if nothing were the matter with him. His face radiated the same simple charm, love and purity. I could even detect a streak of compassion and forgiveness in that face."

The previous night Gandhi's body had been laid at an angle on the roof of Birla House and floodlit. It was brought down at midnight and then reinstated in the morning so that everyone who passed by could see it.

The body was taken to be burned, laid on a gun-carriage drawn by ropes. The two-mile long cortège took nearly five hours to reach the cremation ground at Rajghat on the Jumna.

There was no room for G.D. on the carriage, which bore the Congress leaders and other close associates. He began to follow in the procession but became increasingly lost among the million or more marchers. In the end he gave up and returned alone to the house that would always be associated with Gandhi and himself.

Seven years after Gandhi's death, in January 1955, Pyarelal wrote to G.D. saying that he had come across notes of the conversation between G.D. and Bapu on the day of G.D.'s departure for Bombay during Gandhi's last fast. "On re-reading it," Pyarelal wrote in a postscript to his enclosing letter,

I am struck by its great value – it is a priceless nugget of burnished gold as a "slow-motion" picture of Bapu's soul at one of the greatest moments of his career and also of the process of purification at work in the midst of that atmosphere of insanity and blood lust that had turned man brute and less than a brute those days.

G.D. had called on Gandhi to ask whether, since he was going away, Gandhi would not grant him the favour of ending his fast. His information was that things were greatly improved in Delhi.

Gandhi replied,

Whenever I took to fasting I always looked forward to its termination. This happened in Calcutta as well. I am incapable of self-deception, so whenever I saw anyone approaching I would imagine him to be the harbinger of tidings that would enable me to end the fast. That feeling of anticipation is absent this time. There is no expectation of good news, therefore none of the jubilation at the prospect of a happy termination of the fast. Here comes Ghanshyamdas, presumably with a request to terminate my fast. Isn't that so? . . . If I gave up the fast the good work now in the process of fruition would come to an abrupt end. Delhi needs a lot of cleansing. If Sardar is freed from his preoccupation in Delhi his task will be easier. Then he will be able to go wherever his presence is needed.

G.D. said that what had happened in Pakistan had made him lose confidence in the Muslims. When one was angry one could not rise above prejudices. But the purification and self-cleansing that Gandhi called for was dependent on his own survival. Gandhi replied, "I have not given up the will to live. I have such faith in God that if I feel myself to be in good health even my kidneys improve."

G.D. said, "My heart is here. Sardar's face, that iron man's face, wears a forlorn look. He said if I felt like going I was at liberty to do so. My heart was full of anguish. Why should this fast be prolonged?"

Gandhi urged G.D. to carry out his business engagements. "Things will go on normally. But wherever I go this cleansing process must continue."

One of the things Gandhi had insisted on during his fast – and which had angered Hindu extremists more than anything – was that India should immediately pay the equivalent of £40,000,000 to Pakistan, their entitlement in the share-out of pre-partition India. The payment was authorized as Gandhi's condition began to deteriorate. His last words to G.D. before saying goodbye to him were "That was the only thing that could be exploited. By making this payment India has added inches to its stature. If they feel like fighting our soldiers will

Business Partners. G.D. and Edgar F. Kaiser.

Rajahkrishna with G.D.

Nehru at Pilani. G.D. introduces
the Prime Minister to the
delights of transport by camel.

G.D. and D.P. Mandelia, his close associate
for fifty years.

The Pilani educational complex, G.D.'s "desert rose".

In later years G.D. spent his evenings reading, painting and learning languages.

The family man. G.D. at home.

Businessman and visionary, G.D. looked the part, equally at ease
in Western or Indian dress.

feel they are fighting with our money well spent. Fight on. But for how long will you continue to fight?"

The assassination of Gandhi ended a thirty-two-year association, the correspondence side of which had begun in 1924. In a speech made in 1981 without notes, and in Hindi, under the auspices of Sangit Kala Mandir, Calcutta, G.D. had begun his remarks on Gandhi by saying that after a thousand years when people remembered Gandhiji it would not be because of his struggle for freedom or the Bardoli *Satyagraha*. "He will be remembered for what he gave us; the ideology he gave us; the inspiration he gave us; the new direction he gave us."

The greatest message which Gandhiji gave, G.D. observed, was "Be fearless, Be prepared for going to gaol. But do not sacrifice Truth and do not sacrifice non-violence."

"I never perceived anger in him," G.D. continued. "I always saw a fountain of love in him. On the eve of independence, or soon after, he observed that he was happy we had got our freedom but he was sorry to see such a great empire liquidated."

It was the humanity in Gandhi, not his political wisdom, or his religious qualities, that attracted G.D., that in his own words "possessed him".

G.D., twenty-five years younger than Gandhi, was properly the disciple. But their correspondence was not one-sided, and G.D., once he had established confidence in the relationship, held his own in argument. His attitude fell far short of idolatry, for all the affection and admiration that flowed between the two. Gandhi's letters, G.D. observed, were not just those of "a great man or Mahatma but of a saintly man and the outpourings of a friendly soul".

In his preface to the four volumes of letters, Kaka Saheb Kalelkar, one of the few surviving co-workers of Gandhi from the earliest days, described the mood of India in 1915, when Gandhi returned from South Africa, as one of "utter despair".

In India, he wrote, Gandhi travelled

177

from the Himalayas to Rameshwaram, explaining to the people his vision of satyagraha. Soon the heartbeats of Gandhiji had their echo in the pulse of the people and both were tuned to the same wavelength. . . . Among the chosen few close workers who came in contact with Gandhiji at that time, the place of Shri Ghanshyamdasji is a special one.

In his analysis of the relationship between Gandhi and G.D., Kalelkar lays stress on those aspects that had nothing to do with money. Other rich men, notably Jamnalal Bajaj, gave immense sums to Gandhi schemes and institutions. But it was the dedication of G.D. to Gandhi as a man, the devoting of a large amount of his time to Gandhi's well-being and the interpreting of his political, philanthropic and educational ideas that singled him out. The vast sums of money were doled out unquestioningly and without wish for account, but it was G.D.'s own disciplined involvement in Hindu–Muslim unity, the removal of untouchability, the development of village industries and khadi – even to the extent of himself spinning – that drew from Gandhi a special response. This, too, was despite G.D.'s own disagreement with Gandhi over economic matters and his intense dislike of the civil disobedience movement.

G.D. has been described as an "extension of Gandhi's conscience" as well as an interpreter of it. However it is labelled, this friendship between one of the great figures of this century, certainly one of the most influential in the history of India, and a Marwari industrialist from a remote corner of Rajasthan, was a profound and fruitful one. Their correspondence reveals that it was also touching and delightful.

Hidden Hand

At the time of Gandhi's death G. D. Birla was fifty-four. With Independence he had no further need to spend months of his time on fatiguing negotiations between the British and Indian leaderships. The most important tasks ahead, ones to which he had already given much thought, were to do with production and capital. "We were importing food on a large scale," he wrote, "without either producing exports to pay for it or having markets in which to sell such exports as we could produce. Consequently, in order to make payments we were using up our sterling balances at a fantastic rate."

It was to explain India's much misunderstood position, as well as in relation to his own industrial requirements, that G.D. visited England in the summer of 1949. It might have seemed that, by comparison with his rôle as an emissary of Gandhi, his public stature would be reduced. In fact, having emerged from the shadow of the Mahatma, G.D. now held far greater importance in his own right. For if India was to survive economically it would have to rely heavily over the next decade on the vision and bargaining skills of such as himself.

It was to Sardar Patel, who, G.D. remarked, "now takes the place of Bapu in my correspondence", that he described some of his meetings. In the last stages of the Independence negotiations Patel had been the dominating figure, wholly Hindu in his approach but of bulldog appearance and stature. "He is more of a man than most of these Hindu politicians," Wavell observed, "though he has no sense of compromise or generosity towards Moslems." Wavell had been suspicious of all relationships between what he called the Congress High Command and Big Business, seeing the hidden hand of Birla behind every move relating to Liaquat Ali Khan's controversial and punitive (as far as big business was concerned) 1947–8 Budget. In *The Viceroy's Journal* Wavell confided, "the Budget is a clever one, in that it drives a wedge between Congress and their rich merchant supporters, like Birla".

Wavell's attitude, not unique among British officials, towards Indian industrialists had for some years been unnecessarily suspicious, as if the expressed desire for independence through support of the Congress and the need for economic prosperity were in themselves conflicting and dishonourable instincts.

Lord Linlithgow, in a "most secret and personal" communication to all provincial governors on 2 November 1942, had written:

> I am anxious that every possible step should be taken to trace and bring home to those concerned the part played by "Big Business" in the recent disturbances [following the Quit India resolution and the arrest of Congress leaders]. It has always been known that Congress has depended for financial assistance on a number of wealthy capitalists and the D.I.B. has recently asked Central Intelligence Officers to probe further into the matter with the assistance of Provincial Special Branches. I enclose a copy of a memorandum which he has sent to them giving examples of the manner in which this financial assistance is believed to have operated during the last few months.
>
> A further and even more important possibility is that there is a clique of financiers who, taking a leaf out of Japan's book, and even possibly with Japanese assistance, are endeavouring to use the Congress organisation and the political ferment which it has brought about to establish for themselves a position of financial domination in India comparable to that obtained by the "Big Four" in Japan. . . . It is generally assumed that the Hindus are naturally sympathetic towards the Buddhist culture of Japan and would welcome its support against the Muslims if the Japanese came to India. There may be some such feeling, but it may well have been fostered by the Birla Brothers with a view to their ulterior objects.

Linlithgow continued, stressing the need for delicacy in handling investigations, "I contemplate that a stage might be reached when we could strike against the Birla Brothers and other leading financiers engaged with them in the conspiracy." Linlithgow hints further at a "plot" and the importance of all information "bearing on the financial support which the Indian mercantile community has been giving to Gandhi, the Congress, and the present Congress movement, and the motives underlying it".

What was this conspiracy and plot? It is never made clear. G.D. was disingenuous on occasions as to whether he was financing Congress or not – drawing a distinction where there may have been none between Gandhism and the Congress – and Gandhi, despite later avowals to the contrary by G.D., had moments when he was convinced the British would be defeated. But "conspiracy" and "plot" seem loaded terms to use in relation to someone with whom the Viceroy had enjoyed frank and friendly relations.

The reaction of the government's Intelligence Bureau was along more sensible lines. Having quoted G.D.'s interview with the *New York Times* in February 1943, in which he maintained that reports of Indian industrialists' help to Congress had been "grossly exaggerated", the Bureau's comment continues,

Probably the best indication, however, of the underlying motives of Big Business is to be found in the "Master Plan" for post-war reconstruction recently published by a group of Bombay businessmen, of whom no fewer than five – J. R. D. Tata, Sir Adeshir Dalal, Kasturbhai Lalbhai, Sir Shri Ram, and G. D. Birla – have been mentioned in this note. This plan discloses an ambitious scheme of benevolent capitalism working through a "National Government with full freedom in economic matters", under which it is proposed to expand industry, agriculture and services enormously, to the moderate benefit of India's millions and to the immense profit of Indian "Big Business".

The note concluded,

As to the relationship between "Big Business" and Congress, the available evidence does not appear to justify any assumption that "Big Business" has secretly been using Congress as an unsuspecting instrument towards the achievement of its own ends, or vice versa, but rather that the two have been working together in a partnership of convenience with no illusions on either side.

The Intelligence Bureau compared the support given by industrialists and financiers to Congress with that given by their Russian equivalents to the Mensheviks before the Revolution, involvement with political aspirations being based on the speculation that "fabulous profits" would follow the attainment of power.

As far as the "Bombay Plan" itself was concerned, its reception in Whitehall was mixed. The Wavell papers contain a report on an interview with G. D. Birla on 6 March 1944, in which Wavell describes G.D. as "an interesting and intelligent personality". In the discussion G.D. had emphasized that power – hydroelectric or coal-generated – was the first requirement and recommended the appointment of a Member of Council for Reconstruction. It was at this meeting that G.D. told Wavell he was wrong if he thought that Gandhi ever doubted Britain's ability to win the war; "the problem was more a psychological one."

In 1945 Wavell, on home leave, described in his journal a meeting of the India Committee.

I made a statement on the whole problem of India's industrial development and claimed sympathetic hearing and treatment for the Government of India's proposals. Amery tried to make out that the hampering effect of the safeguard clauses was hypothetical . . . he was prolix and unconvincing and was shot down from all sides. Cripps produced his usual conciliatory compromise draft . . . Grigg then made a fiery statement condemning the whole policy of Indian industrialisation as wrong, fulminating against Birla and Co., and talking of betrayal of Indian people, etc. Amery replied at full length and as usual soon bored most of the Committee.

... Then John Anderson practically supported Grigg and said that the proposals were not in the interests of the Indian masses and that the Indian aim was really the elimination of British business and British personnel. Cripps spoke sensibly ... pointing out that it was not for us to tell the Indians what they wanted.

Wavell, it is clear, had much to contend with in the India Committee, himself fighting a rearguard action for Indian interests in a fashion scarcely suspected in India. As he observed in his journal, the government had the choice between continuing to treat India as a colony, ignoring public opinion at home and abroad, and backing their policy by force; or, alternatively, treating Indian aspirations with sympathy and goodwill and in the long run gaining morally and materially:

> At present we are professing a policy of freedom for India and in practice opposing every suggestion for a step forward ... it was futile to talk of protecting the Indian masses against the policy of industrialisation (as Grigg and Anderson had) when improvement in the standard of living and social services could only be gained by increased wealth, and when all vocal opinion in India was in favour of it.

Wavell, out of sorts at being obliged to kick his heels to little effect for six weeks in London, finally departed with a formula devised by Cripps that left matters open. "I have gained that much at least," Wavell recorded.

In India Wavell received suggestions from Amery to consider Sir Mirza Ismail as a possible Member of Council for Reconstruction. "It may well be that with a really big task to fire his ambition and show that he can do better in practice than Birla & Co., he may run straight and forgo his tendency to try and play up to Congress."

Amery was anxious that the government's own plans for reconstruction should compare favourably with anything proposed by Congress or dreamed up by Indian industrialists.

> I am all for welcoming it [the Birla/Tata proposal] in general terms and making these big industrialists feel that the

Government of India is both more capable and more willing to help on the industrialisation and development of India than Congress could ever be with their fixed obsession about immediate and unqualified political power.

On 5 April 1944, Amery wrote again to Wavell. "I do not see why Birla or Roy or anybody else should draw up more entertaining and interesting pictures of India's future than the Government itself."

Nearly a year later, Amery, in a letter to Wavell on 25 January 1945, showed himself still vexed over possible conflicts between Indian and British business interests. "The Indians are in some cases trying to improve their bargaining position by representing to the United Kingdom interests that if they do not come to terms they will be squeezed out of India by discriminatory legislation after the war."

The Secretary of State for War, at the meeting of the Indian Committee of the War Cabinet on 16 May 1945, expressed even more vehement doubts: he wished to challenge the whole policy underlying the Government of India's proposals.

These proposals were the result of pressure from a very small group of western Indian and Marwari industrialists, hostile to this country, and anxious to establish their own exclusive control in the Indian industrial field. He felt strongly that industrialisation would aggravate rather than cure India's troubles. Industrialisation could be justified only if an industrialised India could compete with foreign products without the assistance of tariffs. She had now some twenty years of protective measures, but it was only over iron and steel that she was able today to compete on equal terms with the outer world. He could not regard it as likely that interests such as Tatas and Birlas would cooperate with British commercial interests if once they got into an impregnable position.

Such views, consequent on the desire to continue to control the purse strings, illustrate the problems that beset successive Viceroys in their dealings with Indian industrialists and businessmen. Suspicion about their motives was never far from the surface, as, for example, when Linlithgow cabled Sir J. A. Herbert, Governor of Bengal, in 1943: "I am disturbed to hear reports (which I recognise may be incorrect) that Birla and Marwaris have apparently been allowed by your government to take over a substantial responsibility for opening communal kitchens in Calcutta, selling rice at concession rates etc."

Linlithgow seemed more concerned at this moment of famine with the image of the government than with any amelioration of the situation.

The Governor in his reply made no bones about what he considered the propriety of what was going on:

> It has always been the practice in Bengal to encourage philanthropic and charitable assistance in times of scarcity and in accordance with this principle, our Civil Supplies Department issued instructions some time ago to the effect that Government would provide foodgrains at concession rates to philanthropic organisations for distribution in the Calcutta area and outside. . . . It is in terms of these instructions that the distribution of gruel by various organisations (including Birla and certain Marwaris) is being carried out; and all these arrangements are under official supervision . . . I do not myself think that arrangements of this kind can reasonably be thought to constitute a reflection upon Government's ability to distribute food or an abdication of functions properly appertaining to itself.

The British were not alone in ascribing the basest motives to any Indians of sufficient stature to engage their interest. Dr Henry F. Grady, an American with the ear of the President and visiting India in connection with the procurement of supplies from India for the war effort, expressed his views on various matters to Sir Roger Lumley, Governor of Bombay, who in turn communicated them to the Viceroy. Among these were that Indian industrialists "were out for profit, and nothing else, and that to hand over to them any important part of the supply effort would be disastrous . . . they were a hopeless crowd". After a meeting with Gandhi in Bombay

Grady reported to Lumley that "the old man had seemed, to him, to talk complete hogwash". Linlithgow's minuted comments on Grady's eloquent appraisals ranged from "splendid" and "pleasing" to "good" and "better still" (as applied to Gandhi).

Wavell was no less suspicious of Marwari businessmen. Nevertheless, when Amery consulted him over Queen Mary's wish to invite either Birla or Tata to lunch when the next Indian delegation came to London, he felt able to reply

> I think Queen Mary would find G. D. Birla better company than J. R. D. Tata if she wishes to invite one of them to lunch. Tata is a pleasant enough fellow to meet, but I have not found him communicative, and as a casual acquaintance he is much the same as any other wealthy young man who has had a conventional education and turns himself out well. Birla, on the other hand, is a less conventional type. He has plenty to say and whatever one may think of Marwari businessmen and their ways, he is well worth talking to. I think Queen Mary would have a very dull lunch with Tata and quite an interesting one with Birla.

Birla House

G.D.'s first letter to Patel, in May 1949, described another meeting with Churchill whom he found "as misinformed about India as before". When G.D. told Churchill that, though India was stemming the tide of communism and was more peaceful than anywhere in the world at that moment, he did not know what would happen after ten years, since their present leaders were old and they needed quick industrialization and strong defence, Churchill replied, "I should not look ten years ahead, one is enough."

Churchill at this meeting expressed confidence that the Conservatives would soon be back in power. He asked G.D. if India had a national anthem and whether it had a good tune. "Why don't you play with your own national anthem *God Save The King*? These small things help a lot."

Eden, who had recently been to India, was "nice and cordial" and in response to G.D.'s request for military and industrial co-operation promised he would talk to the relevant people. "Now that India had decided to remain in the Commonwealth, they would all co-operate."

In July, after a visit to America, G.D. reported to Patel:

About Kashmir they are all very much worried. While the people here appreciate the position of Jammu and the Buddhist area, they do not understand why we should insist on a substantial Muslim area like the Kashmir valley being included in India . . . everybody seems to be in favour of some sort of partition.

Remarking on the seriousness of England's economic position G.D. observed that "what is most remarkable is the way they are fighting it out, in a very scientific manner with grim determination".

As well as having discussions with Attlee, Cripps, Bevin and Sir John Anderson among others, G.D. had "a few talks with businessmen and they were not disappointing . . . there are better possibilities for investment from England than from America".

When G.D. returned to India it was to a life in which there was no longer a Bapu to write to and worry about, and no longer a British presence with policies to react against. From now on Indian industrialists had to deal with an Indian Prime Minister, one with fairly fixed socialist convictions and little experience of economic affairs. G.D., without political or nationalist involvements to distract him, was able to concentrate henceforth on the expansion of his business interests. Looking increasingly beyond India's borders he travelled every year in connection with developing new outlets and studying modern production techniques.

There were, however, domestic matters to attend to, one of which was the future of Birla House, New Delhi. On 7 May 1948, Nehru, in a letter marked "Personal and Secret", wrote to G.D. at Birla House, Mussoorie. "My dear Ghanshyamdasji," he began

> You know that ever since Bapu's death there has been a strong and persistent agitation about Birla House [in the Assembly and at Party Meetings]. . . . There was almost a unanimous sense among our members that Birla House, because of the tragedy that occurred there, should belong to the nation. I did not think this was the correct approach to the problem and I tried my utmost, with a great deal of success, to prevent the question being raised in the House.

What Nehru, after some hesitation because of the delicacy of the matter, proposed was that

> Birla House, that is the entire building, should not be touched and should remain in your personal use, but the

188

place in the garden where Bapu used to have his prayer meetings and the place where he was shot might be separated from the house and the rest of the garden and used as a memorial or a place where people could visit.

It was Nehru's idea that a "small pillar or column" might indicate the spot where Gandhi fell and that the memorial area should be connected separately with the public road. "The first question to be decided is whether you wish some such thing to be done."

G.D. replied,

In a sense a decision on this subject is for me quite an easy one. As I told Sardarji, and as, I believe, he has told you already, I am entirely at your or his disposal. Either of you has merely to give the word and you will not find me hesitant to comply despite my undoubted and deep sentimental attachment to the house. Nevertheless, I should not be human if I did not have an emotional approach to the question.

It was, undeniably, in emotional terms that G.D. rejected any idea of dividing the property. "The House and the premises as a whole treasure Bapu's sacred memory and I would prefer that the whole rather than a part remains an object of hallowed memory."

Having expressed a willingness to leave both house and grounds "if the interests of the nation demand it", G.D. outlined something of what the place meant to him. "Bapu came for the first time to occupy this house in 1932. Except for a short period when he stayed at the Harijan Colony or the Bhangi Colony, he consistently stayed in this house."

After listing some of his more eminent guests over the years, including Nehru himself, G.D. continued:

Many important political decisions of far-reaching consequence have been taken in this house, which undoubtedly has added to its importance and its historical value. . . . The first meeting of the Congress Cabinet was held in this house immediately the Congress assumed power in 1946. I have passed the best part of my life in this house. . . . Every tree has been planted and nursed under my care. I have seen the trees growing, blossoming, and giving fruits. I know the individual history of each tree. . . . The house has thus become for me a store-house of memories and recollections which constitute for me a book into which I can delve deep to recall, with pride, with deep emotion, with a sense of glory and with profound sentiment, a past that has gone to build up every fibre of my frail body and every tissue of my mind.

What appears to have upset G.D., though Nehru in his letter made no mention of it, was the suggestion in certain quarters that Birla House should be compulsorily acquired and compensation paid "if necessary".

Nehru had sent Sardar Patel, who happened also to be staying at Birla House, Mussoorie, a copy of his letter to G.D. Patel's response was unequivocal: "I cannot conceive of a more objectionable way of perpetuating Bapu's memory or of bequeathing to the Nation and to posterity a reminder of that Great Tragedy."

He went on,

I have known Ghanshyamdas for more than twenty-five years. The relations between Bapu and him were those of a father and son; he had a spiritual bond with him which Bapu fully recognised and Ghanshyamdas maintained to the full and to the very end. But never throughout our long connections has he taken any undue advantage of these ties or exploited them. . . . Had it been otherwise both Bapu and myself would have been the last persons to have spared him. It is, therefore, impossible for me to be a party to the proposal which, in my opinion, involves violence of the worst kind to the feelings of both Ghanshyamdas and Bapu.

Patel raised further questions: whether, if the government yielded to pressure, they or a trust would be responsible, and what precise use the house would be put to, regardless of the cost of maintenance. "Further, I feel that, if we take the house over, we should in all decency give Ghanshyamdas a suitable alternative site . . . making full allowance for his public and private needs."

Nehru, in his reply to G.D., fairly pointed out that he had not suggested that Birla House should be given up, merely that the place of assassination could be made available to the public. "A very large number of people look upon that place as some kind of a shrine and I must confess that, irreligious as I am, I share that feeling and if I pass that way I bow my head."

Later that month Nehru went up for a few days to Mussoorie where he and G.D. discussed the matter. Nehru repeated his earlier statement that there could be no question of coercion and that it was entirely up to G.D. to decide.

Subsequently, G.D. wrote to the Prime Minister saying that he would fall in with the original suggestion. It had been his original intention, he wrote, to offer the house to the government as a residence for the Prime Minister, but he had learned from Patel that Nehru had decided on other quarters and in any case did not wish to live where Gandhi had died.

On 3 June, on his return from Ooty, Nehru wrote thanking G.D. for his co-operation and confirming his own intentions. "I think that all that is necessary is for you to make it easy for visitors to go to that part of the garden. No formal separation or isolation of it is necessary. No legal change is necessary; nor need any formal announcement be made."

It was as an entirely informal arrangement, therefore, that visitors were able to visit the place where Gandhi held his prayer meetings and where, as an apostle of religious tolerance, he was shot.

This arangement did not satisfy everyone, but since it was in line with the original suggestion no one had much right to complain. In due course G.D. built himself a new house, Mangalam, opposite the entrance to the Lodi Gardens. In 1971 Birla House was turned into a government-run Gandhi Museum. Curiously, there is no mention of the name Birla, simply that it was the former residence of an Indian business-man and the place of Gandhi's assassination.

During the twenties and thirties there had been a certain coolness between Nehru and G.D., based at least partly on differing political convictions and their different backgrounds. Nehru was patrician, an intellectual, a radical; G.D. was self-educated, if not quite self-made, a Marwari, a capitalist. When Nehru and Patel, in the run-up to Independence, were getting on badly, it was to Patel that G.D. became especially close and it was in Patel that he confided as formerly he had in Gandhi.

Nehru's early stated views on economics were those of an orthodox, doctrinaire socialist, with no experience of trade or industry. G.D. believed in increased production as a cure for most evils, the amassing of wealth as a necessary means towards the creation of new enterprises, the raising of standards of living, a reduction in unemployment. With such divergent views – though with less difference in their ideas as to what constituted a just society – it was scarcely surprising that they rarely sought each other's company. Nehru was a practising politician, G.D. a politician only by alignment.

Inevitably their paths crossed. "It was in the year 1924," G.D. was to write later,

> that I first had an opportunity to talk and meet with him. It was the year when Gandhiji was released from gaol on account of being operated on for appendicitis and was brought to Juhu . . . As I called on him there Gandhi asked me, "Have you ever met Jawaharlal?" to which I replied, "Yes, but I have never had a chance to talk directly to him." In that case, Gandhi said, go and meet him now and try and make friends with him.

Nehru was on the veranda sitting reading the *Gita*. "Looking at him," G.D. observed, "I realised he carried a freshness and the beauty of youth. At the same time I could feel the distance between us."

That distance always remained, in one degree or another. Comparing Malaviya's mind with clear and transparent water in a lake and Gandhi's with the pure and holy flowing water of the Ganges, G.D. likened Nehru's to a vast ocean "which inspired me, attracted me but made me remain in awe of him, as a result of which I could never reach anywhere near him".

Mahadev Desai's view of Nehru as being essentially a philosopher and aesthete who would never do anything ugly, seemed just to G.D. He concurred, too, in the view that Nehru was a liberal at heart, not a revolutionary as he often made out, and that decision-making did not come easily to him. Nehru was a man of ideas, Gandhi had said, Patel a man of action.

Nehru, G.D. observed, had the simplicity of heart of a poor man but the arrogance of a wealthy one. "There is sorrow in his smile, politeness in his challenge, enthusiasm in his weariness."

In the same article G.D. expressed reservations.

Our mythological stories justify any means to achieve noble ends. Gandhi however condemned unjust methods even in just causes. If Jawaharlal Nehru is able to use just means for just causes in international affairs that will be his greatest achievement. But as yet it doesn't seem to be so.

Another example of their polite but distant relationship comes in a letter G.D. sent to Patel in July 1946. G.D.'s car had broken down on the way from Allahabad to Benares, as a result of which he had to return to Allahabad in an Ekka (horse-drawn cart), a journey of fifteen miles which took him two hours in scorching heat. The first house he recognized on the outskirts of the city happened to be Nehru's. The driver declined to approach the house as he said only cars, and not Ekkas, were allowed past the gate. Eventually G.D. got in and had his name announced. Nehru was lunching and after seeming startled at the sight of his unexpected visitor arranged food and a bath, remaining to make polite conversation while G.D. ate. "He was extremely courteous to me," G.D. wrote to Patel, "there was nothing I could complain about. However, what was lacking was any spontaneity; it was all too formal, without warmth. He had no time or inclination for anything approaching shop-talk."

A more childlike side to Nehru's character emerges from a much earlier letter, written to G.D. in 1942.

> When in Allahabad I do not go out very much but sometimes I have to. Now difficulties are arising owing to the lack of petrol. Personally I do not possess a car but my brother-in-law, Ranjit Pandit, has one and I have the use of it. Even that is becoming difficult now because of the petrol situation. I therefore propose to revert to my old habit of using a bicycle. I do not want, as far as possible, to buy a foreign cycle. I had hoped to be able to get the New Hind Cycle but it does not appear to be available in the market. Could you kindly let me know where I can get it?

No doubt G.D., one of whose companies was the manufacturer, had one sent round immediately.

After Independence the letters between G.D. and the Prime Minister were almost entirely on business matters; concerning visits by Nehru to Pilani and the Birla-owned Hindalco aluminium works at Renukoot: requests by G.D. for political briefing before his visits to Moscow and Washington, where he was to address groups of high-powered businessmen and meet government officials; letters from G.D. accompanying large cheques to the Prime Minister's Relief Fund and containing suggestions as to how the donations could best be used; requests from Indira Gandhi on behalf of the government to borrow the Birla plane to transport supplies for refugees in Tezpur.

In 1961 the Dalai Lama had written to G.D. in connection with some land near Mysore, under the impression that it was going to be used for the purpose of settling Bengali refugees and not, as he had hoped, refugees from Tibet. This particular area of land was in fact being used for an experiment in growing flax, which was at that time imported. "I am not awfully anxious to give away the land," G.D. wrote to Nehru's secretary,

> not because of its value, but because we are making an important experiment. I should, however, like to go by

the advice of the Prime Minister in this matter. If the Government feels that by giving away this land we may be doing something towards the solution of the Tibetan refugees, then, of course, I will have no hesitation in giving the land to the Dalai Lama.

The experiment was allowed to continue.

Just as, in the thirties, G.D. had travelled back and forth to London as an intermediary between Gandhi and the British Government, so now he made journeys through the United States, Europe and elsewhere trying to explain India's economic situation, needs and general policies to audiences not always already sympathetic. *Time* magazine, for example, was consistently hostile to the Nehru government in the early sixties. Since G.D. had met Henry Luce, he wrote to him at some length, despite doubts in the Prime Minister's office about whether it would do any good. Luce replied amicably:

First of all, I am indebted to you for giving me such a clear and authoritative impression of what has been happening in India. Most of what you say accords with our impressions here, but it is useful to have confirmation from you.

Secondly, I must assure you that my colleagues and I entirely agree with your general thesis about Communist China and about India. And we have been saying that India has been pursuing a democratic policy and way of life.

All this being the case, I am sorry you have not liked the tone of some recent *Time* reporting. This is partly because of our references to past policy. I can assure you that, from now on, from week to week we shall be happy to report signs and evidences of India's progress towards meeting the challenge to her democratic sovereignty both on her borders and within.

Let me thank you again for writing me as you did.

With a circulation of four million, and over seven million for *Life*, its Luce stable-mate, *Time*'s goodwill towards India was important. A detectable change of attitude followed rapidly in both journals.

The Americans had shown anxiety about the fulsome reception of Russian ministers in India, following Nehru's warm reception in Moscow. G.D. was at pains on his 1956 visit to America to put India's position *vis-à-vis* trade with the Soviet Union into correct perspective. There were questions relating to the need for foreign loans, equipment and technical advice. On all these matters G.D. wrote to the Prime Minister for an official line, so that his own views about what India stood for and wanted should not be at variance with government policy.

The same situation had arisen in 1954 in relation to Korea, when Nehru gave G.D. a run-down of his views on Western mistakes in the Far East. The British approach at Geneva, Nehru believed, was "far more realistic" than the American.

The Americans think they can solve any problem with money and arms. They forget the human element. They forget the nationalistic urge of people. They forget the strong resentment of people in Asia against impositions.

France has behaved with extreme folly in Indo-China ... The Allies of America in Asia are Chiang Kai-Shek, Syngman Rhee and Bao Dai – and no one can be impressed by them. They represent reaction in every sense of the word and, if democracy is supposed to have these champions, then democracy has little future.

About democracy Nehru observed in the same letter,

I cannot ensure democracy or any particular form of Government in the other countries of Asia. For the matter of that, I cannot guarantee it in India. I can only try for it, as I can try elsewhere in Asia ... We should like democratic forms of Government but they will only come if the people of the country also want them. The policy of America in the East and of France in Indo-China has given every help to the non-democratic elements, and indeed to Communism.

Armed with such frank information about Nehru's view of the East–West conflict, it was inevitable that G.D. had to tread warily abroad if India's economic requirements were not to be ignored.

If G.D. and the Prime Minister could never quite agree about the degrees of latitude essential to private enterprise in industrial matters they had a friendly correspondence about rose-growing, varieties of mango, and the problem of Kashmir, and were not hesitant to comment on professional matters within the other's sphere of interest. Thus G.D. felt it advisable to draw the Prime Minister's attention to an outstanding debt of £10 million due from Burma, while Nehru took it upon himself to write a personal and confidential letter relating the government's view of a labour dispute in Birla factories at Hyderabad.

It was G.D.'s practice to send Nehru a handsome cheque on his birthday, for him to use as he thought fit. In 1959 his cheque for 70,000 rupees was returned by Nehru with a polite note. A cheque for a similar amount was sent to Nehru a year later, only this time made out to the "Prime Minister's National Aid Fund". It was accepted.

The relationship between Nehru and G.D., coolly harmonious during Gandhi's lifetime, subsequently underwent certain strains for which neither was responsible. By the time that Nehru became Prime Minister the Birlas were rapidly overtaking the Tatas as India's most powerful business family, their turnover in the region of £45 million. Almost immediately an Income Tax Investigation Commission was set up to inquire into their affairs and in 1950 it reported that the following Birla concerns, among others, were guilty of varying degrees of evasion: Birla Brothers Ltd., Birla Cotton Mills, Orient Paper Mills, Cotton Agents Ltd.

A suit was subsequently filed in the Supreme Court challenging the Commission's constitution. It was successful and the Commission was declared void. The government took no further action, notwithstanding that an advocate of the Calcutta High Court published two immensely detailed books between 1950 and 1957 alleging serious infringements of the law by Birla companies. In 1969, after Nehru's death, the Dutta Industrial Licensing Committee had its findings drawn to the attention of the government by a group of anti-Birla left-wing MPs and a judicial commission of inquiry into Birla affairs was set up.

Inevitably, the scale and range of Birla enterprises created enemies among orthodox socialists, of which Nehru in his early days was certainly one. This enmity was based on principle and had nothing to do with the Birla contribution to the national wealth or conditions in Birla factories. Birla profits were largely ploughed back into their enterprises and though there were Birla Houses of some style in Calcutta, New Delhi and Bombay, and up country in Mussoorie, Ranchi and Nainital, G.D. himself, though he made different arrangements for his heirs, never amassed a private fortune nor earned a large taxable income.

During Nehru's time as Prime Minister, G.D. continued to raise money for Congress. By now Birla philanthropy had become legendary, not only through the work of the Birla Education Trust and the expanding network of scholastic and scientific institutions at Pilani, but for its contribution in the way of hospitals, medical aid, temples, the establishment of industrial and technological museums and, in Calcutta, of the only planetarium in the country. Over and above this there were countless donations to private charities, in keeping with the austere personal habits of a family who, for all the opulence of their houses, scrupulously observed religious ritual, were vegetarian, and neither smoked nor drank.

Nevertheless, though Nehru in office grew increasingly disposed towards a mixed economy of the kind envisaged by Birla and Tata in their 1944 blueprint, the existence of capitalist enterprise on the Birla scale brought about attacks on the system, with Nehru himself often awkwardly placed between his loyalty to a long-standing comrade in the nationalist struggle and loyalty to his socialist colleagues in government. With Gandhi and more recently Patel dead – the latter also spending his last days in a Birla House – Nehru was G.D.'s only close link with the historic past. It was not the easiest of situations. In 1969 Mrs Gandhi, with no such ties, took a less complicated decision, abolishing all managing agencies, which were worth nearly £300 million at the time to the Birlas.

Nehru himself had given no government blessing to G.D.'s efforts to move into the steel industry, hitherto the preserve of the Tatas. The Germans were eager to co-operate but G.D.'s request in 1953 for a line on government policy resulted in confirmation that the production of steel would be kept in the public sector.

There were compensations. In general terms the fifties were golden years for Marwari enterprises, and for none more than the Birlas. Their relationship to the pattern of Marwari migration in the twentieth century is crucial, both in its conformity and its divergences. From the day G.D.'s grand-father Shivnarain first settled in a co-operative Pilani-organized *basa* in Bombay when he arrived there in the 1860s – a method of introduction to city living followed by G.D. himself when he came to Calcutta to set up on his own – the fortunes of the Marwaris have been closely linked to, and ultimately affected by, those of the Birlas.

The Marwaris, who migrated south from Rajasthan to Bom-bay and Mysore, and also more extensively south-east along the Ganges to Bengal, often on river-boats, benefited not only from their initial, favourable position on the old caravan routes and their traditional expertise in speculation but, in the case of Bengal, by entering into a community almost unworldly in its commercial detachment.

The Birlas first came to prominence at a time when fortunes could still be made from opium, grown in Malwa and on the Deccan plain, and later in East Bengal. By the time G.D. got started opium exports, by comparison with the situation in his grandfather's day, had been decimated and indigo had ceased to be viable altogether. On the other hand the export of raw cotton, oil seeds, jute, rice and tea had increased out of all recognition. Marwaris acted as agents to old-established British firms dealing in these areas, as also for goods imported on the strength of them.

By the time G.D. was born Marwaris had been operative in Calcutta for nearly forty years, in the later stages shouldering out Bengalis as the main agents. It was only in his own time, however, that Indians set up in London, Birla Brothers' office for the export of jute set up in 1917 being the first. The Birlas, among other Marwaris, were the first to deal in hessian, and also, with Tata, to trade with Japan.

By the time the Birlas, mainly under G.D., began to move from trading and broking into industry, the Tatas had long been established in steel, electric power and the vegetable oil industries. By the end of the 1939–45 war the vast gulf between the leading Parsi firm and the leading Marwari house had been dramatically reduced and by 1980 there was little between them.

No sooner had G.D.'s own first jute mill gone up in 1919 in Calcutta, than a fellow Marwari, Sir S. Hukumchand, with an Indore banking background, set up another. More Marwari-owned mills followed in the next decades. These were the first mills of any size to be owned by Indians.

In the twenties, Marwaris moved extensively into cotton, Birlas again being the first in the field with their Delhi and Gwalior textile factories. In the thirties, as the effects of the Depression wore off, the Birlas built sugar mills and more textile and engineering plants. By now the government had been obliged, under nationalist pressure, to make things easier for Indian traders and industrialists, though there was still resistance from British firms and discrimination against them, just as G.D. had found in his very first venture in Calcutta.

Both wars provided a climate and a situation in which business could flourish. The Marwaris, in particular, were not slow to take advantage of the increased demand for all their services, and the Birlas emerged from the 1914–18 war four times as powerful as they had been at the start.

In the first post-war period the conflict between the old-fashioned, traditional Marwaris – strictly orthodox in religion, even to the extent of supporting restrictive and backward customs, unsympathetic to the Congress movement and nationalist aspirations, cautious about involvement in industrial ventures – and the Birla-led, religiously reformist, socially enlightened and nationalist-minded group came to a head. It was resolved ultimately in favour of the latter, though there were ambiguities and even dissenters within families.

Neither G.D.'s father, Raja Baldeodas, nor his elder brother, Jugal Kishore, had further ambitions in business. Having demonstrated their ability as brokers, and, in Jugal Kishore's case, an adventurous streak that opened up Far Eastern markets, both were in the process of withdrawing from active life. In the family house at Benares, with its shutters opening on to wide sweeps of the Ganges, G.D.'s father settled to a life of contemplation, gentle walks in the nearby gardens and daily discussions with priests and men of learning. The Birlas as a family had always been disciplined in their habits, their daily lives governed by rituals and routine. The closeness in feeling between family members and loyalty between generations ensured that, however much they might privately differ over specific issues, as a family they showed no dissension. If G.D. took the initiative in opposing orthodox Marwari viewpoints he did not lack support from his father and elder brother. Even after 1956, when Raja Baldeodas died aged 93, the Benares house was a regular port of call for sons, daughters and grandchildren, their visits making certain that the increasingly ascetic widow was never left alone. She lived to be over a hundred, bathing every day in the Ganges until her death in 1963.

Having suffered in 1923 a rebuff from orthodox Marwari *banians* in his effort to represent the Marwari Association in the Central Legislative Assembly, G.D. had founded the Indian Chamber of Commerce, the rift between the two bodies lasting virtually until the outbreak of war.

This did not prevent Marwaris on both sides profiting from the encouragement given to local industry after the 1935 Government of India Act, the awarding of contracts now entirely in Indian hands. They benefited, too, as did all Indian-owned businesses, from the abandonment of the gold standard.

The war, with its increased need for production, gave the Marwaris fresh opportunities, many of them taking over managing agencies from departing British firms. The Birlas preferred at that time to buy into Hyderabad State concerns, acquiring paper and silk factories among others.

After Independence business houses that had supported the nationalist movement had every reason to receive favourable treatment. Marwaris, more adaptable than most, settled happily into their new relationship, making the best of economic policies initially only reluctantly geared to private enterprise. G.D. complained constantly about the brakes to industrial progress imposed by Government during Nehru's time, and in the early 1970s even more vociferously about Mrs Gandhi's policies.

This was not the only confrontation the Marwaris invited, for shortly before Nehru's death two of the largest non-Marwari houses, those of Tata and Mafatlal, severed their connections on a point of business principle with the Marwari-dominated FICCI, founded by G.D.

Nevertheless, by retaining family control over a vast range of subsidiary enterprises in a fashion impossible for Tata and others, and within the family structure making full use of the accounting procedures, intimate control of cost and output invented by G.D., Marwari firms comfortably outpaced all others. By the middle 1960s the days when Marwaris excelled in the rôle of intermediaries between producers and consumers, exporters and importers, were a distant memory. Just as Marwaris benefited in the pre-1914 period by their staunch support of the Raj, so did they now, as architects of an independent, industrialized India, whose loyalty, under its Birla image, had never been in question during the dark days. Had the traditionalist Marwaris not been outflanked by G.D. at the very outset of his business career this would scarcely have been the case.

By 1965 there were over 150 Birla companies trading, as opposed to a mere 20 in 1945. Marwaris had come to control a substantial part of the non-government-owned or banking corporations.

By 1962, when the centenary of the business set up in Bombay by G.D.'s grandfather, Shivnarain, was celebrated in both Calcutta and Bombay, the Birlas had added cement and aluminium to their other interests. By 1970 their range of concerns, in some of which, like the production of cars, they had virtual monopoly, included newspapers, shipping, textiles, synthetic fibres, cables, tea, chemicals, cement and power.

A Meticulous Planner

In reviewing G.D.'s long association with Gandhi and his constant prodding of secretaries of state, governors and viceroys in the pre-Independence period, it is easy to lose sight of the kind of businessman he was. He was, according to D. P. Mandelia, who joined him in the early days and rose to be his most trusted lieutenant, a meticulous planner rather than a gambler. He embarked on numerous large-scale ventures which needed both initial vision and imaginative administration, but before taking any decisive step he made sure that the financial side was secure, not just at the outset but in the comparative long term. He took care never to put himself or any of his existing concerns at risk. He made quick decisions when it came to it, and then left the details to his managers and technicians. His genius lay, at least in part, in his mastery of a balance sheet.

Perhaps nothing shows up the enterprising industrialist in a more revealing light than a long letter written by G.D. to T. T. Krishnamachari in 1955. Krishnamachari, later Minister of Finance, was at that time Minister for Commerce and Industry.

In a covering note G.D. remarked "If you think it all worthless please throw it away in the waste-paper basket and forget all about it. I felt like reiterating the position and was encouraged to do so by some of our mutual friends." The attention to technicalities, as well as the philosophy of the proposals, is not surprising in one who did his stint on the factory floor of all his enterprises in the early days, ensuring that in any subsequent discussions with his managers, he would be fully *au fait* with the practical details as well as with the theoretical principles involved.

My dear Mr. Krishnamachari,

During the meeting of the Central Advisory Council of Industries while discussing the report of the Reviewing Sub-Committee on licensing, you kindly invited members to make remarks, if any. I did not, however, wish to discuss in the meeting anything that may be construed as of a personal nature. I believed that rather than discuss anything publicly I might be allowed to write to you what I have said to you in person so often and elaborate on the same.

When on general principles the Cabinet turned down my proposal of putting up a blast furnace at Durgapur, you were good enough to ask me to withdraw the proposal. I told you then that as the whole proposition was based on something better than a mere business motive, there was no question of my pressing the point and I left the matter entirely to you. When subsequently a question was put in the Parliament about the same matter, the answer from your Ministry was perhaps still open. But after observing the remarks of the Report of the Licensing Board I thought I may write to you not so much with a view to press my point as to reiterate my position in case you desire to reconsider the proposal.

In the course of various conversations with the Prime Minister during the last four years I have never failed to convey to him my belief that India could never industrialise even in a long period if we simply depended for our requirements of the capital goods on the overseas market. I, therefore, maintained that we must produce capital goods ourselves which, I said, would again to a large extent depend on the adequate supply of steel. Panditji himself on different occasions gave me the example of Japan who, he said, only once imported the equipments and then copied them but never imported twice. I concurred. I had, however, anxiety about the steel position. Although Rajaji made the announcement about the erection of two steel plants nearly eight years back, nothing had happened.

I would have ventured myself to step in the field much

earlier, but I always felt that the task would be beyond my reach. But all the same, I started manufacturing capital goods in Texmaco, Calcutta and Gwalior, and as you know, we made great progress in textile machinery and ordinary type of boilers, and now are taking up jute mills and sugar mills machinery and modern Water Tube type boilers. We aspire also to make other types of equipment as the time goes. Cement, Tea and Paper are already on our agenda. Thus, the idea to make capital goods with our limited resources was taken up as far back as in 1947 and I have always nursed a hope that some day I would take up making equipments for steel plant too.

When, however, I was in Europe last year, some makers of steel plants wondered why I did not take up steel in a modest way. The idea caught me firmly because it was an approach more suitable for the Indian capital market and one which had never occurred to me before. There has always been some awe about the capital requirements of a steel plant. But after having discussed the matter with a few makers I realised that a modest beginning could be made successfully. And I felt that if I entered the business, it would give a good lead to others, thereby accelerating the growth of steel production.

With this object in view, I decided to put up a small blast furnace with an output of 2 lacs tons of pig iron a year, out of which I thought I would convert a part at some stage into steel to be utilised partly in making capital goods in my own factories and partly to make specialised steel in small quantities. The rest of the pig iron, I thought, could be sold in the country. I also thought that I would examine new processes of manufacturing steel, for instance, the Krupp Renn process. Mine was to be a small affair but, in my humble opinion, an important step in the achievement of our objects. This enthused me to apply for the licence.

I believed, as I do now also, that during the next 25 years if we aspire to come up to a comfortable standard of life, we shall have to reach a production of 50 million tons of steel, and beginning from the third Five Year Plan nearly 2 million tons of extra steel will have to be produced every year. This would, on the present estimate, require nearly 120 crores of rupees for each million tons of steel or 1200 crores in every five years. Out of this, at least 600 crores will be needed in foreign exchange. . . .

On the other hand, if each plant needs, say, 2 lacs tons of steel, then we shall be utilising in the manufacture of steel plants 4 lacs tons of steel every year from abroad which, if the equipments were made in India, could be consumed out of our own production. Thus both ways it could be most advantageous to produce our own equipment on which there can be no dispute.

The question, however, was: who should do it? And I said to myself: why not I if it was a service? It would be a real headache and a risk but also a definite contribution to the country. I wrote to you from Europe of my intention in general terms. Then we applied for the licence which was approved, but subsequently turned down on policy grounds.

I understood at that time that no more steel would be allowed to be produced by any private party. But since then extensions, even amounting to new plants, have been allowed to some of the existing firms and rightly so. Whatever be the reason, the fact is that steel would be produced in the next five years even outside the public sector and that is the right decision. The public sector, too, is planning for 3 million tons of steel. And thus let us hope that by 1960 we shall have a less uncomfortable position about steel.

If, however, it was a headache for me to plan a project of the kind last year, it would now be a greater headache since to dispose of the products, at any rate in the initial stage when the new production would be coming on the market, would not be an easy task. But my conviction and faith in the desirability of my proposal remains unshaken. In the first place, I hope to get capital from a certain type of investor which may not otherwise be available to the State, and secondly, internal competition can quicken the pace of growth and efficiency all round. In the long run, under the duress of competition, the tendency would be towards greater research and a greater production of capital goods also. Specialised steel would be taken up quickly. My purpose was to utilise, as far as possible, my own production of pig iron in making either specialised steel or such steel as I could use myself – a field in which Government is not likely to enter.

It may be argued, why not make capital goods and steel plant equipment without myself going into steel? The answer is obvious. It was because we were managing textile, jute and sugar mills, that, even without foreign collaboration, we could successfully make equipment just by copying the foreign products as the Japanese did. Direct experience in steel is of the utmost importance in making steel plants, even without foreign collaboration. Copying may not produce the most modern results but it gives good training. This gives the background for my proposal.

The 1948 policy, I feel, cannot be so rigid. A policy, in the ultimate analysis, is a means to an end, the end being a 25 per cent rise in the standard of living in the first five years and 10 million new jobs. Quick industrialisation is the only answer to the challenge. Anything that can help in achieving the above should not be regarded as going against the 1948 policy.

As explained by Panditji, the socialistic pattern of society is only for a better way of life, viz. greater consumption of consumer goods, better health, more houses and so on and so forth. If, therefore, the Government share my view that my proposal takes us towards the achievement of our objective, then I put myself at your disposal. I can bear with a headache now but not perhaps in a few years time when I am older.

I should, however, like to make it clear that I am not pressing the point just as a business proposition to earn money. No private sector can afford to lose money. As you will agree, there would hardly be much money in this business. While, therefore, I am not out to lose, which I cannot afford to do, my proposition is mainly on the basis of service. I have no desire to embarrass. My advice as coming from one with experience and desire to serve would still be – if it has any value – to allow such small projects to come into existence and then allow them to grow. The State by its very nature of a democratic set-up, I maintain, would not be able to do everything themselves and as quickly as it should be done. It is also a question of experience, talents, organising capacity and of so many other factors.

If you find something worth placing before Panditji in this letter, I hope you would do so. If my suggestion does not attract any favourable response, it would not upset me. The very fact that my views were before the highest authority in itself would give me complete satisfaction. Please excuse this long letter.

The businessman, responsible to his own colleagues and shareholders, and the patriot concerned for national prestige and the welfare of the Indian masses, worked hand in glove. It was one of G.D.'s talents that he could establish an identity of interest between the public and the private with persuasiveness and charm.

In this instance, nothing came of it. It is unlikely that G.D. was much put out. He had outlined what appeared to him a project in the national interest and now it was up to the Government. As he made clear, the money side was unimportant, he had long since had more than enough. In any case, ahead of him was the major industrial achievement of his life, the setting up of Hindalco, the aluminium plant at Renukoot, which, with Gwalior Rayon, was probably of all the Birla enterprises closest to his heart.

There is another aspect to the Birla entrepreneurial and administrative system, developed over generations. For not only are there family ramifications at the head of major and subsidiary concerns but also local ones. The Mandelias, for example, were neighbours in Pilani, and D. P. Mandelia's father, the first of the family to come to G.D.'s notice, was put in charge of the Birla estate in Ranchi. D. P. Mandelia, fourteen years younger than G.D., began work in the organization in 1921 at the age of fourteen. Their closer relationship, which led to Mandelia eventually occupying a position analogous to a Chief of Staff, developed in the early thirties, by which time G.D. had phased out speculation on commodities, the initial source of his wealth, and was turning his attention to industry.

At all levels, the Pilani links are maintained, the brighter pupils being trained at one of the local schools and then absorbed into the business. Unlike, for example, in Tata, where there is little family stake and which is administered through trusts, the Pilani network, itself a kind of seigneurial extension of family, is largely responsible for running the Birla organization, though now less than previously.

If Pilani was never neglected in terms of patronage, G.D. visited the place itself less as he grew older. By now, in addition to the original *haveli*, there was a handsome modern house on the edge of farm country outside the village, close to another built by his old friend D. P. Mandelia. He drove the hundred miles from Delhi once or twice a year, or more often flew in on his private plane, usually staying only a day or two to attend meetings of the Birla Educational Trust or to address students. The village, with its old associations of school under the banyan tree, of drought and camel rides, had in any case been relegated to a subsidiary position. For the last period of G.D.'s life the Pilani educational complex, growing from infant beginnings into the most spectacular institution of its kind in India, did much to take the place of Gandhi and the nationalist cause in his emotional life. Here prime ministers and presidents of India, famous scientists, educationists and politicians, were shown off to the students and the staff, and vice versa. G.D. even persuaded Nehru into joining him on a camel, for the benefit of photographers.

G.D. was fond of quoting from the Bhagavad Gita:

As the Gita says, every man must do his duty, which means, if you are a wealthy man you must do your duty by your wealth. A business man's Karma is to amass wealth and his Dharma is to provide for general welfare. If political action is involved in this, I don't see why I should fight shy of it.

The realization of his plans for Pilani came nearer to a bid for immortality than the kind of political action, expressed mainly in financial terms and with a weather eye cocked on the prevailing wind, that had accompanied his trading ventures. Businessmen are not known for disinterested actions, but the development of Pilani appears to have been a labour of love. Except in so far as it became a useful recruitment area, it had little connection with Birla commercial interests.

It was, in fact, in its initial stages, the dream child of G.D.'s father, Baldeodas, who converted the *pathshala* started in 1901 for his sons into a primary school open to the surrounding villages. By the time the Birla Educational Trust had been created by G.D. in 1929, this primary school had progressed in stages to a middle and high school, and finally an intermediate college. In 1931 a new girls' middle school was established. At regular intervals new institutions were added: an engineering college, a Montessori school, a public school, a college of science and commerce. Finally, in 1964, the Birla Institute of Technology and Science was established with university status, its unique contribution being its integration of practical training in industry into its degree course, a policy in line with G.D.'s own thinking on the subject.

Pilani, as a result of all this, has grown out of desert and drab, arid countryside into a colony of inter-related educational ventures, set in idyllic surroundings, among farms and dairies, trees and water, and graced by hordes of peacocks as well as the most beautiful of all Birla temples. Although the government has taken over responsibility for elementary education, the Birla Educational Trust, in line with the wishes of Baldeodas, continues to maintain numerous nursery and primary schools for the children of neighbouring villages.

Long ago G.D. had given generously to Rabindranath Tagore when Tagore's University of Viswabharathi in Shantiniketan was in serious financial trouble, just as he had earlier to Pandit Madan Mohan Malaviya for Benares Hindu University. Similarly, it is not only at Pilani that the Trust's work can be seen in operation, but in agricultural projects in Bengal and a public school at Naini Tal, in hostels in Bombay and

Madras, in an engineering college at Anand and a college of textile technology at Bhiwani.

The main thrust of the educative principles behind all Pilani institutions has been an attempt to close the gap between the humanities and science, the arts and technology. As such it represents the ideal of a self-educated man who wanted learning to be put to work, the young body to be given the best possible chance in serene surroundings, and the adolescent character to be developed with regard to strict moral principles.

The result is undeniably a privileged education, though one that depends on neither money nor caste. What is impressive about Pilani is its absence of sanctimoniousness, its freedom from rigidly-held views about religion, politics, and social problems. The provision, in the Birla Institute of Technology and Science, of an all-round education, geared equally to higher learning and to earning a living, depends for its success, in the last resort, on devoted and skilled teaching. At Pilani, a privately endowed university, they went out for the best and were lucky enough to get and keep them.

In the last decades of his life, despite an almost imperceptible slowing down towards the very end, G.D. continued to run his vast business empire with the lightest of touches. He was kept informed of everything, wherever he was, either by telex or telephone – daily production figures, schedules, technical problems – and he delivered terse comments as necessary. Nothing was left over for another day. His routine, whether in London, Switzerland, or Bombay, varied little: he walked at first light for two hours, he dealt with his correspondence punctiliously, ate regularly, often took a second long walk and was in bed by nine. He read in the evenings or painted, sometimes he listened to devotional music or studied languages. He took pleasure in his family but had few words of small-talk or gossip.

For G.D.'s eightieth birthday a commemoration volume, *Modern India: Heritage and Achievement*, was published in 1977. Running to nearly 1000 pages and with over a hundred eminent contributors, the volume deals, in the form of personal reminiscence, with every aspect of G.D.'s work – as industrial pioneer, entrepreneur, educationist, freedom fighter, unofficial ambassador, philanthropist, child of Gandhi. The contributors range from distinguished men of affairs, scholars and business colleagues to secretaries and household members.

A critical tone on such an occasion is scarcely to be expected, but the volume is valuable for its generally frank descriptions of the impression G.D. made at first-hand, whether on equals or subordinates.

For example, C. R. Mitra, Director, Birla Institute of Technology and Science, describes his first meeting with G.D. in Calcutta before taking up his post:

> I found the man alert, sharp, suave and yet remote. He only used a few brief words to indicate his welcome . . . In some sense it was an anticlimax. I had pictured him to be a human business-machine; but he avoided any of the business conversation connected with the hiring of a new director. He talked about his dream, about his vision of India and the importance he attached to the youth . . . He moves from idea to idea and mood to mood with ease and comfort.

Mitra describes how, even after several years, a certain unease never left him:

> Whenever I attempted to describe details of such of the new educational programmes that we were proposing I somehow felt the conversation ended abruptly. He often remarked, "I am not the Director, I am only the Chairman." But I soon discovered that in his own way he had absorbed the essence of our proposals without having to trouble about our jargon. I learnt that what I considered as a problem of communication really did not exist.

G.D.'s visits to Pilani could be unnerving and occasionally trying, with a continuous stream of engagements and meetings. In the end Mitra was left with the sense of a warm personality within a forbidding exterior, one who, despite a reputation for being "imperious, arrogant and patriarchal" nevertheless allowed a considerable degree of freedom to those entrusted by him to act on his behalf. "It is indeed a remarkable personality who fiercely sticks to his own life style and yet nourishes the birth of another life style in an organisation over which he presides."

G.D. never interfered with the admission policy or recruitment methods at Pilani, nor tried to argue against changes with which he may not have felt in sympathy. Mitra found ultimately that G.D. did not conform to his idea of the boss of a vast industrial complex, but that this was for different reasons from those he first imagined. For what he provided at Pilani was support even for the most unpopular causes.

As far as business was concerned G.D. himself expressed the Birla outlook in these words:

> It has been the policy of the House of Birla not to build up business with a view to the accumulation of capital but to develop unexplored lines, harness the undeveloped resources of the country, promote know-how, create skilled labour and managerial talents, spread education and, above all, add to the efforts of the leaders of the country who have been struggling to build a new, independent India, free from want, the curse of unemployment, ignorance and disease.

The fulfilment of these lofty aims sometimes found him in conflict with those same leaders of the country who saw in large-scale capitalist enterprises an enemy rather than an ally. But thwarted by government policy over steel, G.D. turned to the next most important metal industry, aluminium. Aware that there was insufficient cotton being grown to meet India's future requirements, and that an increase in cotton growing would make severe inroads into available agricultural land, G.D. turned to synthetic fibres. Many other Birla ventures were launched, as was Hindalco, in uneconomic and inaccessible sites, to fulfil needs rather than to increase profits. The money was already there – "It is easy to make money, but difficult to spend it well" was one of G.D.'s less tactful sayings posted up in Birla factories. Thus cotton led to jute, at the

213

time a European monopoly, and jute to sugar, publishing and, in 1933, insurance. With Independence came textile machinery, plastics, tea, coal, aviation, shipping, banking and motor-cars. Individual Birla concerns diversified, Birla Jute going into rayon, cement and chemicals, Jayshree Tea into fertilizers , shipping and plywood, Kesoram Cotton into pipes and cellophane, Century Mills into synthetic fibres, cement and paper. Two cotton-mills were opened in Ethiopia, more recently excursions made into Thailand and the Philippines. Thus, provision of consumer goods for the mass market went hand in hand with heavy machinery and chemicals.

Inevitably, objections were made to this rapid expansion. Yet it was only through operating on this kind of scale that the Birlas were able to contribute lavishly to so many social enterprises. A new Birla factory in a hitherto deprived and unproductive area meant not only hundreds of new jobs, but new schools, hospitals, recreation facilities, temples. Each venture was a calculated step towards economic emancipation, an attempt to make the country less dependent on imports and foreign capital, and at the same time raise the standard of living. As Gandhi, Nehru, and Patel had used essentially political methods to achieve the benefits of freedom, G.D. determined to organize Indian business and industry for similar ends.

Shyam Sunder Kanoria, a former President of FICCI and the Indian Sugar Mills Association, observed G.D. on an industrial delegation to America and Europe:

I was struck by the difference in nature, outlook and life-style between G.D. and the European and American tycoons we met. It was not a difference in business acumen, for when it came to driving a bargain G.D. could be as hard headed as any of them and usually got the better terms. But what they could never understand was that one who ranked as India's top industrialist should lead a life of such spartan simplicity and be so indifferent to the pursuit of pleasure.

Whatever the entertainment or function laid on for him – the ballet in Moscow, dinners in New York or London – G.D.

would make his apologies and retire at nine. That was his unbreakable rule and nothing was allowed to interfere with it.

In his introduction to the collection of speeches and writings by G.D., published in 1950 under the title *The Path to Prosperity*, Sir George Schuster remarked that despite their superficial differences they felt the same on fundamental issues. G.D.'s contention from the earliest days had been that India could only advance to true welfare by increasing production and that the great national effort required could only be achieved by a National Indian Government. "I am convinced," Schuster wrote, "that Mr Birla is right in the sense that the primary need is to stimulate constructive effort and new enterprise. There may be situations in which deflationary monetary measures may be necessary but any Government authority which relies on these alone will find that the remedy is far worse than the disease."

The emphasis in G.D.'s earlier speeches and writings had been on problems of money and exchange. Gradually he turned his attention to elaborating the belief that, given adequate production and proper planning, consumption and investment would follow naturally. *The Path to Prosperity* runs to 250 pages and it deals, in layman's language whenever possible, with such subjects as labour and capital, sterling balances, inflation, monetary reform and the gold standard, imperial preference, and economic planning. In the last item, a paper given to a joint meeting of the East India Association and the Overseas League in London in 1949, G.D. touches on the question of co-operation with the British, the cause that had occupied his thoughts and drained his energies since he first argued the Gandhi and Congress case in London and the British case in India twenty years earlier. He ended his address:

The fight against poverty in India is a fight against communism in the whole of Asia. The job is essentially for India to do and she will do it. But it belongs no less to the world at large. It belongs to Britain no less than to India.

Britain has a problem similar to ours. While she has smaller resources than ours and greater technical skill we have larger resources but less technical skill. Is it a dream to believe that the fate of India and Britain may be linked together for years to come and that both countries will be called upon to solve their respective problems in the closest friendship and cooperation? You and we have been associated for nearly 150 years. The association was that of ruler and ruled. That is past and with it is gone all the past bitterness. A new relation and with it a great friendship has grown.

In 1983 a second volume containing extracts from G.D.'s speeches and writings was published under the title *Words to Remember*. Less technical in theme, this contained such things as his extempore talk on the subject of Gandhi, a welcoming address to Mrs Thatcher, an inaugural address at the AGM of the Indian Chamber of Commerce in 1974, when, at a time of economic decline in India, he once more pressed the case for increased production against the currently fashionable insistence by professional economists on credit squeeze, higher rates of interest and demonetization. In the same speech he reminded his audience that those who argued that agricultural production was the key to India's problems should realize that agricultural production depended essentially on industrial production, on waterworks, tubewells, fertilizer, on steel and cement for reservoirs.

Words to Remember includes speeches to engineering associations, in which the gradual Soviet move from old-style planning to capitalistic methods is discussed, a talk on Indo–China relations, a detailed analysis of the Third Plan, and extensive quotation from published sources on the British Government's attitude to Indian businessmen and to G. D. Birla in particular.

About G.D., H. V. R. Iengar, a former Home Secretary to the Government of Bombay and Governor of the Reserve Bank of India, observed:

I cannot say that I have discovered the secret of his leadership. He is a very soft-spoken man and gives you the impression that, although he is thinking all the time of the expansion of his business interests, he does so in a very relaxed manner . . . He has given very few speeches about the development of indigenous technology but, in actual practice, he has given the utmost possible encouragement to indigenous technology of which the Mavoor and Harihar [bamboo] projects are shining examples.

It surprised many that G.D. was willing to venture at Mavoor into negotiations with the communist ministry of Kerala, but despite recurrent labour problems this was one of many such initiatives that were not only for the national good but paid off handsomely.

R. K. Sinha, the economist and secretary of the Indian Economic Association, wrote in 1977,

It is significant to observe that more than 40 years ago Sri G. D. Birla emphasised most of the questions relating to our economic and social amelioration which Prime Minister Shrimati Indira Gandhi has so emphatically placed before the country under the 20-point economic programme to tide over the national crises that face us today. Important among them are a change in land laws, liquidation of rural indebtedness, scaling down of rents, establishment of agricultural banks to advance loans and direct subsidies in some form to the dairy and fruit industries, special measures for increasing agricultural production. . . . He was always conscious of the problems of poverty and the need to guard against over-centralisation of production or the creation of any large disparity between the upper and the lower strata of society.

A colleague in the early days of the nationalist movement and subsequently an industrialist, Babubhai Chinai, observed of G.D.,

The dream of a mass consumption society has always propelled him. . . . But the single factor which gave the kind of success that he achieved was his extraordinary ability in human relations in the widest sense of the term. He thought of industry not as composed of land, buildings and machinery but of the calibre of its men, both technical and managerial. He may be intolerant of stupidity or laziness, but he has in him that basic regard for human beings, their failings, their potential and their sufferings which characterises the true democrat. He may have imposed his views on people who had none of their own, but when a man is willing to think he lets him experiment and evolve his own solutions. His attitude towards labour, his personal asceticism and his genuine belief that he is a trustee of the community and he is responsible to it, mark him out as a true disciple of Gandhi. If anything, he is an idealist. His entire conception of the universe around him is in terms of ideals, in terms of right and wrong. In addition he has the rare gift of working out an idea in such detail as to make it possible. That is, perhaps, why he is considered a practical man.

One of the few post-war developments in which the Birlas have not been associated is the hotel business. There was a time in the early sixties when Kanti Desai, the son of Morarji Desai, then Finance Minister and subsequently Prime Minister after the Janata, post-Emergency defeat of Indira Gandhi, tried to interest G.D. in backing certain projects. He himself was not averse to the idea, seeing in it a genuine need, but in the end declined to get involved because, as he wrote to Kanti Desai, of discouragement from his children, who disapproved of him being involved in a business that included drinking and dancing. The surfacing in the 1960s of so puritanical a notion, more in keeping with the traditional Marwari orthodoxy G.D. opposed so strongly in his youth, is curious, as is the fact that G.D. should have been swayed by it. Perhaps, ultimately, his terms of refusal were no more than polite gestures masking a disinclination to be associated with the unreliable Desai, rather than a distaste for the hotel trade in itself. He was, after all, with a permanent suite at Grosvenor House in London, no stranger to hotels himself.

It was, in fact, from Grosvenor House that G.D. wrote to Sardar Patel in 1949 one of those perceptive, analytical letters of the kind he had once addressed to Gandhi and which he continued to write to the very end of his days. In this instance, the theme was one which remains relevant, the dependence in England on the export of skills rather than goods.

Observing that England was being fed only by virtue of the Marshall Plan, and inadequately at that, G.D. remarked:

> If America stops or curtails it, there will be a crisis. When I was here in 1935 I asked Attlee what would happen to England if she lost the Colonies and India and had to depend on herself. He simply shrugged his shoulders. Now that position has been reached. England's own resources are very poor, no food, not enough raw materials. She thus has to depend on foreign trade which means importing raw and unfinished goods and exporting manufactured articles. In other words, the only thing she can export is her skill. When Germany starts producing she will be a serious competitor. If England has to depend only on the export of her skill, that skill must always be far in advance of the skill available in other countries. Inherently the position is unsound.

On that same visit G.D. reported to Patel that he had raised the question of Indo–British collaboration, resources being exchanged for technical expertise. He discussed English reaction to the Kashmir problem and passed on gossip that America was inciting Afghanistan to demand the North-West Frontier and Karachi from Pakistan. "One thing is quite clear, that America is establishing herself in Afghanistan, perhaps as a counter-blast to Russia. I would not be surprised if she may incite Afghanistan to take an aggressive move."

Soon Patel, too, was gone, and the later recipients of G.D.'s confidences were more likely to be members of his family and business associates. In more distant terms than those in which he had written to Gandhi and Patel, he continued to send back confidential reports to Government ministers and the relevant civil servants on what he had seen and whom he had met, whether Khrushchev or Eisenhower, Tito or Marcos, Selassie or Callaghan, as well as industrialists and tycoons with whom he had done business, like Edgar Kaiser. On these generally bi-annual tours lasting several months he always had in mind the industrial needs of India, India's position in the world and how the world regarded India. He was never slow to suggest improvements in policy or ways of communication, nor reluctant to criticize inadequate performance when he came across it in those responsible for representing India. If his touch on his own concerns became gentler, with his son Basant Kumar and grandson Aditya, in particular, playing increasingly important parts in the elaborate dovetailing of the numerous Birla concerns, overseas G.D. was as tireless as ever during the sixties and seventies.

Such honours as came his way he accepted gracefully: the coveted distinction of Padma Vibhushan in 1957, a Doctorate of Laws from Benares University in 1967, a D.Litt. from the University of Rajasthan, where Pilani, his "pet project" as he described it, "had now blossomed like a rose on a patch of the Rajputana desert".

At the age of 88, in 1982, he made his second pilgrimage on foot to the holy temple of Kedarnath, situated at an altitude of over 12,000 feet in the Himalayas. Accompanied by his son, Basant Kumar, his daughter-in-law Sarala, and his secretary for fifteen years, Shyamlal Pareek, G.D. made his final journey to the shrine along steep, stony paths into the snows. He had done what he could.

Last Rites

By the spring of 1983 G.D. had become dependent on his family to a greater extent than ever before. There was no one in politics to whom he was attached, his relations with Indira Gandhi having never been close, and his business equals had long since retired. In January 1982 Brijmohan, the last survivor of his three brothers, had died. They had not, at various times, seen eye to eye, but after the death of their brother Rameshwardas in 1973 they had drawn closer. G.D. himself had suffered a severe heart attack in 1977, and Brijmohan, so unlike him in demeanour and bearing, had sat by his bedside during his days of unconsciousness, allowing only Basant Kumar and Sarala near the patient.

Now in these last months he drifted on his memories, of his second wife Mahadevi in particular. The man who throughout his life had shown little emotion was no longer ashamed to shed tears. He seemed visibly to be preparing himself for death, making his dispositions.

His final years were given up, more than at any other period, to reading. He pored over the Bhagavata and the Mahabharata, and, confronted by what he called the "sheer blank wall, the dark veil hanging in space" of the future, gave himself up to analysing the legends, epics, and religious literature of the distant past. He was struck by the anonymity of the authors. "Vyasa has not told us anything about himself" he wrote in *Krishnam Vande Jagadgurum*, the philosophical commentary he published on his reading,

we do not know about the giant intellects responsible for the Upanishads. We know them as Ishavasya, Kena, Mandvkya or Prasna and that is all we know. This effacement of self,

221

this anonymity is a precedent set up by the great ones since time immemorial and it has been followed faithfully by the later Acharyas like Bhagavan Buddha, Adi Sankara, Ramanuja or Madhva. Even the great souls of comparatively recent times, bhaktas like Tulsi, Kabir and Mira have not spoken about themselves.

The concept of self-effacement took an increasing hold on his thinking and attitude to life. Autobiographies came to seem to him mere delusions, men presenting themselves under favourable disguises. Biographies were little better, satisfying curiosity, but valuable only as warnings. "As the poet so aptly puts it, like the swans which take only the milk leaving the water behind, even so should we deal with the nature of man." There was no prurience in G.D., no taste for anecdote or the small-change of life. What he liked about the sacred books was the indifference of their heroes to worldly fame, their demonstration that evil cannot ultimately triumph and that, no matter how terrible the conflicts, the spirit of man cannot be suppressed. "What I have set down," G.D. wrote at the end of *Krishnam Vande Jagadgurum*, "is what I have tried to learn from a study of the great poems. I have not said anything new." It is a modest disclaimer.

Nevertheless, though he had become more remote and introverted, G.D. did not alter his routine in any significant way. He kept on the move, as he had always done, rarely spending more than a few days in any one place. But whereas in the old days he had travelled the world with only his personal secretary, Raj Kumar Gupta, who was with him for twenty-five years, or Shyamlal, with him for fifteen, he preferred latterly to have his family near him, or, when abroad, the company of several senior Birla executives.

In April 1983 he was at Mangalam, his house in Delhi, leaving it with the arrival of the hot weather for Zug, a modest lakeside town near Zürich, where his European company had been established since 1962 and were moving to new premises. Zug, for tax reasons, had become a popular base for international companies and Tata, for example, had offices there, too. G.D. had use of a flat, above the office, his favourite chair so placed that he could look through pines and birches at snow-coated peaks the far side of the Zuger See. Throughout May various members of his family, his sons, daughters, grandchildren, came to visit him. When they had departed his old friend, the celebrated lawyer B. P. Khaitan, stayed on. G.D. continued to walk the forest roads for nearly two hours every day, returning after his last excursion to watch the sunset stain the lake and its sailing boats. In the evenings he read books on philosophy and religion and tried to improve his French. He regularly telephoned India. Just as at home the purer air of Mussoorie and Gangalahari had refreshed and rested him, so did Zug now offer him peace and calm.

By early June he was at the rather forbidding and impersonal Park Towers flat in the shadow of the Hilton, a flat recently rented by Aditya to replace the suite at Grosvenor House, his regular London haunt. With him he had his own cook and bearer, as well as Shyamlal, his secretary. Also in London for meetings were Ashkaran Agarwal, President of Hindalco, Nandlal Hamirwasia, President of Mysore Cement, and S. K. Sabu, Vice-President of Gwalior Rayon.

The days were taken up with discussions about meeting aluminium production targets, turbine and power problems, and other routine matters relating to Mysore Cement and Gwalior Rayon, the enterprises in which G.D. still took the closest personal interest. G.D. lunched out regularly and took his usual lengthy walks in the parks.

On 11 June, a Saturday, G.D. dealt with the usual telex messages before sitting down to breakfast with Agarwal. Agarwal was out of the flat by 8.30, on his way to Heathrow to catch his plane back to Delhi. Hamirwasia and Sabu now arrived, and G.D., having tried without success to reach D. P. Mandelia and his grandson Aditya by telephone to India, suggested a walk.

They set off, on a cloudy, rainy-looking morning, along Piccadilly. They had entered Regent Street when G.D. began to feel unwell. They called a taxi and G.D. got in, asserting that the attack had passed and he was feeling better.

No sooner, however, had he left the taxi to climb the steps into Park Towers than it was apparent all was not well. G.D.'s breathing became irregular and he almost fell. Sabu and Hamirwasia supported him and led him to a sofa, the one cradling his head while the other went up to the flat to call a doctor and an ambulance.

Within minutes the ambulance arrived and G.D. was taken on a stretcher to the Middlesex Hospital, ten minutes' drive away. He survived the journey, but died soon after admittance.

Next day, by different planes and by various routes, the family arrived at Park Towers: sons and daughters, grandchildren, lesser relatives, as well as his trusted lieutenant, Durgaprasad Mandelia and his wife.

It had always been G.D.'s instruction that, contrary to Hindu custom, should he die abroad, his body would not be taken back to India. As a citizen of the world, his wish was that he should be cremated where he died. Accordingly, after a weekend of chanting, prayer, and readings from the *Gita* in the Park Towers flat, the body was taken on the Monday to Golders Green crematorium.

Again, in a chapel overflowing with mourners and heady with the scent of flowers, there were further chantings of *mantras* and a reading from G.D.'s cherished eighteenth chapter of the *Gita*. His mouth was moistened with Ganges water and leaves of the holy basil laid on it.

The next day the urn containing the ashes was collected by the two sons present, Krishna Kumar and Basant Kumar. That same evening they took off for Bombay.

In Bombay, Calcutta and Delhi in turn, thousands of people filed past the urn to pay homage to the dead man. The President of India came to Gita Bhawan in the Birla Temple, and then, finally, the urn was taken to Pilani, the first and last, the most private amongst the most public of the Birla places.

The final respects paid, the last farewells said, some of the ashes from the urn were taken that same afternoon to the sacred city of Hardwar on the Ganges. There, to the chanting of Vedic hymns, these were scattered over the holy water by Krishna Kumar and Basant Kumar. The remaining ashes were carried, by close members of the family, to Gangotri, the source of the Holy River and a place G.D. loved, and immersed.

Over the next weeks the tributes came in, many of them from world leaders. Then began the attempts to assess the achievements and analyse the consequences. Perhaps the most balanced obituary of all was that of 13 June in *The Times* of London. After listing the range of G.D.'s business interests and mentioning his contribution to public affairs, his rôle as a press lord with the *Hindustan Times* and the *Eastern Economist*, his philanthropic and educationist activities, his importance as a benefactor to Congress and as a friend and interpreter of Gandhi, the writer went on to praise G.D.'s *In the Shadow of the Mahatma* for the "light it threw on the attainment of Indian independence from his own particular angle and also in the Mahatma's character with its amazing mixture of simplicity and finesse". The obituary continued:

> Birla's deep purse was always open to assist Gandhi's schemes of social reform, even when he did not agree with them, and his large donations to Congress Party funds were perhaps prompted equally by patriotism and business acumen. . . . As a financial operator on a countrywide scale he had no equal for quickness of mind and decision. He was a leading signatory in the middle of the war of the famous Bombay Plan envisaging a great advance in the industrialization of his country. If, like other industrialists, he viewed with some misgivings the early tendencies of Mr Nehru's Government towards nationalizing great enterprises, he chose to remain a Congress-backer rather than switch to newer right-wing political groups.

There could be no dispute, even among left-wing critics of capitalism in the radical press, about G.D.'s stature as one of the architects of modern India. There was, however,

225

considerable speculation about the effect G.D.'s death would have on the vast empire he had created.

The independent weekly magazine *Sunday* devoted the best part of its issue of 26 June to G.D., with a photograph of him on the cover overprinted with the words *The King is Dead*. In the cover story, Ian Jack, of the London *Sunday Times*, described calling on G.D. at his Park Lane hotel on the publication of *Bapu* in 1978.

I found a tall, erect man in an expensive English suit, surrounded by the human trappings of a great patriarchy: servants, assistants, relatives. We took tea and G.D. talked with great charm, frankness and intelligence about himself, Gandhi and India – charm, frankness and intelligence being the qualities I'll always remember him for, though no doubt managers of unprofitable Birla plants saw a different side.

Jack later travelled as a guest of G.D. in India, visiting his mills, temples, plants and institutes of higher education. "He was never less than interesting and sometimes he could be fascinating, for he had, after all, been intimately connected with some of the momentous events of the 20th century. He spoke with the frankness of an old man who had nothing to fear." Jack discovered that G.D. preferred to talk about any-thing – "the wider economic scene, world statesmen past and present, Hinduism, the meaning of life" – rather than discuss the inner financial workings of the Birla family. "It was like asking a happy English husband about his sex life. It may be a great source of pleasure but it remains private."

Confirming from G.D. himself that, apart from Jawaharlal, he had no great feelings of warmth for the Nehru family, Indira and Sanjay Gandhi in particular, Jack commented that G.D.'s great range of friendships among disparate-seeming people was possible largely because of what might be called an arith-metical approach.

He would subtract what he didn't like – Gandhi's anti-industrialism, Churchill's economic imperialism and blatant ignorance of India – and then count up the qualities he

226

admired or found useful. He was a very pragmatic man, but unlike many other pragmatic men his pragmatism overlaid a moral base – his *Sanatan Dharma*, the eternal religion of duty.

It was Ian Jack's conclusion that, unlike many of those who came after him, G.D. had not given Indian capitalism a bad name. His belief in profitability was underwritten by the almost religious fervour of his belief in capitalism's redeeming power, not least as a bulwark against communism.

It was typical of this modest man that he should describe himself as being in business, rather than a businessman. "I have been a student all my life," he said in an interview when he was eighty-five. "I am still a student."

Three years earlier, in 1976, he had travelled to the Philippines, an outpost, together with South Korea, Indonesia, Malaysia and Thailand, of the Birla Group's joint ventures in south-east Asia. Just as in the preceding decades he had interested himself in Russia, the United States, Britain and various European countries in the search for new markets and areas of co-operation, so now in his old age did he turn to the East and encourage the younger generations to follow him. "I am an Indian," he said in a speech in Manila,

> but I must tell you that I feel very strongly that I am an Asian. Those in Asia must cooperate with each other. No country can be strong unless it has a strong industrial base. I am interested in anything that creates more wealth, more employment. I am a capitalist but I believe in a socialism which means equal opportunity, more employment and a fairer standard of living for everyone. Socialism should not mean socialising poverty but raising the quality of life.

It was not in G.D.'s nature to leave behind him areas of doubt about his intentions. Long before he died he had laid down guidelines as to succession in the various companies, and spheres of influence were clearly defined. At the time of G.D.'s death he himself was responsible, among the major Birla concerns, for Hindalco, Gwalior Rayon, Mysore Cements and J. C. Mills, four of the largest companies. His second son Krishna Kumar, the only one to be interested in politics, was chairman of six companies, covering shipping, chemicals, engineering and textiles. Basant Kumar Birla's four main companies included Century Spinning, second only in its assets to Hindalco, two other textile companies, and Jayshree Tea. Gangaprasad, the son of G.D.'s younger brother Brijmohan, controlled Hindustan Motors and Orient Papers, and another nephew, Madhoprasad, was in charge of Birla Jute and Bihar Alloy Steels. Among the grandchildren Aditya, son of Basant Kumar, was in charge of Indian Rayon, as well as of several Far Eastern concerns, and was heir apparent to Hindalco. Another grandson Sudarshan Kumar, the son of G.D.'s eldest son Laxminiwas, was chairman of Universal Electric as well as of Digvijay Woollen Mills and Orient Carpets. This list covers only the top twenty or so out of over two hundred industrial units all controlled by Birlas. A statement made in the Rajya Sabha in March 1983 assessed the Birla assets at over two thousand crores of rupees, their post-tax profits of over a hundred crores placing them a close second to Tata.

The period of greatest growth for the Birlas, as for such giant contemporaries as Tisco, Premier Automobiles and Iisco, had been between Independence and the late sixties, halted only briefly by the Sarkar inquiry into Birla affairs and continual sniping in parliament at conglomerates and multinationals. Having survived these, the Birlas flourished more than ever, and seem poised now for even greater expansion.

Although the Birla Group companies became public after the war there was no dilution of Birla control. Rather did each Birla member have the responsibility for running his own smaller group, even in competition with another. G.D. insisted on scrupulous and punctual accountancy, and on as large dividends as the public companies could stand.

It was G.D.'s conviction, not by all means common at the time, that only by removing the British would India have a chance to prosper economically. His support of Congress through thick and thin, and even after Independence when Nehru's socialist policies alienated many Indian businessmen, paid off in the way that loyalty should pay off. In recent years the Birlas have had few political associations, only K. K. Birla actively involving himself, but in a sense they, and the country, have grown out of a situation in which industry needed to promote its virtues.

Subir Roy, analysing G.D. and his legacy in the Indian *Telegraph* of 26 June 1983, summed up the Birla top management style as combining elements of Japanese patriarchy, American efficiency and missionary Soviet zeal. "But this was not all. These three separate elements were amalgamated into a unified whole with certain traditional Indian values like loyalty, good faith and trust." As for G.D.'s personal style, "It was a kind of impatient dynamism that motivated him" a senior manager was quoted as saying. "By impatience I do not mean anything negative but that pressure which keeps everyone on his toes. Not that there was any kind of tension in him. His table was always clear. He was totally relaxed. In fact he would walk from room to room, in and out of other senior people's offices exchanging ideas as they came to him."

It has been said that, in financial outlook, G.D. was essentially conservative. That is conceivably true. But what Subir Roy, in the same *Telegraph* article, described as a combination of religious optimism and adopted modernism stood him in good stead. He trusted his own intuition and he guessed well. It was, however, his own mastery of the basic skills of the trader and the entrepreneur that enabled him to do so.

He was lucky in the sense that his values, despite his accumulation of wealth, were essentially good and unaffected ones, and that his patriotism was of a kind that simplified his motives and canalized his efforts. There were no distractions, no hankering after material possessions or sensual gratification. The result could have been censoriousness or a narrowness of vision but, beyond an almost fanatical insistence on punctuality, he was remarkably free of either.

There are Birlas who have mildly kicked over the traces and paid heavily for it: Gajanan, for example, the son of G.D.'s elder brother Rameshwardas, who was unable to lead the austere life of the Birlas. He lost his standing in family circles as a consequence and with it all his influence. Gajanan's son Ashok, less austere in his tastes than most Birlas, has several smaller Birla units in his keeping, but the main lineal descent is directly from G.D. to his youngest son, Basant Kumar, and to his son Aditya. Daughters traditionally play no part in this baton-passing, and Krishna Kumar, older than Basant Kumar, has only daughters. Laxminiwas Birla, G.D.'s eldest son, and only son by his first wife, has always remained on the margins of the main business enterprises, concerned with the administration of the numerous Birla Trusts, as well as their philanthropic and cultural activities.

Sudarshan, Laxminiwas's son, and Aditya each have a son, so when K.K. and B.K. retire from the scene and they take over the reins, there will be an even younger generation in the offing. A further line of succession runs from Gangaprasad, G.D.'s nephew, to his son Chandrakant; they have in their care Hindustan Motors, manufacturers of the Ambassador car, and various paper and engineering concerns.

No other Indian industrial pattern, least of all that of the Tatas, has been formed in comparable family fashion, the lines of command assured from generation to generation.

It would seem on the evidence unthinkable for a Birla to do other than go into the business, and in the circumstances – since there is a shortage rather than a glut of them for the key posts available – why should he? Yet it is strange that so far no member of the familiy has opted for any of the professions. There are no Birla civil servants or doctors, no lawyers, scientists or academics.

At the end of an article tracing G.D.'s relationship to the pre-Independence Congress party and his skill in "rendering Nehru ineffective", as he put it, Girish Mathur remarked: "Today G.D.'s sons have access to the highest in the country and exercise greater influence on decision-making than anyone else, whatever the professed policy of the government, thanks to the class-conscious approach of G.D. towards the national movement from 1920 onwards."

Whether that is true or not, despite the low profile kept by Birlas in Indian public life, it was certainly due to G.D.'s influence, both over his own colleagues and on those in the Congress high command, that Indian industrialists kept faith with the nationalist movement. He had sought, especially at moments of crisis when bitterness between the British and the nationalists was at its most extreme, a workable solution, a workable relationship, which did not entail loss of honour or principle. His much quoted "pragmatism" enabled him to counsel acceptance of responsibility and office rather than confrontation as a means to achieving ultimate ends, a counsel that needed vigorously promoting among all categories of nationalist, from Gandhi and Nehru downwards.

By "class-conscious approach" Mathur presumably meant the interests of the business community, and it was because G.D. saw their interests and those of independent India as synonymous that he was able to campaign so energetically. There is frequent reference to be found to claims that G.D. "manipulated" Congress and there is no doubt that he had allies in all the top echelons of central and provincial government. But the party that Nehru presided over after 1947 was a socialist party and it was in the realms of economic planning and in G.D.'s vision of the national good, not in furtherance of his own self-interest or that of the capitalist class in general, that his ideas prevailed. If there had been crudity in the earlier thrust to wealth, Gandhi's concept of trusteeship had soon tempered it. The influence that G.D.'s sons have inherited, if indeed this can be seen to spread beyond the natural frontiers of their various concerns, would appear to reflect neither more nor less than that legacy of conciliation G.D. himself conceived to be essential to social progress. He never claimed to be more than a spokesman for his colleagues, but it was precisely in the wisdom of his counsel and his detachment from purely parochial interests that his uniqueness lay. Even in his relationship with Gandhi, as acolyte and banker in turn, he was not the only rich supporter: but he differed from the others in that he was able to articulate, in forceful and dignified terms, the economic principles he believed in, to Gandhi and to the British Government equally. In this sense he raised his stake in the community, and though most of his battles with the

British were inevitably concerned with industrial and currency matters, he nevertheless took it upon himself to argue India's causes in terms of morality as much as expediency.

Industrialists rarely rate more than a footnote, if that, in the history of their time, let alone of their country. Inevitably, G. D. Birla will tend to be remembered as a friend and disciple of Gandhi as much as for his pioneering achievements as an industrialist and as an influential intermediary in India's struggle towards nationhood. Men like the Mahatma, idiosyncratically human as he appears in his correspondence with G. D., are rare and G.D. would not, one imagines, have quarrelled with such an assessment. But men of his own stature are not very frequent either. Whatever footnotes come his way he will have earned them.

Like Gandhi, G.D. was a man of western India, a provincial who became a citizen of the world. He belongs to Rajasthan as Gandhi belongs to Gujarat. They both inherited a local toughness which they were able to bring to bear on the problems of a country torn by racial conflict and stumbling towards identity. G.D. helped by common sense and affection to make Gandhi's saintliness serviceable, to nurse his obstinacy and modify his swings of mood. It was somehow typical of him that, though he believed to the end that the caste system was a stabilizing factor in Indian life, he should have done so much to reduce its injustices. The capitalist was also, in his own idiosyncratic conception, a socialist, the man of affairs a devout believer.

SELECT BIBLIOGRAPHY

Bapu: A Unique Association (four volumes) Bombay 1977

Birla, G. D. *In the Shadow of the Mahatma* Bombay 1968

 The Path to Prosperity 1950

 Words To Remember 1983

 Indian Currency in Retrospect Allahabad 1944

 Krishnam Vande Jagadgurum

 Modern India. Heritage and Achievement. G. D. Birla

  Eightieth Birthday Commemoration Volume 1977

Fischer, L. *The Life of Mahatma Gandhi* London 1951

Gandhi, M. K. *An Autobiography* (two volumes) India 1927, 1929

Hennessy, J. *India, Democracy and Education* Calcutta 1955

Jaju, R. N. *G. D. Birla* New Delhi 1985

Kumar, C. & Puri, M. *Mahatma Gandhi* London 1982

Mansergh, P. N. *Transfer of Power* London

Mason, P. *The Men Who Ruled India* London 1985

Sarkar, S. *Modern India 1885–1947* New Delhi 1983

Timberg, T. A. *The Marwaris* New Delhi

Wacziarg, F. & Nath, A. *Rajasthan: The Painted Walls of Shekhavati* New Delhi 1982

Wavell, Lord *The Viceroy's Journal* Oxford 1973

SOME RELEVANT DATES

1894   Ghanshyamdas Birla born in Pilani to Raja Baldeodas Birla, son of Seth Shivnarain Birla, and Yogeshwari Devi Birla

1900   Baldeodas Jugalkishore & Co. established in Kali Godam, Calcutta
Bhagwani Devi, eldest sister of Ghanshyamdas Birla, marries Krishnagopalji Mohta of Sadulpur

1904   G. D. studies with tutor in Bombay, after which, aged 11, he has no further formal education

1907   G. D. marries Durga Devi, daughter of Seth Mahadev Somani of Chirawa, Rajasthan
Joins his father's firm in Calcutta

1909   G. D.'s son, Laxminiwas, born

1910   Durga Devi Birla dies

1911   Marwari Sporting Club, later the Rajasthan Club, founded in Calcutta
The firm G. M. Birla – Ghanshyamdas Murlidhar – & Co. established

1912   G. D. marries his second wife, Mahadevi, only daughter of Premsukhdas Karva of Sardar Shahar, Rajasthan

1915   G. D. meets M. K. Gandhi, on his return from South Africa, in Calcutta

1916   Chandrakala, G. D.'s first daughter, born

1918   G. D. establishes his jute business in Calcutta
Krishna Kumar, his second son, born

1921   Basant Kumar, G. D.'s third son, born
G. D. establishes Jiyajeerao Cotton Mills and is nominated a member of the Bengal Legislative Council
President, Marwari Business Association

1922   G. D. buys Kesoram Cotton Mills from Kesoram Podar

1923   G. D.'s second daughter, Anusuiya, born
His grandfather, Seth Shivnarain, posthumously awarded the title of Raja

G. D. moves to Birla Park, Calcutta
His friendship with Lala Lajpat Rai begins

1924 G. D.'s third daughter, Shanti, born
For the next two years the Birlas are shunned by the Maheshwari Sabha on account of their progressive views

1925 G. D.'s father, Baldeodas, honoured with the title of Raja by the Bihar and Orissa Government

1926 Hindu–Muslim riots in Calcutta, during which G. D. shelters both Hindus and Muslims
Mahadevi, G. D.'s second wife, dies
M. K. Gandhi stays for the first time in Birla Park, Calcutta

1927 G. D. a delegate to the 10th International Labour Conference at Geneva
Federation of Indian Chamber of Commerce formed, with G. D. as one of the founders
Elected to Legislative Assembly, as Member for Gorakhpur
Purchases *Hindustan Times*, with Madan Mohan Malaviya as first chairman

1928 Birla House, New Delhi, later to become the place of Gandhi's assassination, completed

1929 President of Federation of Indian Chamber of Commerce
Attends Round Table Conference as Representative of Indian business interests
Birla Education Trust formed

1930 Resigns as Member for Gorakhpur in Legislative Assembly

1931 Second Round Table Conference, London, which G. D. attends, travelling with Gandhi on the S. S. *Rajputana*

1932 G. D. declines a knighthood and during the year establishes 400 schools in Rajasthan villages

1933 New Asiatic Insurance formed

1934 Ranchi Zamidari purchased and Gauridutt Mandelia, father of D. P. Mandelia, appointed caretaker

1935/6 Birla Bros acquire their 10th major concern, the total comprising 5 sugar mills, 4 cotton mills, and one jute mill

1936 Ruby General Insurance Company formed

1939 Textile Machinery Company started in Calcutta, under the responsibility of K. K. Birla

1941 Three of G. D.'s children marry, Anusuiya Devi, Shanti Devi and Krishna Kumar

1942 Gandhi arrested in Birla House, Bombay

Hindustan Motors registered
Basant Kumar Birla marries Sarala Devi, daughter of Berar Kesari Brijlal Biyani of Akola

1943   Cimmco established in Gwalior
United Commercial Bank opens

1944   Hindustan Gas and Industries registered
Indian Plastics registered

1945   All India Montessori Conference held in Pilani with Dr Maria Montessori as President
Bharat Commerce and Jayshree Tea and Industries registered

1946   Hyderabad Asbestos registered and, in Jaipur, National Engineering and Industries

1947   Gwalior Rayon and Silk (Wvg) Mfg. Co. started

1948   G. D. presides over a meeting held in Birla House organized by Jawaharlal Nehru and Sardar Patel for the purpose of setting up Gandhi Memorial Fund

1951   Century Spinning acquired from Sir Chunilal Mehta

1955   Digvijay Woollen Mills purchased

1957   Raja Baldeodas Birla dies, aged 93, in Benares
G. D. awarded Padma Vibhushan

1958   Hindustan Aluminium Corporation established in Renukoot in collaboration with Edgar Kaiser, of Kaiser Aluminium, San Francisco

1959   G. D. receives Honorary D.Litt. from Rajasthan University

1961   G. D. visits Moscow

1963   Rani Yogeshwari Devi Birla, mother of G. D., dies aged 100

1964   Pilani School raised to university status and named Birla Institute of Technology and Science

1967   G. D. awarded the degree of Doctor of Law by Benares Hindu University
Jugalkishore Birla, G. D's eldest brother, dies in Delhi

1968   Indo–Thai Synthetics Co. Ltd established in Bangkok

1969   G. D. visits Ethiopia at the invitation of the Emperor

1971   G. D. makes pilgrimage to Kedarnath and Badrinath with his youngest son, Basant Kumar, and daughter-in-law Sarala, and the following year to Gangotri

1974   G. D. invited to Thailand and on his return makes pilgrimage with Basant Kumar and Sarala to Jamnotri

1976   President Marcos invites G. D. to the Philippines

1977   G. D. recovers from severe heart attack

1982 B. M. Birla, his youngest brother, dies in Calcutta

1983 G. D. makes second pilgrimage to Kedarnath on foot, an altitude of over 12,000 feet

G. D. Birla dies in London on 11 June

INDEX

Ahmedabad, 20, 32, 36, 39, 87
Ajmer, 17, 20
Ambedkar, Dr, 76
Amery, Leo, 5, 138, 182–3, 184, 186
Amritsar, 37, 38, 47, 92
Anderson, Sir John, 74, 104, 110, 183, 188
Attlee, Clement, 103, 160, 169, 171, 188, 219
Azad, Maulana Abul Kalam, 150, 157

Babu, Rajendra, 93
Bajaj, Jamnalal, 178
Baldwin, Stanley, 99, 100, 104–5, 126
Basu, Bhupendra Nath, 27
Basu, Mrinal Kanti, 88
Bengal, 14, 35, 36, 61, 113, 119, 128, 137, 155, 163, 166–70, 172, 173, 199, 210
Benthall, Sir Edward, 68, 69, 72, 73
Berlin, 53–4, 154
Bevin, Ernest, 160, 188
Bhiwani, 17, 211
Bihar, 88, 151–2, 166, 167, 170, 228
Birla Aditya, 220, 223, 228, 230
Birla, Ashok, 230
Birla, Baldeodas, 21, 22, 86, 200, 210
Birla, Basant Kumar, 14, 220, 221, 224, 225, 228, 230
Birla, Brijmohan, 221, 228
Birla Brothers, 22, 28, 30, 31, 118, 181, 197
Birla, Chandrakala, 27
Birla, Chandrakant, 230
Birla, Durgadeviji, 24
Birla Education Trust, 198, 209, 210
Birla, Gajanan, 229–30
Birla, Gangaprasad, 228, 230
Birla, Ghanshyamdas (G. D.): and business, 203, 207–8, 211, 213–15; and Congress, 122–3, 130, 142, 228; and Harijan cause, 84, 86; commerce, 24–5, 28; education, 22–4; industry, 29–32, 61–2, 119, 120–1, 156; influence of, 230–3; life, 13–14, 21–2; marriage, 24, 26–7, 44–5; on capitalism, 66, 227; on economics, 70, 71, 74, 80, 81, 216; personality, 212–13, 217–18, 222, 226, 229, 232; travels, 51–4, 66–72, 96–100, 122, 127, 159, 179, 195–6, 227
Birla Houses, 41, 113, 146, 148, 154, 155, 173, 174, 188–90, 198
Birla Institute of Technology and Science, 210, 211, 212
Birla, Jugal Kishore, 21, 22, 23, 26, 50, 200–201
Birla Jute, 31, 214, 228

Birla, Krishna Kumar, 224, 225, 228, 229, 230
Birla, Laxminiwas, 24, 228, 230
Birla, Madhoprasad, 228
Birla, Mahadevi, 27, 44–5, 221
Birla, Rameshwardas, 21, 24, 50, 155, 221, 229
Birla, Sarala, 220, 221
Birla, Seth Shivnarain, 18, 20–23, 34, 199, 202
Birla, Sudarshan Kumar, 228, 230
Bombay, 20, 22, 32, 144, 161, 210, 225
Bose, Sarate Chundra, 110
Bose, Subhas Chandra, 110, 132–3, 146, 151, 154, 155
Brabourne, Lord, 128
Broomsfield, C. N., 39
Budd, Edward, 15
Budge-Budge, 31, 33
Burma, 149, 197
Butler, R. A., 98, 99, 101, 102

Calcutta, 22, 85–6, 119, 141, 142, 148, 152, 164, 173, 185
Catto, Sir Thomas, 101
Champaran, 36, 174
Chelmsford, Lord, 37
Chiang Kai Shek, 148, 196
Chinai, Babubhai, 217
Chowdhury, Phool Chand, 27
Churchill, Winston, 67, 103, 107–8, 126, 138, 146, 151, 160, 187, 226
Craik, Sir Henry, 96
Cripps, Sir Stafford, 146–7, 149, 160, 161–2, 163, 164, 166, 167, 182–3, 188

Dalai Lama, 194, 195
Derby, Lord, 100, 102
Desai, Bhulabhai, 94, 97
Desai, Kanti, 218
Desai, Mahadev, 150, 154, 193; correspondence with G. D., 60, 91, 95, 97, 102, 115, 118, 122, 123, 126, 127, 128, 130, 133, 136, 137, 142, 143, 147, 148; editor of *Harijan*, 139; memorial to, 156; secretary to Gandhi, 34
Desai, Morarji, 218
Dev, Narendra, 174
Dyer, General, 47, 92

Fischer, Louis, 147, 149, 150
Fitzpatrick, John, 14
Fitzpatrick, Vere, 14

238